Anti-Colonialism and the Crises of Interwar Fascism

Anti-Colonialism and the Crises of Interwar Fascism

Michael Ortiz

BLOOMSBURY ACADEMIC
LONDON • NEW YORK • OXFORD • NEW DELHI • SYDNEY

BLOOMSBURY ACADEMIC
Bloomsbury Publishing Plc
50 Bedford Square, London, WC1B 3DP, UK
1385 Broadway, New York, NY 10018, USA
29 Earlsfort Terrace, Dublin 2, Ireland

BLOOMSBURY, BLOOMSBURY ACADEMIC and the Diana logo are trademarks of
Bloomsbury Publishing Plc

First published in Great Britain 2023
Paperback edition published 2024

ISBN: HB: 978-1-3503-3492-2
PB: 978-1-3503-3495-3
ePDF: 978-1-3503-3493-9
eBook: 978-1-3503-3494-6

Typeset by Deanta Global Publishing Services, Chennai, India

To find out more about our authors and books visit www.bloomsbury.com and sign up for
our newsletters.

To Laura, Sofia, and Mia

Contents

Acknowledgments

This book is the product of nearly a decade of struggle, failure, adversity, and more failure. I have accumulated innumerable debts, and fear that passing mention here will not do justice to the friends, family, and colleagues that have supported me along the way. I will nevertheless try.

To begin, I must thank the two people who helped me formulate this project: Susan Kent and David Ciarlo. Several years ago, while a graduate student at the University of Colorado, I was awarded a fellowship to conduct research at the British Library. While examining Indian intervention in the Spanish Civil War, I discovered that leading anti-colonialists often mentioned Spain in conjunction with other conflicts in Ethiopia, China, and Czechoslovakia (during the Munich Crisis). Panicked, I sent an email to Susan asking if I could ignore these conflicts and concentrate exclusively on Spain. Like any good historian, Susan urged me to follow the sources. I will never forgive her for it. She is a far more accomplished historian that I could ever hope to be, and I have treasured her support and guidance. Thank you, Susan.

David warned me not to do this project. He was right. It was too broad for a dissertation—more appropriate for a late-career book. Of course, I had no idea what I was doing. Frankly, I still have no idea what I am doing. Initially, I wrote my dissertation as a history of Indian anti-fascism. But I am not a historian of South Asia! As a result, my dissertation was dreadful. In the lead up to my defense, the modern South Asianist at Colorado, Mithi Mukherjee, confirmed this (thank you, Mithi). Crestfallen, I trudged into David's office. He leaned back in his chair and tented his fingers (much like a super-villain). He then told me that although my protagonists were Indian, their arguments challenged how we understand Europe, so my conclusions should do the same. My brain wept. This brilliant insight saved my dissertation and locked in my focus for the book. Thank you, David.

Of course, I made many mistakes along the way. I pitched this project to several presses, often falling victim to the remorseless scythe of anonymous reviewer number two. Editors often specialize in particular geographies; time and time again, they urged me to write this book as a narrative of Indian anti-fascism. Unsure of what to do, I contacted Susan, who recommended I get in touch with

Maddie Holder over at Bloomsbury Academic. Maddie did something no other editor dared—she listened to my vision for the book. What an iconoclast! Thank you, Maddie.

I must also thank numerous professional colleagues. Most importantly, someone once told me that if a particular person is mentioned in the acknowledgments of a book, they will refrain from writing a review. So to begin, I would like to thank anyone considering writing a negative review of this book!

There are several wonderful historians who have supported me over the years: Douglas Kanter, Patricia Kollander, Ken Osgood, Derrick White, Kenneth (SDK) Posner, Nick Underwood, Mattie Fitch, Scott Miller, Martha Hanna, Virginia Anderson, Paul Sutter, Lil Fenn, Marcia Yonemoto, Sanjay Gautam, Tom Zeiler, Myles Osborne, Lucy Chester, and David Shneer. I cannot thank you all enough. This book would not have been possible without you. Also, if it reviews poorly, you are all to blame.

I would like to thank my former colleagues at the University of Northern Colorado for hiring someone so dangerously unqualified. Fritz Fischer (not *that* Fritz Fischer) and Joan Clinefelter were outstanding mentors, and I could not have survived without the support of Corinne Wieben, T of J Tomlin, Robbie Weiss, Aaron "Habey Habes" Haberman, Kelly Cook, Jiacheng Liu, Jamie Fogg, Michael Welsh, Jacob Melish, and Mary Borg. I must also thank Rob Widell and the Department of History at the University of Rhode Island for taking a chance and hiring me. You probably already regret it! The good news (for you) is that there is no way this book reviews well enough for me to get tenure.

There are numerous friends and colleagues that have supported me in the writing of this book. I will begin with Daniel DuBois, whom I hate. Dan and I have a wager on whose book will sell more copies. Reader, I am not saying that you should buy two copies of this book, merely that you should never under any circumstances purchase his. At each stage of writing, Dan was an invaluable resource—often reading entire sections or chapters (while insisting that I incorporate more Thomas Mann). Thank you, Dan. You will notice that I reference Mann in the first paragraph of the introduction.

Douglas Snyder provided far more support than Dan Dubois. At least twice as much. For years, I have bounced ideas off Doug, sought out his advice on the publishing process, and turned to him during my many, many struggles. Doug will nevertheless be livid that I mentioned him after Dan. Sorry Doug. Thank you, Doug.

Ryan "Ryclops" Gillis knows nothing about history, academia, or life. He is an animator in Los Angeles with a bad back. Over the years, he has served as my "intelligent alien." The term is a misnomer—Ryan is not intelligent. Yet whenever I have wondered whether a non-specialist or non-academic knew of a person, place, or idea, Ryan was there. Thank you, Ryan. I hope you (re)grow a spine.

I would like to thank Travis May and Graeme "Ashcan" Pente, both of whom advised me at several stages along this process. Travis is a dreadful misanthrope and Graeme a burgeoning tyrant. I do not trust either of them yet could not have completed this book without their help. Thank you both.

To my parents, Roberto and Elena, your sacrifices are forever appreciated, even as my career is a massive disappointment to you both. I am so sorry. I hope that this book, which will likely sell more than eight copies, will assuage your pain and sorrow. I love you both. To my siblings, cousins, nieces, nephews, and extended family, I cannot express how much your support has made this book possible. I suspect none of you will read this book and, frankly, I cannot blame you. Just know that you will all buy brand new hardback copies so my parents will cry a little bit less at night. Thank you all.

To my partner Laura, you are everything. You have read so many drafts of this book, you might as well be a co-author. Your insights, suggestions, and critiques have been invaluable throughout this process. Let me also apologize for using so many dashes—I know you hate them. I cannot thank you enough for all that you have done for me. This book would not be possible without your love and support. Thank you.

Finally, to my daughters Sofia and Mia, you do not understand the bizarre (and often brutal) thing that Dad does for a living. Few do. I do not harbor illusions that this book will change the world. There are far better scholars (and scholarship) out there. Yet I hope that one day you will be proud that Dad does what he loves for a living and is trying in the smallest way possible to make the world a better place. I love you both. Thank you for making my life a pit of chaos, dance parties, and love.

Abbreviations

AICC	All India Congress Committee
CCP	Chinese Communist Party
CPGB	Communist Party of Great Britain
CPI	Communist Party of India
CWC	Congress Working Committee
ILP	Independent Labour Party
INA	Indian National Army
INC	Indian National Congress
RDP	Radical Democratic Party

Introduction

Fascism and Imperialism

Winston Churchill trudged toward the Palace of Westminster. An air of exasperation followed him. Exiled from the National Government, Churchill often grumbled at anyone willing to listen to him. On this particular day, in the summer of 1938, his frustration was palpable. Britain appeared on the brink of annihilation. Fascism, a protean ideology forged in the crucible of postwar violence, threatened the liberal-democratic order established twenty years earlier.

In Italy, the birthplace of fascism, Benito Mussolini had overrun the kingdom of Ethiopia, undermining the League of Nations and threatening British interests in Egypt and the Sudan. In East Asia, the Empire of Japan had launched a full-scale invasion of China, endangering British colonial interests along the eastern coast. Finally, in Germany, Adolf Hitler had recently orchestrated the Anschluss, and now turned his irredentist gaze toward the Sudetenland—a corridor along Western Czechoslovakia containing a large ethnic-German population. Europe, it seemed, had embraced a fanatical cult of barbarism.[1]

Standing before the House of Commons, Churchill denounced the retreat of democratic forces and urged all Britons to defend civilization from fascism:

> The vast degeneration of the forces of Parliamentary democracy will be proceeding throughout Europe . . . . For five years I have talked to the House on these matters, not with very great success. I have watched this famous island descending incontinently, fecklessly the stairway which leads to a dark gulf . . . . That is the position, that is the terrible transformation that has taken place bit by bit. We should lay aside every hindrance to endeavour by uniting the whole force and spirit of our people to raise again a great British nation standing up before all the world, for such a nation, rising in its ancient vigour, can even at this hour save civilisation.[2]

Seven hundred miles south, in war-torn Spain, a subject of the British Empire propounded a radically different interpretation of fascism. Unbeknownst to Churchill, Jawaharlal Nehru, one of the leaders of the Indian National Congress

(INC) and the first prime minister of independent India (1947), disembarked from an aircraft in Barcelona. For nearly a decade, Churchill's eschatological (and unfounded) predictions about Indian independence had resulted in his political exile, leaving his anti-Nazi exhortations to fall upon deaf ears.[3] Now, a leading Indian anti-colonialist had come to Spain to challenge Churchill's conception of fascism.

Nehru spent five nights in Spain. Early each morning, a cacophony of air-raid sirens and anti-aircraft guns awoke him. On more than one occasion, he watched from his sixth-floor balcony as fascist bombs consumed the Eixample.[4] Aerial bombing terrified Europeans.[5] Only one year prior (1937), the bombing of civilians in the Basque town of Guernica (Gernika) had sparked widespread outrage. *The Times* reprinted its story every day for more than a week. The Bishop of Winchester denounced the attack as "a cruel, deliberate, cold-blooded act against the laws of God and against every law of civilization and of man."[6] The destruction of Guernica portended a future of "unprecedented viciousness."[7] It threatened the destruction of Europe.

Nehru disagreed. From an anti-colonial perspective, the bombing of Guernica did not presage the war to come, but rather hearkened back to Europe's wars of imperial expansion:

> We are deeply moved by these aerial bombardments in Spain and China. And yet aerial bombing is no new thing for us. The evil is an old one, and because it went unchecked it has grown to those vast and terrible dimensions. Have you forgotten the bombing on the Northwest Frontier of India, which has been going on now for many long years and still continues. . . . This was called police action, and [the British Government] insisted on its maintenance. The evil went unchecked, and if it has grown now is it surprising? On whom lies the responsibility?[8]

At the same time Italian, German, and Spanish-nationalist forces targeted innocent civilians in Spain, British colonial planes terror bombed the Waziri and Mahsud peoples of Waziristan, along the Northwest Frontier of British India. How, Nehru often questioned, did British bombings along the Northwest Frontier differ from those in Spain? Innocents in both Guernica and Waziristan suffered, yet European popular opinion only denounced the former. For Nehru, this discrepancy underscored the hypocrisy of Churchill's appeal to defend civilization from fascism. British "civilization" had created an exploitative, racist, and violent regime that brutalized the Indian subcontinent. It murdered innocent civilians in much the same way Italians, Germans, and Spanish-nationalists had at Guernica. Churchill, however, decried fascism as alien—something unmoored from Western liberal traditions.

Nehru and Churchill articulated radically different interpretations of the same political phenomenon. For Churchill, fascism (Nazism, in particular) was a murderous despotism that threatened the quintessence of British liberalism: parliamentary democracy, empire, and English civilization.[9] Nehru, meanwhile, contended that fascism was simply colonialism practiced in Europe. Both ideologies glorified violence, racism, and exploitation; they were, as Nehru often argued, "blood brothers."[10]

These antithetical understandings of fascism reflected, and continue to reflect, broader debates over the meaning of Europe. Is Europe the arbiter of modernity, progress, and justice? Or is it a vicious exploiter that has enslaved and brutalized nations around the world? Answers to these questions remain complex, and often underscore the heterogeneity of the very idea of Europe. There are, as historians have contended, many Europes, "real, historical, and fantasized."[11] Among scholars, one of the few points of consensus is that Europe was made in the image of a colonizing power. Indeed, "far from being self-generated," Europe "[was] the product of constant, intricate, but mostly unacknowledged traffic with the non-European world."[12] Empire was constitutive to the very idea of Europe. All too often, however, the struggles of colonial populations remain untold.

To date, Churchill's interpretation of fascism has dominated Western understandings of the interwar world. Fascism, particularly Hitler and the Nazis, has been depicted as unalloyed evil.[13] Many contemporary politicians and intellectuals still characterize the Second World War as the "good war"[14] or, at the very least, portray it as a conflict between antipodal forces: the villainous Axis and the virtuous Allies (primarily Britain and the United States). This dichotomization of victor and vanquished has encouraged apologal understandings of the interwar world. Both as a word and concept, Churchill's "fascism" has evolved into an uncomplicated pejorative. It has become a shorthand for evil used by anyone seeking to demonize or discredit an opponent.

This book challenges apologal depictions of fascism, and Europe more broadly, by analyzing the crises of interwar fascism (the Second Italo-Ethiopian War, Spanish Civil War, Second Sino-Japanese War, Munich Agreement, and the outbreak of the Second World War) through the prism of Indian anti-imperialism. It is not a history of South Asian internationalism, nor of the Indian independence movement, nor even of the ways in which Indian anti-colonialists influenced (a nebulous concept) fascist ideologies. Instead, this book examines Indian *understandings* of interwar Europe in order to complicate the ways in which Europeans understand their histories, as well as themselves. For more than a century, scholars have examined various dimensions of the fascist phenomenon. During this time, they have disagreed on several important questions, such as what fascism was, when and where it emerged, and the extent to which it emulated existing political ideologies. This book broadens these questions by examining them from the perspective of Indian anti-colonialists. It is, in essence, a juxtaposition of Churchill's and Nehru's Europes.

Brothers in Misfortune

Historians have long debated several aspects of the fascist phenomenon, including its position within Europe's conventional left-right political axis;[15] the extent to which it existed before the First World War;[16] whether historians should "take fascism seriously";[17] its relationship with totalitarianism and totalitarian theory;[18] the degree to which it constituted a revolt against modernity;[19] its development over the course of the interwar era;[20] and, finally, its evolution (or dissolution) after the Second World War.[21] In recent years, the cardinal debate within fascist historiography has centered on the concept of generic fascism—or the minimum set of characteristics that qualify an individual or movement as fascist. Characterizations have ranged from the straightforward—radical "anti-modernist anti-Marxism,"[22] or a mythical "palingenetic form of populist ultra-nationalism"[23]— to the more labyrinthine.[24] Michael Mann, for example, has contended that fascism constituted organic nationalism, radical statism, paramilitarism, and the transcendence of class conflict, while Stanley Payne has created a typological description of fascism that contains thirteen distinct components.[25]

On the other end of the spectrum, scholars such as Ian Kershaw, Saul Friedländer, and Hannah Arendt have repudiated generic frameworks, criticizing their tendency toward homogenization and insisting on the singularity—and thus, incomparability—of Nazism.[26] Similarly, though less extreme, Zeev Sternhell, Karl Bracher, and A. James Gregor have contended that generic models deepen our understanding of fascism, but must approach "Italy as archetypal and reject Germany as anomalous."[27] Disputes over the fascist minimum, particularly Nazi Germany's place therein, have led some scholars to eschew the concept altogether.[28] Stuart Woolf has argued that excessive use of the term "fascism" has rendered it meaningless, while Gilbert Allardyce famously contended that "there is no such thing as fascism. There are only the men and movements we call by that name."[29]

Taken together, these debates have deepened our understanding of fascism in meaningful ways. Yet, as Robert Paxton has noted, the search "for a perfect definition, by reducing fascism to one ever more finely honed phrase, seems to shut off questions about the origins and course of fascist development rather than open them up."[30] Debates over the fascist minimum tend to atomize the often-dynamic evolution of fascist movements and individuals.[31] They focus on what makes fascism unique; an approach that necessarily discounts the characteristics that fascism shared with conservative, liberal, and Marxist regimes—most notably, at least for the purposes of this study, imperialism.[32]

Until recently, scholars had largely ignored the role that imperial ideologies played in the formation of interwar fascisms. Their justifications, while varied, followed a familiar line of reasoning. Over the course of the nineteenth century, much of Africa and Asia were colonized by various European nation-states. Whether British, French, Belgian, or American, imperial regimes brutalized local populations. Colonizers despoiled natural resources, exploited religious divisions, and suppressed anti-colonial activism, justifying their actions as part of a civilizing mission. Dominated by Western imperialisms, "poorly liberalized"[33] African, Asian, and American colonies evolved differently than their European metropoles, precluding organic fascisms from emerging. As Stanley Payne has contended, colonial territories were "generally under western European tutelage and lacked the national independence or political development to give expression to new political forms."[34]

While extreme, Payne's argumentation illustrates the Eurocentric lens from which scholars traditionally examined interwar fascism.[35] Europeans believed, and in many cases still believe, that political developments at home evolved independently from colonial developments abroad.[36] Seen from this perspective, fascism, as Renzo de Felice has argued, "must be limited geographically, to Western Europe, that is to say, that part of Europe that had undergone a process of liberalization and democratization."[37] Conventional narratives suggest that Europeans controlled interactions between colony and metropole.[38] Imperial actors influenced Europe, but only in specific instances involving violence and disruption the Amritsar Massacre, Rift War, and Fashoda Incident, to name just a few. Beyond these struggles, "empire has no history."[39]

In recent years, colonial, global, and subaltern scholarship have challenged this dichotomization of Europe and empire.[40] Far from an "imagined periphery,"[41] imperialism shaped Western identity, culture, society, gender relations, and politics.[42] "Europe," Nicholas Dirks has argued, "'became' itself through imperial conquest; then it veiled its dependence on the world outside by legitimating and naturalizing empire."[43] British histories, in particular, no longer trumpet the sovereign interpretation: "Insular, presumptively English and safely distant from the taint of colonial possession."[44] Imperialism was constitutive to the making of modern Britain. It was, and continues to be, one of the defining characteristics of what it means to be European, and thus fascist.[45]

Examining the mutually constitutive relationship between Europe and empire has expanded our understanding of interwar fascism in important ways.[46] Recently, historians have put forth a simple, though controversial, question: What if fascism failed to emerge in Europe's colonies because it was already there?[47] That is, what if Western colonialisms served as the ideological and intellectual precursors—archetypes, even—of European fascisms?[48] Mark Mazower, for example, has contended that for Hitler and the Nazis, "empire was an 'ideal'—or, to put it more bluntly, a violent fantasy of racial mastery, a demonstration of prowess of a martial elite bred to lord over hundreds of millions of subjects."[49] Seen through the prism of empire, fascist expansionism in Europe constituted a radical evolution of the imperial rivalries that had animated Western modernity.[50] The Treaty of Versailles stripped the newly created Weimar Republic of its overseas possessions, and so embittered Italian irredentists that many referred to it as a "mutilated victory."[51] At the same time, the victorious Allied powers enlarged their colonial empires.[52] From a colonial perspective, fascists felt as though they "needed to make up for lost time."[53]

Within fascist nation-states, everything—from foreign relations to economic policy and even gender relations—borrowed from imperial ideologies practiced by British, French, and other Western colonialists.[54] In Italy, "fascist policies on gender, war and empire were all closely interconnected."[55] A "larger population, it was argued in Fascist propaganda, was essential if Italy was to fulfil its militaristic and imperial ambitions."[56] Similarly, in Nazi Germany, government officials "constantly invoked the examples offered by other imperial powers."[57] Imperialist notions "of race purity, of women's special duty and ability to preserve Germanness, and of the superiority of German culture and colonization were relatively obvious matches with Nazi thinking."[58] As in India, Algeria, and other European colonies, fascists persecuted internal enemies, particularly those accused of undermining the nation or threatening capital.[59] They also envisioned imperialist expansion as a means of social, economic, and gendered regeneration.[60] In Japan, Manchukuo was seen as "the biopolitical 'lifeline' of Japan, whose elites toyed with novel forms of technocratic planning, resource extraction, and human exploitation (from forced labour from coolies to prostitution, as well as drug trafficking)."[61] Whether adopting particular colonial policies or, as Patrick Bernhard contends, employing them as negative points of reference, Western imperial ideologies influenced fascist aggression in Manchuria, Ethiopia, Republican Spain, China, Czechoslovakia, and elsewhere.[62]

Amid fascist expansion, and particularly after the Italian invasion of Ethiopia (1935), anti-colonialists from around the world challenged "the construction of fascism as a distinctly European phenomenon."[63] In India, Nehru "made the case that India's anticolonialism was linked to antifascist and anti-imperialist struggles in places such as China, Nicaragua, Abyssinia [Ethiopia], Egypt, Republican Spain, and the Gold Coast (present-day Ghana)."[64] Beyond the INC, "few [Indian] communists had any doubt about the existential threat posed by fascism."[65] They knew, Ali Raza has argued, that "the collapse of the Soviet Union and the victory of fascism would not only spell the defeat of socialism—it would also spell the defeat of national liberation struggles around the world."[66] Similarly, outside of South Asia, many Black and African anti-imperialists "experienced the rise of fascism in a personal way and linked it to other instances of racial oppression and imperial aggression."[67] Increasingly, as fascist regimes pursued imperial expansion, many (though not all) anti-colonialists incorporated anti-fascist solidarities within their anti-colonial praxis.[68]

Thus far, the historiographies examining fascist imperialisms (Arendt, Mazower, and Hedinger) and colonial anti-fascisms (Louro, Raza, and Matera) have remained disconnected.[69] To be fair, traversing these analytical categories begets certain challenges: geographic and linguistic barriers; fears of concept deflation (in which fascism's "casual use makes it unavailable for serious political use"[70]); Western historians' insistence that fascism only existed in Europe; regional specializations (in both Europe and South Asia); and nationalist narratives that preclude global and transnational inquiry, to name just a few. As a result of these challenges, no single monograph has examined colonial understandings of the crises of interwar fascism. Scholarship exploring fascist imperialism has ignored narratives of colonial anti-fascism (as well as vice-versa).[71] This disconnect has led to two interrelated gaps in our understanding of interwar fascism.

First, historians have traditionally analyzed colonial anti-fascism through the lens of internationalist solidarity, the nationalist march to independence, or broader narratives of resistance and revolution.[72] While effective, these narratives tend to ignore the ways in which colonial understandings of fascism challenge our conception of interwar Europe. Of course, the burden of reimagining European history should not fall upon analyses of non-Western anti-colonialists and, just as importantly, non-Western scholars. At the same time, "the problem of getting beyond Eurocentric histories remains a shared problem across geographical boundaries."[73] When practicable, I believe that scholars of colonial anti-fascism should transcend historiographical boundaries and engage with narratives of fascist imperialism, in order to (1) determine, beyond colonial contexts, the profundity of colonial anti-fascist thought, and (2) globalize—and complicate—our understanding of interwar Europe.

Second, and in my opinion more problematically, scholarship examining fascist imperialism has yet to critically engage with narratives of colonial anti-fascism. It has employed an "inside-out" methodology that analyzes imperial discourses that pushed European fascisms outward, into Africa, Asia, Europe, and the Americas.[74] By approaching fascist expansionism as a centrifugal European discourse, inside-out scholarship perpetuates—often implicitly—Eurocentric understandings of fascism. In many instances, scholars have explored the ways in which European fascisms affected other parts of the world, but have ignored the inverse—the ways in which these places and their inhabitants understood European fascisms. The disjuncture between colonial and European fascist narratives underscores subaltern arguments that non-Western scholars must become experts on European scholarship but, conversely, that Europe's leading historians are free to ignore the work of their non-Western colleagues.[75] Indeed, "inside-out" methodologies remain one of the primary reasons that "the (still meagre) material on 'global' fascism 'outside Europe' still sees Europe as the natural homeland of fascism."[76]

Addressing these methodological and geographical lacunae, this book analyzes the crises of interwar fascism from the perspective of Indian anti-imperialists. It does not seek to reconceptualize the categories of "fascist imperialism" and "colonial anti-fascism," but rather put them in conversation with one another. It is a history of interwar Europe, as seen from the "outside-in." Long before Mazower, Arendt, and other inside-out scholars, Indian anti-imperialists argued that fascism was colonialism practiced in Europe. To date, however, their contentions have been excluded from mainstream narratives. My approach challenges this provincialism (or Eurocentrism) by analyzing Europe through the lens of non-Western—and specifically Indian—anti-colonialists. Far from universal, Europe "appears different when seen from within the experiences of colonization or inferiorization in specific parts of the world."[77] Analyzing fascism from the outside-in reveals a different Europe—one in which Nazi Germany and imperialist Britain were "brothers in misfortune."[78]

A Colonial History of European Fascisms

Examining Europe through the prism of Indian anti-colonialism blurs the divide between liberal-imperialist and fascist nation-states.[79] Seen from the outside-in, the "Age of Appeasement" (1935–9) was not a titanic clash between Manichean sociopolitical systems, but rather an imperial contest between satisfied and unsatisfied empires. In this book, I contend that the great crises of interwar Europe—the Second Italo-Ethiopian War, Spanish Civil War, Second Sino-Japanese War, Munich Agreement, and the outbreak of the Second World War—were yet another paroxysm of imperial cupidity analogous (though not identical) to the Scramble for Africa and the Treaty of Versailles.[80] Whether fascist, democratic, or imperialist, Europe's great powers (Britain, France, Italy, and Germany) collectively negotiated the fate of smaller nations. Together, they resembled a constellation of synergetic yet antagonistic nation-states with one thing in common: the procurement and maintenance of empire.

To date, many popular and historical narratives of interwar Europe have minimized its complexity by dichotomizing fascism and liberal-imperialism. The Nazis epitomized villainy; thus, their opponents personified virtue. Even today, historical narratives across Europe and the United States often characterize the interwar world through binaries: freedom or fascism, righteousness or evil, progress or reaction, and, finally, imperialist or anti-imperialist. Understanding fascism, liberal-imperialism, and (inevitably) the Second World War in this way misrepresents the victors as well as the vanquished. They were more similar than either would have cared to admit.[81]

In Kenya in the 1950s, British colonialists tortured local populations in concentration camps, well after the horrors of the Holocaust had become known.[82] Claiming themselves the vanguard of a superior civilization, French colonialists brutalized civilians during the Algerian War of Independence (1954–62).[83] Finally, American colonialists enslaved millions of Africans and orchestrated the systematic extermination of native populations.[84] Though ahistorical, these examples underscore the limitations of characterizing liberal-imperialist regimes as defenders of freedom and democracy. From a colonial perspective, they resembled something far closer to European fascisms. This conclusion, though fundamentally incompatible with inside-out histories of Europe, is nevertheless meant to be read alongside them. There were, as Dipesh Chakrabarty has argued, multiple Europes—many of which were paradoxical or even irreconcilable. Analyzing the similarities between fascism and liberal-imperialism was unthinkable within Europe and unmistakable within its empires.

Such fluidity underscores the extent to which Europe appeared different from the outside. This book, consequently, examines one aspect of a provincialized Europe. It is a colonial history of European fascisms.

Examining the similarities between fascism and liberal-imperialism creates an uncomfortable comparison. Whereas fascism has been universally stigmatized (or reduced to a pejorative), imperialism has triumphed. Neocolonial discourses have been legitimated and normalized. As a result, associating fascism with the victors of the Second World War—particularly Britain and the United States, whose governments exist today—will likely spark controversy. To be clear, I am not conflating fascism with liberal-imperialism. Simple comparisons ignore population dynamics and sociocultural nuances, while often homogenizing imperialist and anti-imperialist ideologies.[85] Throughout the interwar era, similar miscalculations emboldened fascist seizures of power—particularly in Germany.[86] I maintain, moreover, that the scope and severity of fascist atrocities eclipsed those committed by imperialists. The Holocaust remains a singular tragedy. Nevertheless, fascism and liberal-imperialism were interrelated. Colonial violence, exploitation, and repression animated fascist expansionism. To understand one, we must explore the other.

In examining European fascisms from the outside-in, my methodology does not seek to replace a Eurocentric approach with a similarly problematic Asian-centric approach.[87] Rather, I hope to highlight the complexity of Europe's pasts by challenging the assumptions of Western historical narratives, which, as Pankaj Mishra has contended, "are no longer a reliable vantage point and may even be dangerously misleading."[88] I believe that to understand interwar Europe, and the crises of fascism in particular, outside-in perspectives must be analyzed alongside traditional, inside-out narratives. The major developments of the interwar era "were the products of global connections and forces rather than simply emanating from events and actors in Europe and the United States."[89] Analyzing the interrelation between fascism and liberal-imperialism is just one example of the ways in which traditional European narratives were often global phenomena.

Indian Anti-fascism

I have chosen India because it is the context with which I am most familiar, but also because it was the famed "jewel in the crown" of the British Empire. In an oft-cited 1901 letter to Arthur Balfour, Lord Curzon plainly declared: "As long as we rule India, we are the greatest power in the world. If we lose it we shall drop straight away to a third-rate power."[90] India was the greatest colony within the greatest empire the world had ever seen. Perhaps more than anywhere else, India epitomized the subjecthood of British imperialism. The experiences of Indian anti-colonialists offer important insights into the ways in which colonial nations understood interwar Europe, and fascism in particular.

Although diverse, Indian anti-colonial attitudes toward fascism evolved into several broad, often intersecting, positions. Some publicly opposed fascism; others sought to manipulate the international situation to extract concessions from the British government; still others admired the ways in which fascist regimes challenged the British Empire. Finally, many conservatives, particularly Gandhian traditionalists, concentrated on domestic issues and largely ignored the rise of fascism.[91] A comprehensive examination of each of these positions is beyond the scope of this work. My research, consequently, focuses primarily on Indian opposition to fascism—what I call Indian anti-fascism.[92]

Anti-fascists belonged to several different anti-colonial organizations. The largest and most influential was the INC, led popularly by Mohandas K. Gandhi and Jawaharlal Nehru.[93] However, although claiming to serve the entire subcontinent, the elites of the Congress largely ignored "the politics of the people"[94] (or "the domain of subaltern politics"). Leading anti-colonialists such as Nehru were often educated in elite London schools, disdained traditional Indian customs, and were, as many South Asian historians have contended, a colonial bourgeoisie.[95] Throughout the interwar era, amid celebrated civil disobedience campaigns such as the Salt March (1931), the Congress "withdrew its support for peasant movements whenever they threatened Congress's control."[96] More than a decade after independence, in 1960, Nehru still referred to himself as "the last Englishman to rule in India."[97]

Indian anti-fascism was also remarkably homosocial.[98] Indeed, although the men that helmed the Congress forged linkages with women, they also "tried to impose traditional gender roles and values."[99] Anti-colonial women were often restricted to local advocacy and organization (such as the *Mahila Samitis*), while men dominated international relations and foreign policy.[100] Even as women increasingly aspired to leadership roles within the Congress, the "progressive commitments of both [Gandhi and Nehru] were constrained by their traditional if nationalist ideas of the Indian woman."[101] Trailblazing, avant-garde anti-colonialists such as Sarojini Naidu and Kamaladevi Chattopadhyay "transgressed stereotypical gender roles, but they were few and exceptional."[102] By the late 1930s, as the Congress ruptured along political and ideological lines, "the agenda for women and that for the nation diverged."[103] "The urgency of the nationalist struggle overrode the priorities of the feminist agenda."[104] Accordingly, when I use the phrase "Indian anti-fascism," it primarily describes the elite men of the independence movement, not necessarily the Indian nation.

Though varied, Indian anti-fascists' characterizations of fascism shared a similar, often Marxist, dialectic.[105] Rooted in Europe's intellectual, political, and sociocultural traditions, fascism represented the denouement of colonial violence. For centuries, Europeans had constructed "Europe" upon a foundation of brutalization and repression. Liberalism, in particular, propounded a politics of difference that circumscribed universal liberal ideas (freedom, liberty, and self-determination, among them) to Europe.[106] Colonial "'others' were deemed deficient in normative rationality, and thus unworthy of the political rights and civic inclusions which liberalism in theory offers up."[107] At the same time Whiggish narratives extolled Western liberal and industrial ascendancy, liberal empires exploited resources, cultures, and human ingenuity to fuel an imperial machine that demanded evermore conquest. This process was both ruthlessly efficient and systemized—most famously during the Berlin Conference (1884).

Eventually, as "untouched" or "empty" space across Africa and Asia dwindled, conflict ensued. Rather than perish, however, Europe's age of empire endured the destruction of the First World War. Afterward, the Paris Peace Conference frustrated territorial expansionists in several countries—Italy and Germany, in particular. With little recourse, and facing political, social, gendered, and cultural revolutions (both real and imagined) Mussolini, Hitler, and other fascists embraced radical ideologies that circumvented expansionist restrictions by bringing colonialism home to Europe. From an anti-imperialist perspective, fascism was colonialism practiced in Europe. Fascists appropriated the violence, exploitation, and racio-religious stratification of liberal-imperialism (or "democratic-imperialism"[108]) and practiced it in Europe, in what had traditionally been the liberal-democratic sphere. As Chattopadhyay put it:

> Hitler is introducing the colonization method to Europe and because it is in Europe you see the horror of it. . . . In India we have known concentration camps and bombs from planes flying over our villages killing our women and children. . . . We have suffered dictatorship in India and from a democratic institution, the British parliament. We need no propaganda to know Nazism.[109]

Initially, the old liberal empires (particularly Britain, France, and the United States) adopted conventional methods of coexisting with rival colonial empires—negotiation, intimidation, association, or isolation. The new fascist empires, however, often demanded territorial expansion at the expense of the old empires. Fascist Italy invaded Corfu (1923), manipulated the Albanian economy (1926–7), and terrorized the Senussi of Libya (1923–32). After the Nazi seizure of power, Hitler rearmed the Wehrmacht (1933), remilitarized the Rhineland (1936), and would soon menace Austria and Czechoslovakia. Finally, the Empire of Japan overwhelmed Manchuria (1931), invaded Jehol in Northeast China (1933), and created a puppet state (eventually known as *Mengjian*) in Inner Mongolia (1936).[110] Each of these expansionist—or at the very least, irredentist—ambitions threatened British, French, and American imperial hegemony. As antagonisms mounted, Europe's colonial powers increasingly prepared for war. The old empires would fight the new empires.

~

Indian anti-fascism spanned the globe. Rather than examine each individual articulation, this book is divided into five interrelated case studies, each of which investigates a different fascist regime from the perspective of Indian anti-fascists (as well as their wider political context).[111] Chapter 1 explores the Second Italo-Ethiopian War (1935) from the perspective of Rajani Palme Dutt, one of the leaders of the Communist Party of Great Britain. Together with Indian anti-fascists around the world, Palme Dutt denounced Benito Mussolini, the League of Nations, the British Empire, and the unconscious imperialism of European anti-fascists.[112] Scholars have traditionally examined the ways in which the Second Italo-Ethiopian War crystallized the divide between the (soon-to-be) Axis powers and the Anglo-French alliance. Seen, however, from the perspective of Indian anti-colonialism, the conflict also exhibited the interrelation between fascism and liberal-imperialism. British, French, and German nonintervention in Ethiopia represented yet another instance of New Imperialist collaboration. Fascist and liberal-imperialist powers collectively negotiated—or, at the very least, tolerated—colonial aggression abroad so as not to spark a continental war over "black Africa."

Chapter 2 examines the Spanish Civil War (1936) from the perspective of Jawaharlal Nehru. Only months after the fall of Ethiopia, a group of military generals organized a coup against the Second Spanish Republic. Scholars have since debated whether Anglo-French nonintervention in the Spanish Civil War was a desperate attempt to prevent another world war or a nefarious scheme to support Nationalist General Francisco Franco.[113] In India, anti-fascists contended that Anglo-French nonintervention reflected the interrelation between fascism and liberal-imperialism. Nehru, in particular, characterized the Spanish Civil War not as a conflict between fascism and communism—as it was often popularly understood—nor even a struggle between democracy and militarism. Rather, it was part of a global war of self-determination that encompassed the Congress-led campaign for independence. Wedded to imperialist oppression, and thus hostile to self-determination, Britain and France pursued nonintervention. Their colonial interests, Nehru maintained, bound them to Europe's fascist powers.

Chapter 3 analyzes the Second Sino-Japanese War (1937) from the perspective of Subhas Bose, a leading anti-colonialist and eventual leader of the Indian National Army. Less than one year after the outbreak of the Spanish Civil War, the Empire of Japan invaded China. Scholars have traditionally portrayed the British Government's response to the conflict as supportive of China yet limited in its support due to a variety of factors, including an overextended military, the policy of appeasement, and a preoccupation with the rise of Nazi Germany. In India, anti-fascists contended that British colonialism was largely responsible for the Japanese invasion of China. Certain parts of China—Hong Kong and the treaty ports, in particular—were controlled by the British government. Bose contended that these holdings, and British imperial hegemony more broadly, had inspired Japanese expansionism, and underscored the extent to which Japanese fascism sought to emulate British imperialism.

Chapter 4 explores the Anglo-German Munich Agreement (1938) from the perspective of Mohandas K. Gandhi. For nearly a century, historians have characterized the Munich Agreement as a betrayal of time-honored principles, a shrewd political maneuver that facilitated rearmament, a product of limited military and political alternatives, or a reflection of British anti-communism. Each of these arguments has portrayed the Munich Agreement as an anomalous or, at the very least, exceptional event in the history of Britain. However, from the perspective of Indian anti-colonialists, it was yet another instance of British colonialists negotiating the sovereignty of another nation. Led by Gandhi, Indian anti-fascists contended that the Munich Agreement reflected the similarities between British colonialism and German Nazism, insomuch as it was great-power imperialism practiced in Europe.

Chapter 5 examines the outbreak of the Second World War in Europe (1939) from the perspective of M. N. Roy, famed revolutionary and the founder of the League of Radical Congressmen. Beginning with the German invasion of Poland, Europe's great powers waged war against one another. Historians have generally depicted this war as a clash between disparate sociopolitical systems or, as British prime minister Neville Chamberlain contended, a war "against brute force, bad faith, injustice, oppression and persecution." By contrast, Indian anti-fascists characterized the conflict as a civil war between rival imperialisms. Unlike many Marxists, however, Roy contended that supporting British imperialism would precipitate Indian independence, insomuch as the nature of the conflict—its scope and destructiveness—would render Britain morally, economically, and politically insolvent. Seen from the outside-in, the German invasion of Poland engulfed Europe in a punishing civil war that would inaugurate the era of decolonization.

In each of these case studies, it is important to note that concepts such as fascism, socialism, liberalism, and imperialism were understood in different, often contradictory, ways. Fascism and anti-fascism, in particular, were multivalent political ideologies that evolved with and against the contours of interwar internationalism. "What was so unique about the 1920s and 1930s," Michele Louro has argued, "was the ability to move across and within . . . categories and to rethink solidarities beyond the rigid frameworks afforded by strict orthodoxies or institutionalization."[114] There was no monolithic Indian anti-fascism. The individuals examined in these case studies possessed kaleidoscopic Weltanschauungen. Some, like Bose, did not necessarily consider themselves anti-fascist (and would go on to support fascist regimes). Others, like Roy, alleged that Gandhi and the INC were fascist.[115] Additionally, whereas Nehru and Gandhi were internationally acclaimed, Roy—and to a lesser extent Dutt—had by the outbreak of the Second World War become marginal political figures. When relevant, I have attempted to engage with these narratives. Yet many of the political debates animating Indian anti-imperialism are beyond the scope of this work. My lodestar remains analyzing fascism through the prism of Indian anti-colonialism. Whether acclaimed or inconspicuous—erroneous or sibylline—Dutt, Nehru, Bose, Gandhi, and Roy propounded ideas that deepen our understanding of interwar Europe.

~

During his trip to Barcelona, Nehru attended an anti-fascist reception held in his honor. Standing before Republican president Manuel Azaña, he proclaimed that India and Spain were part of the same struggle; both nations "were fighting for their independence, even if in a different manner."[116] While at times misguided, this conviction deepens our understanding of interwar Europe. Seen from the outside-in, fascism and liberal-imperialism appeared interrelated. Mussolini, Hitler, and other fascists radicalized colonial ideologies and practiced them in Europe. Fascism, accordingly, laid bare the hypocrisy of imperial claims to a superior civilization. Colonialism was a savage institution; many colonialists, however, ignored or rationalized this savagery until it threatened Europe.

Only months before his death, Nobel Prize–winning poet Rabindranath Tagore condemned the vacuousness of European civilization. Gleaming city-centers, he argued, had been constructed upon a foundation of terror. Inevitably, Europe would crumble, revealing a rotten core:

> When the stream of their centuries' administration will have run dry at least, what a waste of mud and filth they will leave behind them. I had at one time believed that the springs of civilisation would issue out of the heart of Europe. And today when I am about to quit the world, that stubborn faith has gone bankrupt altogether.[117]

The Europe Tagore denounced has yet to fully enter the mainstream of Western histories.[118] This book addresses this imbalance by examining interwar Europe from the perspective of Indian anti-colonialisms.

Notes

1 Thomas Mann, "An Appeal to Reason," in *The Weimar Republic Sourcebook*, ed. Anton Kaes, Martin Jay, and Edward Dimendberg (Berkley: University of California Press, 1994), 154.

2 Quoted in William Manchester, *The Last Lion, Winston Spencer Churchill: Alone, 1932–1940* (New York: Dell Publishers, 1989), 297.

3 Arthur Herman, *Gandhi and Churchill: The Epic Rivalry That Destroyed an Empire and Forged Our Age* (New York: Bantam Books, 2008), 418.

4 Catalan for "expansion," the Eixample is a district in the center of Barcelona.

5 Ian Patterson, *Guernica: And Total War* (London: Profile, 2008); Robert Stradling, *Your Children Will Be Next: Bombing and Propaganda in the Spanish Civil War, 1936–1939* (Cardiff: University of Wales Press, 2008).

6 Quoted in Nicholas Rankin, *Telegram from Guernica: The Extraordinary Life of George Steer, War Correspondent* (London: Faber & Faber, 2013), 5.

7 Basque president José Antonio Aguirre famously described the attack as a campaign of "unprecedented viciousness." See: Andrew Durgan, *The Spanish Civil War* (Basingstoke: Palgrave Macmillan, 2008).

8 Jawaharlal Nehru, "The Bombing of Open Towns," in *Jawaharlal Nehru: The Unity of India: Collected Writings 1937–1940* (New York: The John Day Company, 1942), 281.

9 Churchill believed that fascism undermined British global ascendancy—enshrined, as it was, over the course of the nineteenth century. He consequently advocated

confronting fascism, even as his own party espoused a more conciliatory approach. Richard Toye, *Churchill's Empire: The World That Made Him and the World He Made* (London: Pan Books, 2015).

10 Jawaharlal Nehru, "Food for Spain," in *The Unity of India*, 266.

11 Dipesh Chakrabarty, *Provincializing Europe: Postcolonial Thought and Historical Difference* (Princeton: Princeton University Press, 2008), xiv.

12 Peter Hulme, "Subversive Archipelagos: Colonial Discourse and the Break-Up of Continental Theory," *Disposition* 14, no. 36/38 (1989): 3. First seen in Antoinette Burton, "Introduction: On the Inadequacy and the Indispensability of the Nation," in *After the Imperial Turn: Thinking with and through the Nation*, ed. Antoinette Burton (Durham: Duke University Press, 2003), 3.

13 There are, of course, several notable exceptions. Perhaps most famously, A. J. P. Taylor contended that Hitler lacked a premeditated plan of aggression and blundered into the Second World War. A. J. P. Taylor, *The Origins of the Second World War* (London: Hamish Hamilton, 1961).

14 Studs Terkel popularized the phrase in his 1984 Pulitzer Prize–winning book: *"The Good War": An Oral History of World War II.*

15 Renzo de Felice, for example, has contended that Mussolini still considered himself a socialist in 1919. Renzo de Felice, *Interpretations of Fascism* (Cambridge, MA: Harvard University Press, 1977). See also Zeev Sternhell, *Neither Right Nor Left: Fascist Ideology in France* (Princeton, NJ: Princeton University Press, 1996).

16 Geoff Eley has contended that "Rather than any longer-term societal pathologies or deep-historical structures of political backwardness . . . it was the contrasting outcomes of the war and the associated political settlements that primarily enabled the opening toward fascism." Geoff Eley, *Nazism as Fascism: Violence, Ideology and the Ground of Consent in Germany 1930-1945* (London: Routledge, 2013), 207. First seen in David Roberts, *Fascist Interactions: Proposals for a New Approach to Fascism and Its Era, 1919-1945* (New York: Berghahn Books, 2016), 5. By contrast, Zeev Sternhell has argued that "In the fascism of the interwar period, in Mussolini's regime as in all other western European Fascist movements, there was not a single major idea that had not gradually come to fruition in the quarter of a century preceding August 1914." Zeev Sternhell, *The Birth of Fascist Ideology: From Cultural Rebellion to Political Revolution* (Princeton: Princeton University Press, 1995), 6.

17 Roberts contends that taking fascism seriously entails moving "beyond an earlier tendency to dismiss fascism, in a moralistic and triumphalist way, as a mere 'historical negativity.'" Roberts, *Fascist Interactions*, 6-7. See also Adrian Lyttelton, *The Seizure of Power: Fascism in Italy 1919-1929* (London: Weidenfeld and Nicolson, 1973); Michael Mann, *Fascists* (Cambridge: Cambridge University Press, 2006). Richard Bosworth, *The Italian Dictatorship: Problems and Perspectives in the Interpretation of Mussolini and Fascism* (London: Arnold, 2007).

18 Hannah Arendt, *The Origins of Totalitarianism* (London: Penguin Classics, 1951); Carl J. Friedrich and Zbigniew Brzezinski, *Totalitarian Dictatorship and Autocracy* (New York: Praeger, 1965); Carl Friedrich and Zbigniew Brzezinski, "Fascism as Totalitarianism: Men and Technology," in *The Place of Fascism in European History*, ed. Gilbert Allardyce (Englewood Cliffs, NJ: Prentice Hall, 1971), 67–85.

19 Barrington Moore, *Social Origins of Dictatorship and Democracy: Lord and Peasant in the Making of the Modern World* (Boston: Beacon Press, 1966); Ernst Nolte, *Three Faces of Fascism: Action Francaise, Italian Fascism, National Socialism* (New York: Henry Hold & Company, 1966) Barrington Moore, "Fascism as the Heritage of Conservative Modernization," in *The Place of Fascism in European History*, 127–43; Wolfgang Sauer, "Fascism as the Revolt of 'the Losers,'" in *The Place of Fascism in European History*, 162–74; Roger Griffin, *The Nature of Fascism* (New York: Routledge, 1991); Roger Griffin, *Fascism* (Oxford: Oxford University Press, 1995); Stanley G. Payne, *A History of Fascism, 1914–1945* (Madison: University of Wisconsin Press, 1995); Philip Morgan, *Fascism in Europe, 1919–1945* (New York: Routledge, 2002); Mann, *Fascists.*

20 Philip Morgan has created an analytical framework that divides the rise of interwar fascism into two waves separated by the Great Depression. Robert Paxton, by contrast, has constructed an anatomy of fascism that contains five potential stages of development: (1) creation, (2) rooting in political systems, (3) the seizure of power, (4) the exercise of power, and (5) either radicalization or entropy. Robert Paxton, *The Anatomy of Fascism* (New York: Vintage Books, 2004).

21 Federico Finchelstein, *From Fascism to Populism in History* (Berkeley: University of California Press, 2017); Ishay Landa, "The Magic of the Extreme: On Fascism, Modernity, and Capitalism," *The Journal of Holocaust Research* 33, no. 1 (2019): 43–63; Nicos Poulantzas, *Fascism and Dictatorship: The Third International and the Problem of Fascism* (London: Verso Books, 2019); Enzo Traverso, *The New Faces of Fascism: Populism and the Far Right* (London: Verso, 2019).

22 Ernst Nolte, "Fascism as an Antimodernist Revolt," in *The Place of Fascism in European History*, 151. It should be noted that Nolte has rejected anti-Marxism as a comprehensive explanation for fascism. Instead, he defines fascism as "anti-Marxism which seeks to destroy the enemy by the evolvement of a radically opposed and yet related ideology and by the use of almost identical and yet typically modified methods, always, however, within the unyielding framework of national self-assertion and autonomy." Nolte, "Fascism as an Antimodernist Revolt," 151. See also Ernst Nolte, *Die Krise des liberalen Systems und die faschistischen Bewegungen* (München: Piper, 1968).

23 Griffin, *The Nature of Fascism*, 44.

24 One of the more convincing interpretations of fascism was put forth by George Mosse, who contended that rather than a consistent articulated philosophy,

fascism revolved around a series of mobilizing passions. George Mosse, *The Crisis of German Ideology: Intellectual Origins of the Third Reich* (New York: Grosset & Dunlap, 1964). First seen in Paxton, *Anatomy of Fascism*, 41.

25 Mann, *Fascists*, 5–8. Payne's definition of fascism includes three sections. "First, there were the fascist negations: antiliberalism, anticommunism, and anti-conservatism (though with the understanding that fascist groups were willing to undertake temporary alliances with groups from any other sector, most commonly with the right). Second, there was fascist ideology and goals: the creation of a new nationalist authoritarian state based not merely on traditional principles or models, the organization of some new kind of regulated, multiclass, integrated national economic structure (whether called national corporatist, national socialist, or national syndicalist), the goal of empire or a radical change in the nation's relationship with other powers, and the specific espousal of an idealist, voluntarist creed (normally involving the attempt to realize a new form of modem, self-determined, secular culture). Finally, there was fascist style and organization: An emphasis on esthetic structure of meetings, symbols, and political choreography stressing romantic and mystical aspects, an attempted mass mobilization with militarization of political relationships and style and with the goal of a mass party militia, the positive evaluation and use of, or willingness to use, violence, an extreme stress on the masculine principle and male dominance (while espousing the organic view of society), the exaltation of youth above other phases of life and emphasizing the conflict of generations (at least in effecting the initial political transformation), and a specific tendency toward an authoritarian, charismatic, personal style of command, whether or not the command is to some degree initially elective." Stanley Payne, *Fascism: Comparison and Definition* (Madison: University of Wisconsin Press, 1983), 7–8.

26 Arendt, *The Origins of Totalitarianism*; Carl Friedrich, *Totalitarianism; Proceedings of a Conference Held at the American Academy of Arts and Sciences, March 1953* (Cambridge: Harvard University Press, 1954); Ian Kershaw, *The Nazi Dictatorship: Problems and Perspectives of Interpretation* (London: Edward Arnold, 1985); Ian Kershaw, *Hitler, the Germans, and the Final Solution* (New Haven: Yale University Press, 2008). In his excellent work, David Roberts notes that with some notable exceptions, "German students of Nazism have tended not to treat generic fascism." Roberts, *Fascist Interactions*, 8. Prominent exceptions include Arnd Bauerkämper and Wolfgang Wippermann.

27 Roberts, *Fascist Interactions*, 8. Zeev Sternhell famously contended that "fascism can in no way be identified with Nazism." Zeev Sternhell, *The Birth of Fascist Ideology: From Cultural Rebellion to Political Revolution* (Princeton: Princeton University Press, 1994), 5. See also A. James Gregor, *Interpretations of Fascism* (Morristown, NJ: General Learning Press, 1974); Antonio Costa Pinto, *Salazar's*

Dictatorship and European Fascism: Problems of Interpretation (New York: Columbia University Press, 1995); Richard J. B. Bosworth, *The Oxford Handbook of Fascism* (Oxford: Oxford University Press, 2009).

28 Roberts describes Nazi Germany as "the elephant in the room; can we even dare to talk about the generic or aggregate in light of all-too-obvious sense in which Nazi Germany ended up overwhelming?" Roberts, *Fascist Interactions*, 8.

29 Gilbert Allardyce, "What Fascism Is Not: Thoughts on the Deflation of a Concept," *The American Historical Review* 84, no. 2 (1979): 368. See also Stuart Woolf, *Fascism in Europe* (London: Methuen, 1981).

30 Paxton, *Anatomy of Fascism*, 14.

31 Impermanence defined fascist ideology. As Stanley Payne has noted, "definition bedeviled the original Italian Fascists from the beginning, since they developed a formal codified set of doctrines only ex post facto, some years after Mussolini came to power, and then only in part." Payne, *Fascism: Comparison and Definition*, 4. Similarly, Matthew Lyons has contended that fascism must be understood as a protean phenomenon: "Like liberalism and socialism, then, fascism may be said to exist 'in multiple variations . . . [to evolve] dynamically to address new historical conditions,' and to appeal to further audiences in a wide breadth of ways." Matthew Lyons, "Two Ways of Looking at Fascism," *Socialism and Democracy* 22, no. 2 (2008): 123.

32 Payne's approach illustrates the ways in which the search for a fascist minimum has largely precluded broader analyses of fascism and imperialism: "Fascism is said to have been imperialist by definition, but this is not entirely clear from a comparative reading of the programs of diverse fascist movements. Most were indeed imperialist, but all types of political movements and systems seem to have produced imperialist policies, while several fascist movements had little interest in and even rejected new imperial ambitions. All, however, sought a new order in foreign affairs, a new relationship or set of alliances with respect to contemporary states and forces, and a new status for their nation in Europe and the world." Payne, *Fascism: Comparison and Definition*, 10.

33 Griffin, *The Nature of Fascism*, 146. Griffin nevertheless contends that fascism was not an intrinsically European phenomenon.

34 Payne, *A History of Fascism*, 354. Similarly, Walter Laqueur has contended that "One of the few issues on which there was a consensus at the time was the assumption that fascism was a European phenomenon. This seems true even now in regard to 'historical fascism.' At that time, fascism in very backward countries was technically impossible because the masses could not be mobilized and propaganda and terror were not yet sufficiently effective." Walter Laqueur, *Fascism: Past, Present, Future* (Oxford: Oxford University Press, 1997), 14.

35 See Arendt, *The Origins of Totalitarianism*; Friedrich, *Totalitarianism*; Kershaw, *The Nazi Dictatorship*; Gregor, *Interpretations of Fascism*; Payne, *A History of Fascism*;

Sternhell, *The Birth of Fascist Ideology*; Griffin, *The Nature of Fascism*; Morgan, *Fascism in Europe*; Mann, *Fascists*; Eley, *Nazism as Fascism*; Paxton, *The Anatomy of Fascism.*

36 Chakrabarty, *Provincializing Europe*, 3–26.

37 Renzo de Felice and Michael Ledeen, *Fascism: An Informal Introduction to its Theory and Practice* (New Brunswick: Transaction Books, 1976), 89. De Felice has also contended that fascism possessed an "inseparable link with the crises (moral, economic, social and political) of European society following the First World War." Quoted in: Paxton, *Anatomy of Fascism*, 297.

38 As Dipesh Chakrabarty has contended, European liberal, conservative, and Marxist conceptions of uneven development have been globalized, rather than understood as a provisional way of organizing information. Chakrabarty, *Provincializing Europe*, xi. See also Edward W. Said, *Orientalism* (New York: Pantheon Books, 1978); Partha Chatterjee, *Nationalist Thought and the Colonial World: A Derivative Discourse?* (Minneapolis: University of Minnesota Press, 1986); Frederick Cooper, and Ann Laura Stoler, *Tensions of Empire: Colonial Cultures in a Bourgeois World* (Berkeley: University of California Press, 1997).

39 Antoinette Burton, *The Trouble with Empire: Challenges to Modern British Imperialism* (New York: Oxford University Press, 2015), 1.

40 It is important to note that these arguments are not necessarily new. Franz Fanon, for example, contended in 1961 that "Europe is literally the creation of the Third World." Frantz Fanon, *The Wretched of the Earth* (New York: Grove Press, 1963), 58. See also the scholarship of Rozina Visram, Peter Fryer, Partha Chatterjee, Bernard Cohn, Frederick Cooper, Albert Hourani, Albert Memmi, Edward Said, Susan Kent, Dipesh Chakrabarty, Ranajit Guha, Kathleen Wilson, Michael Fisher, Ann Laura Stoler, Antoinette Burton, Lyn Innes, and Elleke Boehmer, to name just a few.

41 Sasha Davis, *The Empires' Edge: Militarization, Resistance, and Transcending Hegemony in the Pacific* (Athens: University of Georgia Press, 2015), 64.

42 As Antoinette Burton has argued, distinctions between colonizer and colonized "needed constant vigilance." Burton, *The Trouble with Empire*, 7.

43 Nicholas Dirks, *The Scandal of Empire: India and the Creation of Imperial Britain* (Cambridge: Belknap Press, 2006), 329.

44 Antoinette Burton, "Connective Tissue: South Asians and the Making of Postcolonial Histories in Britain," in *India in Britain: South Asian Networks and Connections, 1858–1950*, ed. Susheila Nasta (Basingstoke: Palgrave Macmillan, 2012), 194.

45 Tim Jacoby has contended that European fascisms drew inspiration from transnational and global discourses: "Seeing fascism as quintessentially European overlooks the fact that its ideological development was subject to a wide range of influences from outside the continent. This includes the social dynamics behind

the rise of Japanese military power (demonstrated by its victory over Russia in 1905) and the mythical communitarianism of Indian Aryanism. Moreover, even if the predominantly European character of fascism is accepted, this does not . . . necessarily mean that other countries 'could not experience relatively similar socio-economic strains." Tim Jacoby, "Global Fascism: Geography, Timing, Support, and Strategy," *Journal of Global History* 11, no. 3 (2016): 454. Similarly, in an article describing the relationship between fascism and imperialism, Reto Hoffman has argued that "as the historiography on the imperial turn has shown, imperialism forged national identities—and nationalism. Whether it was victories over 'natives,' colonial literature, or racial thinking, imperialist practices had a profound impact on metropolitan culture and helped to create popular consent around the nation." Reto Hoffman, "The Fascist New-Old Order," *Journal of Global History* 12, no. 2 (2017): 167. See also: Roger Eatwell, "Explaining Fascism and Ethnic Cleansing: The Three Dimensions of Charisma and the Four Dark Sides of Nationalism," *Political Studies Review* 4, no. 2 (2006): 263–78.

46 In recent years, scholars have increasingly explored the extent to which fascist movements communicated with one another. Driven, Bernhard has contended, "not only by strategic considerations, but also by a shared racist ideology, these regimes collaborated and learned from each other precisely because they understood that they needed each other to overthrow the existing post-war order established by the Treaty of Versailles, and to fight against 'international Jewry,' which the Nazis believed threatened the racial integrity of their own people." Bernhard, 207. See also: Ana Antic, Johanna Conterio, and Dora Vargha, "Conclusion: Beyond Liberal Internationalism," *Contemporary European History* 25, no. 2 (2016): 359–71; Giorgia Priorelli, "'The Founders of a European Era'? The Fascist and Falangist Plans for Italy and Spain in the New Nazi Order," *Modern Italy* 24, no. 3 (2019): 317–30.

47 In posing this question, many scholars have moved beyond debates over generic fascism and begun examining "fascism in the empire and, conversely, the empire in fascism." Reto Hoffman and Daniel Hedinger, "Editorial—Axis Empires: Towards a Global History of Fascist Imperialism," *Journal of Global History* 12, no. 2 (2017): 163.

48 Louise Young, *Japan's Total Empire: Manchuria and the Culture of Wartime Imperialism* (Berkely: University of California Press, 1998); Stein Ugelvik Larsen, *Fascism Outside Europe: The European Impulse against Domestic Conditions in the Diffusion of Global Fascism* (New York: Columbia University Press, 2001); Federico Finchelstein, *Transatlantic Fascism; Ideology, Violence, and the Sacred in Argentina and Italy, 1919–1945* (Durham: Duke University Press, 2009); Shelley Baranowski, *Nazi Empire: German Colonialism and Imperialism from Bismarck to Hitler* (Cambridge: Cambridge University Press, 2011); Daniel

Hedinger, "Universal Fascism and Its Global Legacy: Italy's and Japan's Entangled History in the Early 1930s," *Fascism* 2, no. 2 (2013): 141–60; Haggai Erlich, "The Tiger and the Lion: Fascism and Ethiopia in Arab Eyes," in *Arab Responses to Fascism and Nazism*, ed. Israel Gershoni (Austin: University of Texas Press, 2014), 271–88; Birthe Kundrus, "Colonialism, Imperialism, National Socialism: How Imperial Was the Third Reich?" in *German Colonialism in a Global Age*, ed. Geoff Eley and Bradley Naranch (Durham: Duke University Press, 2014), 330–46; Benjamin Zachariah, "A Voluntary Gleichschaltung? Indian Perspectives Towards a Non-Eurocentric Understanding of Fascism," *Journal of Transcultural Studies 2014* 2 (2014): 63–100; Reto Hofmann, *The Fascist Effect Japan and Italy, 1915–1952* (Ithaca, NY: Cornell University Press, 2015); Jens Steffek, "Fascist Internationalism," *Millennium: Journal of International Studies* 44, no. 1 (2015): 3–22; Jacoby, "Global Fascism: Geography, Timing, Support, and Strategy"; Madeleine Herren, "Fascist Internationalism," in *Internationalism: A Twentieth Century History*, ed. Glenda Sluga and Patricia Clavin (Cambridge: Cambridge University Press, 2017), 191–212; Michael Ebner, "Fascist Violence and the 'Ethnic Reconstruction' of Cyrenaica (Libya), 1922–1934," in *Violence, Colonialism and Empire in the Modern World*, ed. Philip Dwyer and Amanda Nettelbeck (London: Palgrave Macmillan, 2018), 197–218; Roberta Pergher, *Mussolini's Nation-Empire* (Cambridge: Cambridge University Press, 2018); Holger Weiss, "Against Japanese and Italian Imperialism: The Anti-War Campaigns of Communist International Trade Union Organizations, 1931–1936," *Journal of Social History and the History of Social Movements* 60 (2018): 121–46; Giuseppe Finaldi, "Fascism, Violence, and Italian Colonialism," *The Journal of Holocaust Research* 33, no. 1 (2019): 22–42; Sean Andrew Wempe, *Revenants of the German Empire: Colonial Germans, Imperialism, and the League of Nations* (London: Oxford University Press, 2019); Kasper Braskén, "'Whether Black or White—United in the Fight!' Connecting the Resistance against Colonialism, Racism, and Fascism in the European Metropoles, 1926–1936," *Twentieth Century Communism* 18 (2020): 126–49; Rachel O'Sullivan, "Integration and Division: Nazi Germany and the 'Colonial Other' in Annexed Poland," *Journal of Genocide Research* 22, no. 4 (2020): 437–58; Thomas Linehan, *British Fascism 1918–39: Parties, Ideology and Culture* (Manchester: Manchester University Press, 2021); Sven Reichardt, "Fascism's Stages: Imperial Violence, Entanglement, and Processualization," *Journal of the History of Ideas* 82, no. 1 (2021): 85–107.

49 Mark Mazower, *Hitler's Empire: How the Nazis Ruled Europe* (New York: Penguin Press, 2008), 2. See also Hannah Arendt's "Boomerang Thesis," in *The Origins of Totalitarianism*.

50 Axis imperialism, Reto Hoffman has contended, "was not the repudiation of liberal imperialism but its consummation." Hoffman, 167. Additionally, it is important

to remember, as Patrick Bernhard has argued, that "many Nazi leaders were born in the late nineteenth century, during the heyday of European imperialism." Bernhard, 208.

51 Famed Italian poet Gabriele D'Annunzio popularized the phrase "mutilated victory."

52 Mazower, *Hitler's Empire*, 2. During the Paris Peace Conference, Britain acquired Transjordan, Iraq, the Palestine Mandate, and many former German colonies.

53 Mazower, *Hitler's Empire*, 2.

54 Hedinger, for example, has characterized fascist imperialisms as postcolonial phenomena: "Seen from the perspective of the dreams shared by the three Axis powers, I suggest that it would be more fitting to speak of 'post-colonial imperialism.'... When I use the term 'post-colonial' here, I underscore a connotation far less positive than that associated today with 'post-colonial studies,' because the post-colonial order which the Axis powers strove to establish was always coupled with the desire to revive imperial rule. Their efforts were directed against other empires, primarily the British, and were not in favour of those being repressed. In the world of nascent decolonization and genuine anti-colonial movements, such ideas were surely anachronistic. But for many in the 1930s they looked new, suitable for carrying imperialism over into a post-colonial world." Daniel Hedinger, "The Imperial Nexus: The Second World War and the Axis in Global Perspective," *Journal of Global History* 12, no. 2 (2017): 191.

55 Perry Wilson, "Empire, Gender and the 'Home Front' in Fascist Italy," *Women's History Review* 16, no. 4 (2007): 487. See also: Gaia Giuliani, *Race, Nation and Gender in Modern Italy: Intersectional Representations in Visual Culture* (New York: Palgrave Macmillan, 2019).

56 Ibid.

57 Bernhard, 208. Similarly, Hedinger contends that the imperial nexus not only brought the Axis powers together but also bound ideology (fascism) to geopolitical aims (imperialism)." Hedinger, "The Imperial Nexus," 186.

58 Lora Wildenthal, *German Women for Empire, 1884–1945* (Durham: Duke University Press, 2001), 201. During the Nazi Regime "violence, death, and sex were closely intertwined and seemingly dependent on each other. . . . Sexual violence [was] a result of militarized, hetero-nationalist hegemonic masculinity and act[ed] as an expression of supreme dominance." Franziska Karpiński and Elysia Ruvinsky, "Sexual Violence in the Nazi Genocide: Gender, Law, and Ideology," in *Genocide: New Perspectives on its Causes, Courses and Consequences*, ed. Uğur Ümit Üngör (Amsterdam: Amsterdam University Press, 2016), 149.

59 Hoffman, "The Fascist New-Old Order," 167.

60 Liam Liburd, "Beyond the Pale: Whiteness, Masculinity and Empire in the British Union of Fascists, 1932–1940," *Fascism: Journal of Comparative Fascist Studies*

7, no. 2 (2018): 275–96; Lorenzo Fabbri, "Queer Neorealism: Luchino Visconti's Ossessione and the Cinema Conspiracy Against Fascism," *Screen* 60, no. 1 (2019): 1–24; Julie Gottlieb, *Feminine Fascism: Women in Britain's Fascist Movement, 1923–1945* (London: Bloomsbury, 2021).

61 Hoffman, "The Fascist New-Old Order," 175. See also Ethan Mark, "Fascisms Seen and Unseen: The Netherlands, Japan, Indonesia, and the Relationalities of Imperial Crisis," in *Visualizing Fascism: The Twentieth Century Rise of the Global Right* (Durham: Duke University Press, 2020), 183–210; Edwin Michielsen, "Fighting Fascism with 'Verbal Bullets': Kaji Wataru and the Antifascist Struggle in Wartime East Asia," *Fascism* 9, no. 1–2 (2020): 9–33.

62 Bernhard contends that the architects of the Nazi empire in Eastern Europe modeled much of their administration on fascist Italy's conquest of Libya. In this "instance of inter-imperial borrowing, Fascist Italy offered a 'blueprint' to the Nazis." Additionally, "while the Nazis took a broad look at international colonialism, they differentiated considerably between the various national experiences. French and British empire-building, for instance, did not receive the same attention as Italian and Japanese colonial projects." Hoffman and Hedinger, "Editorial—Axis Empires," 164.

63 Kasper Braskén, David Featherstone, and Nigel Copsey, "Introduction: Towards a Global History of Anti-Fascism," in *Anti-Fascism in a Global Perspective: Transnational Networks, Exile Communities, and Radical Internationalism* (New York: Taylor and Francis, 2020), 2.

64 Michele Louro, *Comrades Against Imperialism: Nehru, India, and Interwar Internationalism* (Cambridge: Cambridge University Press, 2018), 2.

65 Ali Raza, *Revolutionary Pasts: Communist Internationalism in Colonial India* (Cambridge: Cambridge University Press, 2020), 220.

66 Ibid., 218.

67 Marc Matera, *Black London: The Imperial Metropolis and Decolonization in the Twentieth Century* (Berkley: University of California Press, 2015), 63.

68 One notable exception is Subhas Bose (see Chapter 3).

69 Liam Liburd, and Paul Jackson, "Debate: Decolonising Fascist Studies," *Fascism* 10, no. 2 (2021): 323–45.

70 Benjamin Zachariah, "Global Fascism and the *Volk*: The Framing of Narratives and the Crossing of Lines," *Journal of South Asian Studies* 38, no. 4 (2015): 609.

71 Richard Overy, *Blood and Ruins: The Great Imperial War, 1931–1945* (London: Penguin Books, 2021).

72 For scholarship that explores India and Indian internationalism, see Maia Ramnath, *Decolonizing Anarchism: An Antiauthoritarian History of India's Liberation Struggle* (Oakland: AK Press, 2011); Maia Ramnath, *Haj to Utopia: How the Ghadar Movement Charted Global Radicalism and Attempted to Overthrow the British Empire* (Berkley: University of California Press, 2011);

Kama Maclean, *A Revolutionary History of Interwar India: Violence, Image, Voice and Text* (Oxford: Oxford University Press, 2015); Durba Ghosh, *Gentlemanly Terrorists: Political Violence and the Colonial State in India, 1919–1947* (Cambridge: Cambridge University Press, 2016); Louro, *Comrades Against Imperialism*; Raza, *Revolutionary Pasts.*

73 Chakrabarty, *Provincializing Europe*, 17.

74 Exceptions include the scholarship of Stein Ugelvik Larsen, Federico Finchelstein, Benjamin Zachariah, and Jen Steffek.

75 In response, Chakrabarty contends that scholars must provincialize Europe, or "find out how and in what sense European ideas that were universal were also, at one and the same time, drawn from very particular intellectual and historical traditions that could not claim any universal validity." Chakrabarty, *Provincializing Europe*, xiii. See also Said, *Orientalism.*

76 Zachariah, "Global Fascism and the *Volk*," 99.

77 Chakrabarty, *Provincializing Europe*, 16.

78 Nehru, "Food for Spain," 266.

79 I use the terms "liberal-imperialist" and "liberal-imperialism" to refer primarily to the British and French empires. As Martin Thomas has argued, "for most of the nineteenth century and much of the twentieth, the one constant in British and French international politics was the exploitation of non-European ethnic groups through authoritarian systems of political control that denied equivalent civil rights, economic entitlements, and citizenship status to whites and non-whites. Reduced to their absolute essence, varieties of imperial rule invariably replicated these and other forms of discrimination." Martin Thomas, *Fight or Flights: Britain, France, and Their Roads from Empire* (Oxford: Oxford University Press, 2014), 5.

80 I am conscious of the need to disaggregate the terms "imperialism" and "colonialism." In this study, I use imperialism to describe the urge to expand outward—what C. A. Bayly has described as the "ruthless drive for dominance." C. A. Bayly, "The First Age of Global Imperialism, c. 1760–1830," in *Managing the Business of Empire: Essays in Honour of David Fieldhouse* (London: Frank Cass Publishers, 1998), 28. Colonialism, by contrast, was characterized by "territorial conquest, power, violence, domination, and subjugation." Mithi Mukherjee, "'A World of Illusion': The Legacy of Empire in India's Foreign Relations, 1947–1962," *The International History Review* 32, no. 2 (2010): 254. Mukherjee contends that "The British engagement with India was not a homogenous phenomenon but rather characterized by two competing but also collaborating political discourses: the 'colonial' (the major) and the 'imperial' (the minor). Whereas the 'colonial' stressed territorial conquest, power, violence, domination, and subjugation, the 'imperial' stressed justice as equity for the colonized, represented by the figure of the imperial monarch as arbiter of conflicts between the British administration

and the Indian people, and between different groups of Indians." Mukherjee, "A World of Illusion," 254. See also: Michael Adas, "Imperialism and Colonialism in Comparative Perspective," *The International History Review* 20, no. 2 (1998): 371–88; Caroline Elkins and Susan Pedersen, eds., *Settler Colonialism in the Twentieth Century* (London: Routledge, 2005); Marguerite Waller, and Sylvia Marcos, eds., *Dialogue and Difference: Feminisms Challenge Globalization* (London: Palgrave Macmillan, 2005); Barbara Bush, *Imperialism and Postcolonialism* (London: Routledge, 2006); Ania Loomba, *Colonialism/Postcolonialism* (London: Routledge, 2007); Lorenzo Veracini, "'Settler Colonialism': Career of a Concept," *The Journal of Imperial and Commonwealth History* 41, no. 2 (2013): 313–33; Dane Kennedy, *Decolonization: A Very Short Introduction* (Oxford: Oxford University Press, 2016); Goldie Osuri, "Imperialism, Colonialism and Sovereignty in the (Post)Colony: India and Kashmir," *Third World Quarterly* 38, no. 11 (2017): 2428–43; Krishan Kumar, "Colony and Empire, Colonialism and Imperialism: A Meaningful Distinction?" *Comparative Studies in Society and History* 63, no. 2 (2021): 280–309.

81 As Susan Kent and Marc Matera have argued, "an understanding of the world divided into two camps vying for the loyalty of one-time colonies and soon-to-be nation-states is often projected back onto the 1930s from the postwar period." Marc Matera and Susan Kent, *The Global 1930s: The International Decade* (London: Taylor and Francis, 2017), 13.

82 David Anderson, *Histories of the Hanged: Britain's Dirty War in Kenya and the End of Empire* (London: Weidenfeld and Nicolson, 2004); Caroline Elkins, *Imperial Reckoning: The Untold Story of Britain's Gulag in Kenya* (New York: Henry Hold and Company, 2005).

83 Alistair Horne, *A Savage War of Peace: Algeria, 1954–1962* (New York: The Viking Press, 1977).

84 Benjamin Madley, *An American Genocide: The United States and the California Indian Catastrophe, 1846–1873* (New Haven: Yale University Press, 2017).

85 Fascist governments generally persecuted minority populations, while imperial regimes represented a minority population. Finchelstein, "On Fascist Ideology," 325–6. See also: Nicola Labanca, "Studies and Research on Fascist Colonialism, 1922–1935: Reflections on the State of the Art," in *A Place in the Sun: Africa in Italian Colonial Culture from Post Unification to the Present*, ed. Patrizia Palumbo (Berkeley: University of California Press, 2003), 38–9.

86 Catherine Epstein, *The Last Revolutionaries: German Communists and Their Century* (Cambridge: Harvard University Press, 2003); Richard J. Evans, *The Coming of the Third Reich* (London: Allen Lane, 2003).

87 Pankaj Mishra, *From the Ruins of Empire: The Intellectuals Who Remade Asia* (New York: Farrar, Straus and Giroux, 2012), 8.

88 Ibid.
89 Matera and Kent, *Global 1930s*, 12.
90 Quoted in Alfred Martin Wainwright, *The Role of South Asia in British Strategic Policy 1939–1950* (Madison: The University of Wisconsin Press, 1989), 2.
91 There is an extensive body of literature examining each of these positions. For an introduction, see Michael Brecher, *Nehru's Mantle: The Politics of Succession in India* (Westport: Greenwood Press, 1976); Michael Brecher, and Krishna Menon, *India and World Politics: Krishna Menon's View of the World* (London: Oxford University Press, 1988); Akhil Gupta, "Blurred Boundaries: The Discourse of Corruption, the Culture of Politics and the Imagined State," *American Ethnologist: The Journal of the American Ethnological Society* 22 (1995): 375–402; Manu Bhagavan, *Sovereign Spheres: Princes, Education and Empire in Colonial India* (Delhi: Oxford University Press, 2003); Mushirul Hasan, and Margrit Pernau, *Regionalizing Pan-Islamism: Documents on the Khilafat Movement* (New Delhi: Manohar, 2005); Sunil Amrith, "Asian Internationalism: Bandung's Echo in a Colonial Metropolis," *Inter-Asia Cultural Studies* 6, no. 4 (2006): 557–69; Nicholas Owen, *The British Left and India: Metropolitan Anti-Imperialism, 1885–1947* (New York: Oxford University Press, 2007); Chakrabarty, *Provincializing Europe*; P. B. Mehta, "Still Under Nehru's Shadow? The Absence of Foreign Policy Frameworks in India," *India Review* 8, no. 3 (2009): 209–33; Mithi Mukherjee, "Transcending Identity: Gandhi, Nonviolence, and the Pursuit of a 'Different' Freedom in Modern India," *The American Historical Review* 115, no. 2 (2010): 453–73; Mukherjee, "'A World of Illusion': The Legacy of Empire in India's Foreign Relations, 1947–62"; Srinath Raghavan, *War and Peace in Modern India* (Basingstoke: Palgrave Macmillan, 2010); Sunil S. Amrith, *Migration and Diaspora in Modern Asia* (Cambridge: New York, 2011); Manu Goswami, "Imaginary Futures and Colonial Internationalisms," *The American Historical Review* 117, no. 5 (2012): 1461–85; Mithi Mukherjee, *India in the Shadows of Empire A Legal and Political History, 1774–1950* (New Delhi: Oxford University Press, 2012); Manu Bhagavan, *India and the Quest for One World: The Peacemakers* (Basingstoke: Palgrave Macmillan, 2013); Manu Goswami, *Producing India: From Colonial Economy to National Space* (Chicago: University of Chicago Press, 2013); Burton, *The Trouble with Empire*; Ali Raza, Franziska Roy, and Benjamin Zachariah, ed., *The Internationalist Moment: South Asia, Worlds, and World Views, 1917–39* (New Delhi: Sage, 2015); Venkat Dhulipala, *Creating a New Medina: State Power, Islam, and the Quest for Pakistan in Late Colonial North India* (New Delhi: Cambridge University Press, 2016); Kishwar Sultana, *Politics of the All-India Muslim League, 1924–1940* (Karachi: Oxford University Press, 2016).
92 My interpretive framework draws upon the definition of anti-fascism proposed by Nigel Copsey, who has argued that "anti-fascism is defined as a thought, an

attitude or feeling of hostility towards fascist ideology and its propagators which may or may not be acted upon." Nigel Copsey, *Anti-Fascism in Britain* (London: Routledge, 2017), 4. Maria Framke similarly uses the term "Indian anti-fascism" in her article: Maria Framke, "Political Humanitarianism in the 1930s: Indian Aid for Republican Spain," *European Review of History* 23, no. 1–2 (2016): 63–81.

93 Far from homogenous, various factions within the Congress articulated competing interpretations of anti-imperialism. See: Sourendra Ganguly, *Leftism in India: M. N. Roy and Indian Politics 1920–1948* (Calcutta: Minerva Publishers, 1984); Satyabrata Rai Chowdhuri, *Leftism in India, 1917–1947* (New York: Palgrave Macmillan, 2007); Mukherjee, "Still Under Nehru's Shadow?"; Bhagavan, *India and the Quest for One World.*

94 Ranajit Guha, "Introduction," in *Subaltern Studies 1: Writings on South Asian History and Society* (Delhi: Oxford University Press, 1982), 4. Gayatri Spivak has contended that the "politics of the people" was "both outside ('this was an autonomous domain, for it neither originated from elite politics nor did its existence depend on the latter') and inside ('it continued to operate vigorously in spite of colonialism adjusting itself to the conditions prevailing under the Raj and in many respects developing entirely new strains in both form and content') the circuit of colonial production." Gayatri Chakravorty Spivak, "Can the Subaltern Speak?" in *The Post-Colonial Studies Reader*, ed. Bill Ashcroft et al. (London: Routledge, 1995), 26.

95 Chatterjee, *Nationalist Thought and the Colonial World*; Ranajit Guha, *Dominance Without Hegemony: History and Power in Colonial India* (Cambridge: Harvard University Press, 1997); Gayatri Chakravorty Spivak, "*Can the Subaltern Speak?*" in *Can the Subaltern Speak?: Reflections on the History of an Idea* (New York: Columbia University Press, 2010).

96 Margery Sabin, "In Search of Subaltern Consciousness," *Prose Studies* 30, no. 2 (2008): 181–2. See also Uday Chandra, "Rethinking Subaltern Resistance," *Journal of Contemporary Asia* 45, no. 4 (2015): 563–73.

97 Many scholars of South Asia have contended that Nehruvian internationalism perpetuated imperial discourses. Mithi Mukherjee, for example, has contended that "India's foreign policy under Nehru . . . was based on a juridical discursive framework that assumed that any dispute between two nations would be resolved by a neutral and impartial third party, the United Nations' Security Council, thus conceptually excluding the possibility of war. This approach to foreign relations . . . was not grounded in the principle of Gandhian nonviolence. It was a legacy of empire." Mukherjee, "A World of Illusion," 253.

98 Raka Ray, *Fields of Protest: Women's Movements in India* (Minneapolis: University of Minnesota Press, 2000); Bandana Purkayastha, Mangala Subramaniam, Manisha Desai, and Sunita Bose, "The Study of Gender in India: A Partial Review,"

Gender & Society 17, no. 4 (2003): 503–24; Patricia Jeffrey and Amrita Basu, eds., *Appropriating Gender: Women's Activism and Politicized Religion in South Asia* (London: Routledge, 2011); Nitya Rao, *"Good Women Do Not Inherit Land": Politics of Land and Gender in India* (London: Routledge, 2017); Jessica Hinchy, *Governing Gender and Sexuality in Colonial India* (Cambridge: Cambridge University Press, 2019); Durba Mitra, *Indian Sex Life: Sexuality and the Colonial Origins of Modern Social Thought* (Princeton: Princeton University Press, 2020).

99 Samita Sen, "Toward a Feminist Politics? The Indian Women's Movement in Historical Perspective," in *The Violence of Development: The Politics of Identity, Gender & Social Inequalities in India* (London: Bloomsbury Academic, 2002), 473.

100 Priyamvada Gopal, *Literary Radicalism in India: Gender, Nation and the Transition to Independence* (London: Routledge, 2005); Angela Woollacott, *Gender and Empire* (London: Bloomsbury, 2006); Mary Procida, *Married to the Empire* (Manchester: Manchester University Press, 2017); Sumita Mukherjee, *Indian Suffragettes: Female Identities and Transnational Networks* (Oxford: Oxford University Press, 2018); Anu Aneja, ed., *Women's and Gender Studies in India: Crossings* (London: Taylor & Francis, 2019).

101 Elleke Boehmer, *Stories of Women: Gender and Narrative in the Postcolonial Nation* (Manchester: Manchester University Press, 2013), 72.

102 Sen, 477. See also: Rajan Mahan, *Women in the Indian National Congress, 1921–1931* (Jaipur: Rawat Publications, 1999).

103 Ibid., 478.

104 Ibid.

105 There were, of course, exceptions. See Raza, et al. *The Internationalist Moment.*

106 Like fascism, liberalism "was a protean phenomenon, a shape-shifting amalgam of philosophical arguments and political-economic practices encompassing diverse views on the self, society, economy, and government." Duncan Bell, *Reordering the World: Essays on Liberalism and Empire* (Princeton: Princeton University Press, 2016), 19. Similarly, Matthew Fitzpatrick has contended that "abstract definitions of liberalism have generally failed to be of enduring use, given the diverse contexts within which it has found enthusiastic adherents, even within an area as small as Europe. Fittingly, the notion of 'classical liberalism' refers more to a corpus of texts than any particular project of rule." Matthew Fitzpatrick, "Introduction," in *Liberal Imperialism in Europe*, ed. Matthew Fitzpatrick (London: Palgrave Macmillan, 2012), 6. See also Uday Singh Mehta, *Liberalism and Empire: A Study in Nineteenth-Century British Liberal Thought* (Chicago: University of Chicago Press, 1999), 4; Priya Satia, *Time's Monster: How History Makes History* (Cambridge, MA: Harvard University Press, 2020), 64.

107 Theodore Koditschek, *Liberalism, Imperialism, and the Historical Imagination: Nineteenth-Century Visions of a Greater Britain* (Cambridge: Cambridge University

Press, 2011), 5. See also John Hobson, *The State and International Relations* (Cambridge: Cambridge University Press, 2000), 64–104; Tarak Barkawi and Mark Laffey, "Introduction: The International Relations of Democracy, Liberalism, and War," in *Democracy, Liberalism, and War* (London: Lynne Rienner Publishers, 2001), 1–24; Robbie Shilliam, *German Thought and International Relations: The Rise and Fall of a Liberal Project* (London: Palgrave Macmillan, 2009), 3–29; Martin Hall and John Hobson, "Liberal International Theory: Eurocentric But Not Always Imperialist?" *International Theory* 2, no. 2 (2010): 210–45; Robbie Shilliam, ed., *International Relations and Non-Western Thought* (London: Routledge, 2010); Robbie Shilliam, *Decolonizing Politics: An Introduction* (London: Wiley, 2021).

108 Many anti-colonialists used the term "democratic-imperialism" to describe the hypocrisy and violence of liberal-imperialism.

109 Kamaladevi Chattopadhyay, "Extract from Honolulu Star-Bulletin," April 30, 1941, India Office Records (IOR) L/PJ/12/625, British Library (BL).

110 In carving out these spheres of influence, "what the three powers shared during the 1930s was the idea of reinventing imperialism and bringing it nearer to home, so that the nation could be reborn and thereby survive a worldwide struggle." Hedinger, "The Imperial Nexus," 192.

111 Although many scholars have contended that Nationalist Spain and the Empire of Japan were not fascist, Indian anti-imperialists characterized the wars against them as anti-fascist. Accordingly, this book uses the term "fascist" when describing the governments of Spain and Japan.

112 Barbara Bush, *Imperialism, Race and Resistance: Africa and Britain, 1919–1945* (London: Routledge, 1999), 29.

113 There is, of course, a considerable amount of middle ground between these arguments.

114 Louro, *Comrades Against Imperialism*, 7.

115 Michael Ortiz, "'Disown Gandhi or be Damned': M.N. Roy, Gandhi, and Fascism," *Journal of Colonialism and Colonial History* 21, no. 3 (2020).

116 "A Press-Clipping Article Entitled 'Nehru in Barcelona' by Peter Casamada," 1989, Miscellaneous Items 141, Nehru Memorial Museum and Library (NMML).

117 Rabindranath Tagore, *Eighty Years* (London: The India League), 15.

118 Burton, "Connective Tissue," 194.

1

"It Is Us Today. It Will Be You Tomorrow"[1]

India and the Second Italo-Ethiopian War

The war drums are sounded.
Men force their features into frightfulness and gnash their teeth;
and before they rush out to gather raw human flesh for death's larder,
they march to the temple of Buddha, the compassionate,
to claim his blessings,
while loud beats the drum rat-a-tat
and earth trembles.

—Rabindranath Tagore[2]

In September 1935, as the Royal Italian Army mobilized along the border zone between Ethiopia and Italian Somaliland, Sir Stafford Cripps addressed a gathering of British leftists at a Socialist League conference in London.[3] A Marxist and Labour MP, Cripps frequently denounced British imperialism, and would even organize an unsuccessful anti-fascist popular front to wrest majority control from the National Government. Standing before middle- and working-class leftists, Cripps condemned the impending Italian invasion of Ethiopia. However, rather than advocate for anti-imperialist and anti-fascist mobilization, he urged listeners to support British nonintervention. "I may be asked, can Italian aggression be stopped? The answer is, I am afraid, that in an imperialist world imperialist methods will be used . . . . The only contribution we can really make to the solution of this problem is to build up as rapidly as we can a convinced socialist opinion in this country."[4] Even before the outbreak of war, Cripps had forsaken Ethiopia.[5]

Weeks later, Rajani Palme Dutt addressed a special national conference of the Communist Party of Great Britain (CPGB).[6] Like Cripps, many in the CPGB, Independent Labour Party (ILP), and the Socialist League supported the National Government's policy of nonintervention in the Second Italo-Ethiopian War.[7] Frustrated, Dutt accused the British Left of supporting an imperialist ethos: "With regard to Abyssinia [Ethiopia], they profess to be concerned, they pay lip-service, but the vital issue of the struggle of the Abyssinian people for independence has no real living existence for them, is remote and secondary, a mere counter, a pretext of imperialism."[8]

With some notable exceptions—Nancy Cunard, Victor Gollancz, Reginald Sorensen, Ellen Wilkerson, and Ben Bradley, to name just a few—many British leftists willfully ignored Ethiopia.[9] Dutt contended that an "unconscious imperialism"[10] blinded them to the significance of the conflict.[11] In addition to an isolated fascist-imperialist adventure, the Second Italo-Ethiopian War also represented the denouement of New Imperialist collaboration.[12] White Europe, Dutt argued, was loathe to risk a war over Black Africa:

> [British] imperialists . . . could stop the whole thing if they wanted, without any issue of war. Why do they hesitate? Why, in spite of the protestations of sympathy with Abyssinia, did they refuse to send arms to Abyssinia? Because they can see the issues following the situation as clearly as we can. They did not want to send arms to a colonial people at any price. They are afraid of colonial peoples getting arms. They do not want Italy to be defeated because that means a defeat and a check to reaction all over Europe.[13]

Dutt's frustrations reflected the ways in which, seen from the outside-in, fascism and liberal-imperialism appeared interrelated. When Italy invaded Ethiopia, the British government—supported by many Marxists, liberals, and leftists—pursued nonintervention.[14] However, only months after the fall of Addis Ababa, a civil war erupted in Spain. Although Whitehall once again remained neutral, the British Left scrambled to defend the Second Spanish Republic.[15] Why Spain? Why not Ethiopia? The answer, according to Dutt, was that whereas within Europe distinctions between fascist, conservative, Marxist, and liberal were unmistakable, outside of Europe they were inconsequential. Seen from India, Britain, the arch-imperial power along the Sinai Peninsula, differed little from Italy, the proto-imperial power in the Horn of Africa. Both nations brutalized local populations within their spheres of influence. Whatever their political differences—and within Europe, there were many—outside of Europe, imperialist Britain and fascist Italy resembled one another.

Scholars have traditionally characterized the Second Italo-Ethiopian War, together with the Japanese invasion of Manchuria (1931) and the German remilitarization of the Rhineland (1936), as the dawn of fascist expansionism.[16] Compelled, among other things, by irredentism, Social Darwinism, and paradoxical notions of a "permanent revolution,"[17] Italian fascists demanded the Horn of Africa, challenging the status quo created by Britain and France.[18] However, from Dutt's perspective, the Italo-Ethiopian War, rather than dividing fascist and democratic Europe, exhibited the similarities between them.[19] In this chapter, I contend that at the same time it inaugurated the era of fascist expansionism, the Second Italo-Ethiopian War also revivified the New Imperialist covenant—the collaborative yet adversarial entente that rapidly expanded European colonial empires while preventing a continental war.[20] Whitehall conceded, or tacitly supported, the Italian invasion of Ethiopia, just as it had during the First Italo-Ethiopian War (1895).[21]

The Eyes of Satan

The Second Italo-Ethiopian War culminated nearly five decades of imperial aggression. In February 1896, the armies of King Menelik II occupied a strategically advantageous position near the Ethiopian town of Adwa.[22] Acting upon intelligence misrepresenting the geography of battle, Italian General Oreste Baratieri ordered his colonial troops—including several thousand Eritrean Ascari—to confront Menelik.[23] While marching through the night, numerous Italian brigades isolated themselves from the main attack force. Taking advantage of the situation, the Ethiopian army swept through and overpowered the detached brigades, before striking at what remained of Baratieri's army. By the end of the Battle of Adwa, Menelik's forces had inflicted a "rankling embarrassment"[24] upon Italy. In an age of unprecedented imperial expansion, Ethiopia defended its sovereignty.[25]

After seizing power, fascist-imperialists were determined to avenge Adwa.[26] In 1928, the Royal Italian Army constructed a stronghold at Walwal, in the Ogaden—a boundary zone between Ethiopia and Italian Somaliland. Six years later, Ethiopian soldiers marched to Walwal and demanded that Italian forces withdraw to Somalia. The Italian commander, Captain Roberto Cimmaruta, refused. Two weeks later, a clash between Italian-Somali and Ethiopian soldiers left more than one hundred dead. Italy demanded a formal apology, while Ethiopian emperor Haile Selassie appealed to the League of Nations.[27]

In the months after the Abyssinian Crisis, Italian troops mobilized along the disputed border zone. Emperor Selassie appealed once more to the League of Nations, which held a special session to address the incident.[28] In June, British Secretary of State for Foreign Affairs Anthony Eden tried and failed to broker a peace settlement between Italy and Ethiopia. Soon thereafter, British prime minister Stanley Baldwin publicly declared an arms embargo against both nations—allegedly in response to Mussolini's decree that the sale of arms to Ethiopia would be considered an "unfriendly act."[29] As tensions rose, negotiations between Italy, Ethiopia, and the League foundered. By September, Emperor Selassie had begun mobilizing his large, but poorly equipped, army.[30]

On October 3, 1935, the Kingdom of Italy invaded the Ethiopian Empire. The League of Nations determined that Mussolini was the aggressor and imposed sanctions on Italy. The League, however, "cannot be treated as if it were a state . . . [but rather] a force field, one made up of shifting alliances, networks, and institutions, which a host of actors entered and sought to exploit."[31] Anxious over German rearmament, Britain and France hoped Italy would join the Stresa Front—a short-lived anti-Nazi coalition.[32] The British Foreign Office, in particular, was "convinced that the Duce was prepared to form a common front against the Hitlerian threat to European security."[33] Whitehall, consequently, did little to implement League sanctions. Important raw materials such as oil were exempt, while Britain allowed Italian military convoys to pass through the Suez Canal.[34]

In December, British foreign secretary Samuel Hoare and French prime minister Pierre Laval proposed ending the war by partitioning Ethiopia. Mussolini would have received Ogaden and Tigray, leaving Emperor Selassie with a "corridor for camels."[35] Public outcry in Britain ultimately disgraced the Hoare-Laval Pact. Labour, the archbishop of Canterbury, and even several prominent conservatives publicly denounced it.[36] Meanwhile, the Royal Italian Army advanced westward. In May 1936, Marshal Pietro Badoglio captured the Ethiopian capital of Addis Ababa. Back in Rome, Mussolini publicly declared that "Adwa has been avenged." After the war, Italian colonial officials merged the former Ethiopian Empire with Italian Somaliland and Italian Eritrea, creating the colony of Italian East Africa.

~

The Second Italo-Ethiopian War was a pivotal moment in world and, in particular, anti-colonial history.[37] It undermined the League of Nations, enslaved the last free nation-state in Africa, shattered the tenuous peace imposed by the Versailles Agreement, and—together with the Spanish Civil War—crystallized the divide between the Anglo-French alliance and what would become the Axis powers.[38] It sparked anti-colonial protests from Delhi to Damascus to Detroit.[39] "What was very much at stake," Neelam Srivastava has argued, "was a debate about the meaning of 'civilization' and 'barbarism,' and the very meaning of the 'civilizing mission' itself, which was, of course, the ideological underpinning of European imperial projects."[40] In Geneva, exiled emperor Haile Selassie warned the League of Nations of a gathering storm:

> That is why I decided to come myself to bear witness against the crime perpetrated against my people and give Europe a warning of the doom that awaits it. . . . I assert that the problem submitted to the Assembly today is a much wider one. It is not merely a question of the settlement of Italian aggression. It is collective security: it is the very existence of the League of Nations. . . . In a word, it is international morality that is at stake.[41]

After his speech, Selassie warned that fascist cupidity would soon turn inward, to Europe itself. "It is us today," he argued, "it will be you tomorrow."[42]

The fall of Addis Ababa radicalized Black and pan-African internationalisms, inspiring anti-imperialists such as Jomo Kenyatta, C. L. R. James, and Amy Ashwood Garvey to challenge Italian imperialism.[43] London, in particular, transformed from a colonial metropole into a "locus of resistance to empire."[44] By adopting nonintervention and eschewing League sanctions, Britain condoned the Italian invasion of Ethiopia.[45] Many Black anti-colonialists contended that the Second Italo-Ethiopian War further evinced "the vacuity of racialized Western liberal democracy, belying the claim to any differences between Hitler, Mussolini, and the British and French Empires."[46] George Padmore, for example, argued that at home Europe's great powers were divided into "Versailles" and "anti-Versailles"[47] blocs; outside of Europe, however, these distinctions blurred.[48] Liberal, conservative, and fascist nation-states each demanded colonial empires. Beginning with the Berlin Conference (1884), this mandate was systematized through great-power diplomacy, nonintervention, and the League of Nations.

From a global perspective, Black and pan-African resistance to Italian fascism remains the most significant anti-imperialist narrative, but not the only one.[49] Building upon the Afro-centric scholarship of Robert Hill, Minkah Makalani, and others, this chapter examines the ways in which Indian anti-imperialists similarly challenged fascist imperialism.[50] In India, Jawaharlal Nehru, Rabindranath Tagore, and anti-colonialists within the INC adopted anti-fascist rhetoric similar to that of activists in "Black London."[51] In Europe, Rajani Palme Dutt denounced the unconscious imperialism of the British Left. Around the world, "the Indians who condemned the Italian attack on Ethiopia and claimed sympathy with its people felt, or at least asserted, a commonality of interests, future expectations and even ancestry with Ethiopians."[52] Ethiopia mattered to

Indian anti-imperialists; it was not, as one Royal Air Force pilot put it, "this silly African business."[53]

Prior to the Second Italo-Ethiopian War, many Indian anti-colonialists had admired Italian fascism. On the surface, Mussolini had stabilized the economy and unified the nation.[54] In an era in which European imperialisms appeared unassailable, Mussolini's anti-British temerity attracted anti-colonial admiration from around the world. Several prominent Indians visited Italy. Benoy Kumar Sarkar propounded corporatist economic theory in Calcutta and delivered lectures at both the University of Milan and the University of Rome.[55] In 1931, after the Second Round Table Conference, Mohandas K. Gandhi—the political and spiritual leader of the Congress-led campaign for independence—visited Rome.[56] He toured government buildings, inspected a Blackshirt youth honor guard, and met with Mussolini.[57] Although their conversation only lasted ten minutes, the two leaders were amicable. Afterward, Mussolini praised Gandhi as a "genius and a saint,"[58] and lauded his "ability to challenge the British Empire."[59] In response, Gandhi hailed Mussolini as "one of the great statesmen of our time."[60]

In a letter reflecting on his time in Rome, Gandhi described the grandiosity and inscrutability of fascist Italy:

> Mussolini is a riddle to me. Many of his reforms attract me. He seems to have done much for the peasant class. I admit an iron hand is there. But as violence is the basis of Western society, Mussolini's reforms deserve an impartial study. . . . What strikes me is that behind Mussolini's implacability is a desire to serve his people. Even behind his emphatic speeches there is a nucleus of sincerity and of passionate love for his people. It seems to me that the majority of the Italian people love the iron government of Mussolini.[61]

Shortly after Gandhi departed Rome, *Giornale d'Italia* published an interview misquoting him as "sympathetic to fascist opinions"[62] and alleging that he "sanctioned the use of violence."[63] The interview rankled British colonial authorities, members of the Congress, and anti-fascists across Europe. Even after Gandhi denounced the interview as "wholly false,"[64] critics decried his credulity in accepting Mussolini's invitation. *La Libertà*, the anti-fascist newspaper founded by Italian exiles in Paris, characterized Gandhi's visit as the product of "ingenuità," or naiveté.[65] Days later, Gandhi remarked to his personal secretary, Mahadev Desai: "His [Mussolini's] eyes are like those of a cat, did you notice?"[66] "More like the eyes of Satan,"[67] Desai responded. Gandhi did not disagree.

In a similar episode, Professor Carlo Formichi of the Philological Society of Milan invited world-renowned and Nobel Prize–winning poet Rabindranath Tagore to visit Italy in 1926.[68] At the time, the Poet's "visit was one of the major events of the century. There was eager expectation of the meeting of the philosopher poet Rabindranath with the fascist dictator Mussolini."[69] Tagore was an "Oriental Sage, a Seer, a Prophet"[70]—a towering international figure. As with Gandhi, Tagore's experience of fascist Italy represented a critical propaganda opportunity for Mussolini.

After their brief meeting, Tagore praised Mussolini. "I dream," he announced in a statement to the press, "of the day when the immortal spirit of Italy will usher in a new dawn of civilization."[71] Privately, however, Tagore harbored serious "doubts about the real character of Fascism."[72] Before returning to India, he visited Romain Rolland in Switzerland. A novelist, essayist, and fellow Nobel Prize winner, Rolland convinced Tagore that fascism suppressed freedom and worshipped violence. "I did not want devils," Rolland later wrote to the Poet, "misusing your sacred name in the annals of history . . . The future (the present already) will show you that I have acted as your faithful and vigilant guide."[73] After meeting with Rolland, Tagore returned to India an anti-fascist, though still occasionally expressed admiration for Mussolini.[74] "I have to pass," he wrote to Rolland in July, "through a purification ceremony for the defilement to which I submitted myself in Italy."[75]

In the years before the Second World War, Tagore's writing developed a more critical lens. In addition to pleading for mercy for the suffering—long a staple of his poetry—he condemned the immorality of empire. Tagore, in this regard, espoused a political ecumenicism distinct from Gandhian nationalism.[76] Shortly after the outbreak of war, Gandhi declared his sympathy for Ethiopia. "I cannot be indifferent about the war that Italy is now waging in Abyssinia."[77] Gandhi, however, largely avoided engaging with international developments. He was "not well informed about international affairs; nor had he any experience of them. Nor indeed was he particularly interested in them."[78] Tagore, by contrast, possessed an Internationalist outlook. A self-described peripatetic litterateur, he empathized with liberation movements in Ethiopia, Spain, Egypt, China, and British Palestine.[79]

In 1930, Tagore visited the United States. Standing before Franklin D. Roosevelt, Henry Morgenthau, and Sinclair Lewis at a dinner party in New York, he decried the exploitation of Western industrialization: "This epoch belongs to the West and humanity must be grateful to you for your science . . .

[But] you have exploited those who are helpless and humiliated those who are unfortunate with this gift."[80] Tagore's criticisms of the West encompassed not only imperialism and nationalist exclusion but also "crafty politicians, deceptive council chambers, the voracity of the strong—all these caught the poet's discerning eye."[81]

Fascism, in particular, troubled the poet. Mussolini had "pounced on helpless Abyssinia with impunity."[82] In response, Tagore criticized not only fascist "savagery" but also the "timid" imperialists, Britain and France:

On its one side a defiant savagery
and the growl of homicidal drunkenness,
on the other timid powers tied to the load
of their carefully guarded hoardings,
meekly settling down to a silent safety of acquiescence
after miscalculated bursts of impatience.
At the old nations' council-chambers
plans and protests are pressed flat between the tight-shut prudent lips.
In the meanwhile across the sky rush with their blazing blasphemy
the soulless swarms of vulture machines
carrying their missiles of ravenous passion for human entrails.[83]

By 1935, however, the era of Gandhi and Tagore had nearly come to an end. Beginning in the 1930s, a younger generation of anti-colonialists began to lead the Congress campaign for independence. Many in this rising generation— including Jawaharlal Nehru, Subhas Bose, Ram Manohar Lohia, and Jayaprakash Narayan—embraced Marxist-Leninist anti-imperialism. During his 1929 presidential address to the All India Congress Committee (AICC), Nehru openly professed his faith in Marxism: "I am a socialist and a republican, and am no believer in kings and princes, or in the old order which produces the modern kings of industry."[84] In 1933, after Gandhi suspended a civil disobedience campaign, Bose publicly declared: "Mahatma Gandhi has failed. The time has therefore come for a radical organisation of the Congress on a new principle and with a new method. For bringing about this reorganisation a change of leadership is necessary."[85] The rise of Nehru and Bose, together with the end of Depression-era isolationism, the outbreak of political and military crises around the world, and Gandhi's retirement from active Congress membership (1934), created a generational and political divide within the Congress. Increasingly, young anti-colonialists embraced socialism, not Gandhian swaraj, as their liberating creed.[86]

An Unregenerate Past

In 1946, Rajani Palme Dutt visited the headquarters of the Communist Party of India (CPI). His timing was serendipitous. In a paradigm-shifting speech, Soviet premier Joseph Stalin had recently characterized the Second World War as a global anti-fascist struggle: "[It] assumed from the very outset the character of an anti-fascist war. . . . The entry of the Soviet Union . . . could only augment—and really did augment—[its] anti-fascist and liberating character."[87] Stalin's argument contradicted the orthodox—or Stalinist, as many described it—argument that the Second World War encompassed two distinct conflicts.[88] The first, begun during the German invasion of Poland, was an internecine struggle between Europe's imperialist powers: Britain, France, Italy, and Germany. The second, inaugurated by the Nazi invasion of the Soviet Union, was a war of liberation between global forces of progress (communism) and reaction (fascism).

Fiercely loyal to the Soviet Union, Dutt justified Stalin's reappraisal of the Second World War, contending that the Soviet leader had simply broadened the lens from which he analyzed the war of liberation. From an international perspective, Dutt argued, the global anti-fascist war did not begin in 1941, with Operation Barbarossa, but rather in 1931, with the Japanese annexation of Manchukuo:

> When did the Second World War begin? Everybody knows it did not begin in 1939. It began before that. . . . We are all aware how we have traced its development right from its inception over Manchuria in 1931, growing and expanding from that to Abyssinia, to Spain, Austria, Czechoslovakia, and broadening out into the character of a full world war. . . . The struggle of the Abyssinian people, supported by the international progressive forces all over the world, against Italian Fascism was a liberation struggle against Fascism.[89]

According to Dutt, the war of liberation encompassed the Great Patriotic War, the Second World War, the Second Sino-Japanese War, the Spanish Civil War, the Second Italo-Ethiopian War, and the Japanese invasion of Manchuria.

Dutt's uncritical revisionism epitomized his devotion to Stalin. Throughout his career, he justified, or attempted to reconcile, the ideological contradictions of Soviet policy.[90] During the Great Purge (1936–8), Dutt, in the words of one critic: "Repeated every vile slander against Trotsky and his followers and against the old Bolsheviks murdered by Stalin through the 1930s, praising the obscene parodies of trials that condemned them as 'Soviet justice.'"[91] Dutt's loyalty to Stalin was consequential. In the era of fascism, he was perhaps the most important member of the Communist Party of Great Britain. He sat on the Executive Committee, formulated party policy, and edited *Labour Monthly*, the CPGB's unofficial magazine.

Dutt also served as the CPGB's leading theoretician on colonial matters. While in Brussels (1924–36), he represented a critical link between the Comintern, CPGB, and "communist politics in many parts of the British Empire—notably the Indian subcontinent, where the Communists were particularly dependent on his advice and guidance from a very early stage in their development."[92] The publication of *Modern India* (1926) established Dutt as one of the foremost experts on the Indian campaign for independence.[93] In 1929, his notoriety further exploded when the prosecutors of the Meerut Conspiracy Case identified him as one of India's leading insurrectionists.[94] Throughout his decades-long career, Dutt remained an unwavering ally of the Communist Party of India. Even "[Jawaharlal] Nehru—whom he had known since childhood—turned to him for advice on communist policy, and his influence extended far into the Congress left which Nehru led."[95]

Amid the rise of fascism, Dutt propagated the Third Period thesis espousing ideological militancy and denouncing social fascists.[96] During the 1929 General Election, he criticized the "imperialist" ideology of the second Labour government: "The Labour Party . . . its whole programme and policy is based on the capitalist State and the maintenance of imperialism; it is dominated and led by the Labour imperialists."[97] After the Nazi seizure of power (1933), however, the Comintern reversed course. Georgi Dimitrov and other Comintern officials acknowledged that the policy of denouncing non-Bolshevik leftists—anarchists, syndicalists, liberals, and Marxists, among them—had fractured anti-fascist coalitions, emboldening fascists to seize power.[98] Beginning in 1934, and formalized at the Seventh World Congress (1935), the Comintern encouraged the formation of popular fronts—broad political coalitions that would jointly resist the fascist menace.

Only two months after the Seventh World Congress, the Royal Italian Army invaded the kingdom of Ethiopia. In a test of the new Comintern line, Dutt would have to embrace many of the leftist groups he previously criticized.[99] He did so not only out of devotion to the Soviet Union but also because Ethiopia mattered to him. This was the paradox of Dutt. He willfully, often ruthlessly, sanctioned the worst atrocities of the Stalin regime. Of all the members of the CPGB, he was, in the words of one historian, "the least redeemed by human qualities."[100] At the same time, Dutt supported Haile Selassie and the kingdom of Ethiopia. More so than many socialists in Europe, he promulgated the anti-imperialist tenets of

Marxist-Leninist political theory. "The colonial struggle," he contended, "cannot be dismissed as being outside the class struggle of the workers: it is an integral part of it: the struggle of the workers for their own objectives and the struggle for national liberation must proceed side by side."[101]

~

With the outbreak of the Second Italo-Ethiopian War, Dutt criticized not only Italian imperialism but also the abortive Versailles system, Anglo-French nonintervention, and the ineffectual League of Nations. From his perspective, Ethiopia fell victim not only to fascist expansionism but also liberal-imperialist connivance: "While, therefore, the dynamic war-making forces, Germany, Japan and Italy, occupy to-day the immediate international foreground in the drive to war, a correct estimate of forces must devote no less careful attention to the role of the most powerful imperialist forces, Britain, the United States and France."[102] At the same time Whitehall and the Foreign Office criticized the Italian government, they proposed the partition of Ethiopia, permitted Italian warships to pass through the Suez Canal, and promptly recognized the creation of Italian East Africa. Moreover, while initially outraged, leftists and the media quickly lost interest in the conflict.[103] Britons, Dutt argued, tacitly supported— or, at the very least, ignored—the Italian invasion of Ethiopia.

Seen from India, Italian expansion within the Horn of Africa was not, as many in England considered, a "distant conflict"[104] nor was Ethiopia, in the words of Evelyn Waugh, a "barbarous"[105] country. More than 1,000 Indians lived in the Horn of Africa, including at least 500 in Ethiopia. Most were textile merchants, though some labored as artisans, carpenters, and barbers. During the initial invasion, Italian soldiers allegedly killed an Indian civilian in Jijiga, while others, such as Wazir Ali Baig, were expelled from their homes.[106] In a letter written to the All India Congress Committee, Shri Gulabchand Talakchand—a member of the Indian Association of Addis Ababa—denounced the "humiliating and degrading regulations"[107] imposed upon Indians by Italian colonial officials. Classified as "coloured people,"[108] Indians were prohibited from entering hotels, restaurants, and public places containing "white Europeans."[109]

Dutt contended that Italian colonial oppression paralleled that of the British in India. Fascism, he maintained, had radicalized imperial ideologies; it was "the leading expression of modern imperialism, of capitalism in decay, of the most violent policies of capitalism in crisis, [and] therefore means war."[110] Seen from the outside-in, Ethiopia—rather than negotiating between democratic and fascist nation-states—was surrounded by expansionist colonial powers: British-Sudan,

British-Kenya, Italian Somaliland, British Somaliland, French Somaliland, and Italian-controlled Eritrea. In India, Subhas Bose argued that Ethiopia's imperial circumscription was "not a new problem,"[111] but rather "a story of imperialist robbery."[112] To understand the Second Italo-Ethiopian War, he contended, was to grasp the historical profundity of European colonialism.

Delving into the history of the Scramble for Africa, Bose emphasized the frequency with which Ethiopia resisted British, French, and Italian incursions. "One cannot forget," he argued, "the abortive military exploits of [British] Lord Napier of Magdala in Abyssinia or the overthrow of Emperor Theodore by the British."[113] In 1868, Emperor Tewodros (Theodore) II of Ethiopia imprisoned several British subjects after the Foreign Office scuttled a letter he wrote to Queen Victoria (colonial officials purportedly forwarded the letter to India, where it was registered as "not even pending").[114] After a failed relief mission, Robert Napier led British colonial forces in a punitive expedition from India. As the Bombay Army stormed the fortress at Magdala, Tewodros committed suicide, allegedly with a pistol given to him by Queen Victoria.[115]

During the First Italo-Ethiopian War (1895), Italian colonial forces—supported by British colonialists attempting to obstruct French colonial expansion—invaded Ethiopia. Menelik II and the Ethiopian Ras ultimately defended their sovereignty. Since then, Bose argued, "Adowa [Adwa] has been remembered by the Italians as a defeat which has to be avenged."[116] During the First World War, Britain, France, and Italy signed the Treaty of London (1915), which promised Italy "equitable compensation . . . to the frontiers of the Italian colonies of Eritrea, Somaliland, and Libya"[117]—essentially, Ethiopia. According to Bose, the imperialist Entente powers furtively negotiated the fate of an internationally recognized nation-state: "France and Britain bought her [Italy] off. They signed a secret Treaty under which Italian Imperialism was promised that the frontiers of her East African colonies should be extended at the expense of Abyssinia."[118] Ethiopia, Bose contended, represented little more than a bargaining chip in the New Imperialist tête-à-tête between Europe's great powers.

Like Bose, Dutt situated the Second Italo-Ethiopian War within the larger framework of European colonial history. In *World Politics, 1918-1936*, he contended that the postwar Treaty of Versailles actually encouraged fascist imperialism in the Horn of Africa. The victorious colonial powers—Britain, France, and the United States—denied Italy territorial gains promised by the Treaty of London. Famed Italian poet Gabriele D'Annunzio called it a "mutilated victory." At the same time, Britain, and particularly France, punished Germany and the collapsed Ottoman and Austro-Hungarian empires with what John Maynard Keynes deemed a "Carthaginian Peace." Dutt argued that Italy and Germany—Europe's "Have-Not Powers"[119]—systematically undermined the Weltanschauung established at Versailles. Leaders in both countries demanded a greater share of the imperial system that had sustained British military, political, and economic ascendancy:

> The Italian claims to expansion, registered in the London Treaty of Britain, France and Italy in 1915 (although circumvented in respect of Asia Minor by the British-French Sykes-Picot agreement behind Italy's back in 1916), had been in great part thwarted by the dominant Powers at the Peace Conference. As later in Germany, so in Italy, Fascism developed first in these countries, as the weapon of the bourgeoise in a weakened imperialist country, not only against the working-class revolution, but also in order to pursue its offensive war aims against the other Powers, the internal and external roles of Fascism being closely related.[120]

Colonialism promised power, while the imperial ethos demanded evermore colonies. Fascism, Dutt reasoned, emerged out of a fanatical determination to reassert imperial sovereignty.[121] The Treaty of Versailles denied Italy and Germany their colonial empires, radicalizing the means by which they sought to obtain them.

After colonial adventures in Corfu, Yemen, Libya, and elsewhere, fascist Italy invaded Ethiopia.[122] "Italy," Mussolini argued, required more than "a few crumbs from the rich colonial booty gathered by others."[123] Around the world, fear spread that Ethiopia represented "another Belgium," or "a pretext like Belgium"[124]—a casus belli from which a second Great War would erupt. However, none of Europe's great powers "saw the preservation of Ethiopian sovereignty as a vital interest."[125] As Hoare argued before the League of Nations: "The security of the many cannot be ensured solely by the efforts of a few, however powerful they may be."[126] Rather than intervene in the Second Italo-Ethiopian War, the National Government haphazardly adopted three conflicting positions: isolationism, intimidation, and collective security. Dutt contended that each of these approaches exhibited the similarities between fascism and liberal-imperialism.

Isolationists within the Foreign Office advocated strict nonintervention in Ethiopia, or at the very least a negotiated settlement with Italy. Their motivations remain somewhat abstruse. Some sought to reinvigorate the Stresa Front, others hoped to prevent a second Great War, still others contended that Ethiopia mattered little to British strategic interests. In each instance, isolationists often trumpeted a Foreign Office report concluding that Britain lacked any strategic interest in Ethiopia.[127] Interestingly, a spy at the British Embassy in Rome provided Mussolini with a copy of the report. Unfamiliar "with the workings of the British democracy, the dictator confused the expert recommendations with government policy."[128]

Dutt contended that British isolationism ultimately emboldened fascist imperialism. The Hoare-Laval Pact, in particular, demonstrated the extent to which Europe's great powers blithely negotiated the fate of non-European nations.[129] Britain and Italy, Dutt argued, were not ideological adversaries, but rather arch-imperialists recommencing the partition of Africa:

> The main urgent danger at the present moment is not that the imperialist powers of the League are racing to involve their countries in a war with Italy in the name of League sanctions for Abyssinia. On the contrary, they are doing everything to hold up and delay and weaken and minimize any sanctions. They are doing everything to try and reach a corrupt settlement with Italy on the basis of the subjection and partition of Abyssinia.[130]

According to Dutt, isolationists condoned the subjugation of Ethiopia so long as Italy honored British interests.

Imperialists, particularly those stationed in Egypt and the Sudan, sought to intimidate Mussolini.[131] Few, if any, sympathized with Ethiopia; for them, "the crisis was much more about imperial defence than about saving Abyssinia."[132] Many imperialists believed that the Italian invasion of Ethiopia threatened the Suez Canal—the fulcrum of British colonial power. Rumors swirled that Mussolini would eventually attack the Sudan. The colonial secretary, David Ormsby-Gore, warned Prime Minister Baldwin that British nonintervention in Ethiopia would substantiate fascist propaganda depicting "an effete Britain cowering before an all-powerful virile Italy."[133] Dutt contended that Italian expansionism spurred imperialists to brandish British imperial might: "It was the wider strategic interested involved . . . and the wider aims of the Italian offensive, that raised the problem. . . . Control of the Mediterranean and the Red Sea represented for Britain its vital line of communication with its Empire in Africa, the Near and Middle East, India and Australia."[134] If the Italian Empire conquered the Horn of Africa (Eritrea, Ethiopia, French Somaliland [Djibouti], and British Somaliland), as well as Yemen on the southern end of the Arabian Peninsula, it "meant not only a deadly peril to that line of communication, but was also regarded as the starting-point for an ultimate converging attack, from Libya on the west and Abyssinia on the south, for the conquest of the Sudan and Egypt."[135]

In September, the government dispatched more than one hundred British and Dominion warships to the Eastern Mediterranean.[136] After Italian forces crossed the Mareb River, Whitehall rushed Indian troops to Addis Ababa, claiming that their presence would safeguard British interests. "Are the Indian people," Bose questioned, "really so naive that they can be taken in by such a statement?"[137] British troops stationed in Kenya, the Sudan, or Egypt could be marshaled faster than sepoys from the subcontinent. The British government, Bose argued, deployed Indian troops to dissuade further Italian expansion: "Indian troops were sent with the idea of committing Indian support to British policy in Abyssinia and on the other hand, to remind Italy that the vast resources of India are behind Great Britain."[138] Although their intent "was only to use force as a last resort,"[139] imperialists believed intimidation would dissuade additional Italian expansion. Dutt contended that this pugnaciousness, however perfunctory, evinced the interrelation between fascism and liberal-imperialism. Just as they had during the Scramble for Africa, British and Italian imperialists competed for supremacy within the Horn of Africa.

Finally, advocates of collective security contended that forceful League sanctions would discourage Italian aggression. During the Abyssinian Crisis, the League of Nations allegedly "had more than a fair chance of forcing Italy to back down by means of a commercial embargo."[140] However, rather than risk war, the French and British governments implemented languorous sanctions. As Pierre Laval explained to Samuel Hoare: "There ought to be no provocative talk of sanctions and no wounding of Italian feelings."[141] Dutt denounced the timorousness of League—and by extension, British—sanctions. Although envisioned as an arbiter of world peace, the League was "in fact no league of 'nations,' but a grouping of victor imperialist powers and of secondary states."[142] Motivated by self-interest, the League's great powers frequently jeopardized global security.[143] The Mukden Incident (1931), the Chaco War (1932), the Second Italo-Ethiopian War, and the Spanish Civil War (1936) each exposed the limitations of the Covenant.[144]

Around the world, frustration with the League abounded. Azaj Warqneh C. Martin, the Ethiopian minister in London, criticized the vacuity of League collective security:

The League has been talking while Ethiopia burned. The Emperor and our whole people believed in the promises of the League of Nations. How terribly we have suffered! I am right, I believe, in predicting that retribution will fall upon those who permit the oppression of the weak . . . Britain undoubtedly will suffer, and will have to resist the aggression under circumstances very much more perilous than the present.[145]

When Mussolini threatened Ethiopia, the National Government declared that it would not intervene; when *The Times* exposed Italian atrocities, Whitehall proposed the Hoare-Laval Pact; and when rumors claimed that Mussolini would attack the Suez Canal, the League imposed ineffective sanctions. Britain, Martin argued, had forsook the Covenant and betrayed Ethiopia.

The Second Italo-Ethiopian War forced the British government into a difficult decision.[146] It could support the League of Nations and alienate Italy from the Stresa Front, or undermine the League and retain Italy as a bulwark against German expansionism.[147] By pursuing both, Whitehall ultimately accomplished neither. Criticizing Italian atrocities, proposing the Hoare-Laval Pact, and adopting ineffectual sanctions ensured "the worst of all possible outcomes: the League destroyed, and Italy on Germany's side."[148] Whitehall's conflicting responses reflected myriad concerns—the rise of Nazi Germany, maintenance of the Stresa Front, preservation of empire, economic insecurity, and continued existence of the League of Nations, to name just a few—together with a paradoxical set of impulses: protectionism, imperialism, isolationism, anti-communism, Orientalism, humanitarianism, paternalism, and a decidedly anti-war public opinion.[149] On several occasions, King George V threatened to abdicate if Britain declared war on Italy. Whitehall, moreover, was not a monolithic institution; it was comprised of various actors with competing agendas.[150] As prime minister, Stanley Baldwin's "notorious lack of interest in foreign policy rendered him vulnerable to scheming by ministers and senior advisors."[151] These micro-tug-of-wars only begin to explain the British government's contradictory approach to the Second Italo-Ethiopian War.[152] As famed historian A. J. P. Taylor drolly argued: "No one knows why the British Government took the line it did; probably they did not know themselves."[153]

Seen from the outside-in, another interpretation of Britain and the Second Italo-Ethiopian War emerges. Dutt contended that British vacillation between isolationism, intimidation, and collective security exhibited the similarities between fascism and liberal-imperialism:

The existing conflict between the imperialist Powers in possession [Britain] and the "dynamic" or challenging [fascist] imperialist Powers cannot be understood except in relation to the dynamic of imperialist as a whole and its drive for expansion, which leads to the present insoluble problems and contradictions of inter-imperialist relations.[154]

Absent any representation from Addis Ababa, British and Italian colonialists negotiated the fate of a sovereign nation. Whether democratic, conservative, or fascist, Europe's great powers conspired in the colonization of Ethiopia. Africa, as Cain and Hopkins have argued, "was still a continent to be divided and apportioned for the sake of greater European interests."[155]

To some extent, this perspective discounts the Gordian complexity of European politics.[156] Many Indian anti-colonialists only briefly considered Whitehall's manifold considerations—domestic electoral politics, French defeatism, and the looming German threat, to name just a few.[157] Particularly after the German remilitarization of the Rhineland (1936), the British public, "newly aware of the German danger . . . mostly did not now want to risk even a naval war with Italy."[158] Indian anti-colonialists' arguments nevertheless remain useful, insomuch as they underscore the similarities between fascism and liberal-imperialism. In Ethiopia, imperial interests transcended democratic principles, reducing an internationally recognized nation-state to a bargaining chip.[159] As Robert Vansittart, Permanent Under-Secretary of State for Foreign Affairs explained to Hoare: "Italy will have to be bought off—let us use and face ugly words—in some form or other or Abyssinia will perish. That might in itself matter less if it did not mean that the League would also perish."[160] Unwilling to risk war over Black Africa, Whitehall invoked the New Imperialist covenant and, together with Italy, negotiated the fate of Ethiopia.

~

Throughout the Second Italo-Ethiopian War, Winston Churchill languished amid his "wilderness years," due primarily to his aversion toward the Government of India Act, not—as he later claimed—his opposition to appeasement.[161] One day, a French woman accosted him, arguing that Italy's brutalization of Ethiopia mirrored British colonial conquest across Africa and Asia. "Ah, but you see," Churchill responded, "all that belongs to the unregenerate past, is locked away in the limbo of the old, the wicked days. The world progresses."[162] Churchill legitimated the civilizing mission by relegating British colonial conquest to an unregenerate past. This conviction led him and other imperialists to criticize Italian war crimes, often while exalting their own civilized stewardship over colonies such as India. Only weeks before the invasion, Samuel Hoare stood before the League of Nations and argued that "backward nations"[163] such as India were "entitled to expect that assistance will be afforded to them by more advanced peoples."[164]

Subhas Bose criticized Hoare's paternalistic rhetoric, as well as any claim to distinction between fascist Italy and imperialist Britain. Both powers, he contended, committed atrocities to sustain imperial hegemony. Whitehall, however, claimed moral superiority over Italy by propagandizing its civilizing mission in India:

> It is to be greatly regretted that the spokesman of Great Britain at Geneva, with an unabashed impudence, mentioned Britain's treatment of India as an argument to prove her [Britain's] moral superiority over Italy—not withstanding the fact that while he spoke, bombs were raining over the heads of women and children of the frontier province and the Indian Government was forging fresh fetters for the Indian people in the shape of the Criminal Law Amendment Act.[165]

In Ethiopia, the Royal Italian Army poisoned civilians with mustard gas, destroyed Red Cross ambulances, and used aerial bombing as a terror tactic.[166] At the same time, along the Northwest Frontier of India, British colonial forces sequestered troubled regions, destroyed homes, and bombed innocent civilians as part of a ruthless "aerial surveillance regime."[167] From the perspective of Indian anti-colonialists, these parallel campaigns highlighted the nihility of British liberalism, belying any difference between fascism and democratic-imperialism.[168] Indeed, as an aphorism popularized during the First Italo-Ethiopian War contended: "Of a black snake's bite, you may be cured, but from the bite of a white snake, you will never recover."[169]

The West Will Perish

In 1926, Norman Leys published *Kenya*. A British member of the League Against Imperialism, an avowed socialist, and a colonial doctor in Northeast Africa, Leys understood Africa through the lens of a paternalistic Orientalism.[170] Describing the anti-imperialism of John Chilembwe and Harry Thuku, he contended:

> Nor must they [readers] blame the governor or the Colonial Secretary for repressing the rising with slaughter. That is the kindest way of dealing with native risings. The fact that most of the people who engage in them are in no real sense criminally inclined make it no less necessary to shoot them.[171]

Leys epitomized the unconscious imperialism of many English anti-colonialists.[172] During the Second Italo-Ethiopian War, white support of Ethiopia was, "from the standpoint of black socialists, disappointing."[173] Apart from several notable exceptions, "the white Left failed to sustain interest in Ethiopia."[174] Even Labour "was at best silent on the issue [of Empire] and at worst aggressively pro-imperialistic."[175]

White indifference toward Ethiopia frustrated anti-imperialists. Dutt, in particular, accused both the "Right and Left in Britain of having a 'largely unconscious, deeply ingrained . . . imperialist outlook' and reacting negatively to Ethiopia."[176] Dutt contended that Ethiopia represented the "'cockpit' of the colonial struggle and a 'symbol' of the independence of African people."[177] It was not a lost cause, but rather an opportunity to defend freedom from European imperialists:

> The issue of Abyssinia is already our direct concern because it is the issue of a struggle for independence against imperialism, because they represent the last independent African state fighting to turn the tide of the imperialist invasion of Africa, because their cause is followed with the ardent support of all the colonial and semi-colonial peoples all over the world.[178]

Many in the Socialist League, ILP, and CPGB sympathized with Ethiopia but believed it had little chance of success. They hoped that Whitehall would avoid sparking another Great War over a lost cause. Frustrated, Dutt contended that Left defeatism supported fascist imperialism: "Turn to the other side of the controversy—the supposedly 'left' position of the leadership of the I.L.P. [Independent Labour Party] and the Socialist League. They no less reveal the imperialist basis of their position by making the central issue, not Abyssinia and the vital world conflict involved, but how to keep Britain out."[179] Dutt argued that Britain's colonial ethos had embedded itself in popular consciousness, preventing leftists from organizing an anti-imperialist and anti-fascist world front. "There is here in reality no international outlook," he maintained, "but a deeply British outlook."[180]

From the perspective of Indian anti-imperialists, Europe—whether liberal, conservative, Marxist, or fascist—had abandoned Ethiopia. The League of Nations adopted ineffective sanctions; many leftists ignored the conflict; the *Daily Mail* proclaimed that British sympathy was "wholly with the cause of the white races, which Italy is so firmly upholding";[181] Stanley Baldwin appeared disinterested in international developments; the Foreign Office proposed the partition of Ethiopia; and Whitehall "was more embarrassed than sympathetic when Haile Selassie pleaded before the League Assembly."[182] Seen from the outside-in, each of these developments exhibited the similarities between fascism and liberal-imperialism. As Dutt argued in *World Politics*:

> On the side of imperialism, the most important new development of the present stage is Fascism. Fascism appears as the open terrorist dictatorship of capitalism

in extreme decay against the rising revolt of the working class. But Fascism is at the same time the highest expression of organisation for war. These two aspects of Fascism are inseparably interlinked. On the one hand, modern totalitarian war requires the complete crushing of all popular resistance, the wiping out of all independent working-class organisation or even liberal-progressive or pacifist currents, and the organisation of the entire population and economy for war. This is the task of Fascism in the domestic sphere. On the other hand, Fascism, because it cannot solve the economic contradictions of capitalism which underlie its rise, is driven to foreign adventure and war for its attempted solution. This policy is the expression of the policy of the most reactionary, chauvinist and imperialist sections of finance-capital of which Fascism is the organ. Fascism is the most complete organisation of modern imperialism for war.[183]

Many leftists, however, focused only on the destruction of European fascisms. As one particularly sardonic cartoon in the *Evening Standard* quipped: "See no Abyssinia, Hear no Abyssinia, Speak no Abyssinia."[184]

~

Haile Selassie fled Addis Ababa on May 1, 1936. George Steer, a South African–born *Times* correspondent, described him as "a fragile figure.... In the luminous grey before sun-rise he looked out on the dim Shoan plain, cold and sleeping still, and thought in bitter impassivity of this fearful finish. The exhaustion was too much: he hoped that he had not betrayed his people, he only knew that many had betrayed him."[185] Eight days later, King Victor Emmanuel II of Italy was proclaimed emperor of Ethiopia.

Selassie spent five years in England. Due to his "misplaced trust in the League,"[186] he took little with him (famed French anti-fascist André Malraux bought one of his personal planes for use in the Republican Air Force during the Spanish Civil War).[187] While in exile, Selassie wrote his autobiography in Amharic, contested Italian propaganda, and condemned fascist atrocities in East Africa. Italian soldiers, meanwhile, executed two of his sons-in-law, Ras Desta Damtew and Dejazmach Beyene Merid, while his daughter, Princess Romanework, died in captivity on the prison island of Asinara. Disheartened, Selassie warned that fascism would soon imperil Europe: "I must still hold on until my tardy allies appear. And if they never come, then I say prophetically and without bitterness, 'the West will perish.'"[188]

After the Royal Italian Army captured Addis Ababa, Mussolini invoked the New Imperialist covenant. Rather than invade British or French colonial territory, he publicly declared that Italy was a "satisfied power."[189] Europe had finished the Scramble for Africa. Britain, however, confronted the war's many repercussions. In March 1936, as the Royal Italian Air Force bombed Hara and Jijiga, Adolf Hitler remilitarized the Rhineland. Ethiopia, Nehru argued, "showed the world that the League was powerless. Hitler could now defy it without fear."[190] Four months later, Spain erupted in a bloody civil war. Fascist imperialism had spread to Europe.

The British Left eagerly combated fascism in Spain.[191] While righteous, their enthusiasm nevertheless frustrated Black and Indian anti-imperialists. In England, the outbreak of the Spanish Civil War eclipsed the tragedy of Ethiopia. As Stafford Cripps argued in a letter to Sylvia Pankhurst: "I do not believe it is possible to rouse anti-fascist feeling on this issue [Ethiopia] now, while the Spanish issue is just beginning to exercise the minds of the British workers . . . I should hesitate to do anything which would detract from the keenness on the Spanish issue."[192] Leftists volunteered en masse for the International Brigades, yet many ignored Ethiopia. For anti-colonialists, this disparity revealed the imperial ethos animating fascist, liberal, and conservative Europe. As Emmanuel Abrahams of *The Ethiopia League* contended:

> The Italian aggressor as soon as he succeeded to overrun Ethiopia with . . . incendiary bombs and mustard gas, determined to divert the attention of Europe and the world from the scene of horror in Ethiopia . . . set fire to Spain, a European country. The "great" statesmen of Europe, who were only doing lip service to the Ethiopian cause and who in reality did not seem to have cared if the Ethiopians were enslaved or exterminated by a European Power, found a good excuse, as they thought, to forget about the thorny question of that distant land in "darkest Africa . . ." From July 1936 onward, Spain took the place in the news of the world . . . Ethiopia fell in the background and her cry of agony was drowned by the cries of the Spaniards and Chinese.[193]

Dutt and other Indian anti-imperialists supported the Second Spanish Republic. The INC sponsored a medical mission to Barcelona, collected foodstuffs and medical supplies for the International Brigades, and coordinated several All-India Spain Day celebrations to promote awareness of the conflict. Still, the British Lefts' enthusiasm for the Spanish Civil War frustrated Indian anti-imperialists. "The groan of peace in Abyssinia," Rabindranath Tagore contended, "is no less ghastly than the howl of war in Spain."[194]

In India, the Italian invasion of Ethiopia galvanized anti-fascist sentiments within the INC.[195] In April 1936, as Italian General Pietro Badoglio launched the March of Iron Will to Addis Ababa, Nehru succeeded Congress president Rajendra Prasad—a Gandhian conservative preoccupied with domestic issues. One year prior, during Nehru's 1935 visit to London, many anti-imperialist organizations—including the League Against Imperialism—had "called upon Nehru to raise awareness in India of the Abyssinia crisis. Nehru would not disappoint his comrades."[196] As Congress president, Nehru denounced Italy, the League of Nations, the Hoare-Laval Pact, and British nonintervention.[197] "The Congress," he declared in his presidential address, "expresses the sympathy of the Indian nation for the Ethiopian people who are so heroically defending their country against imperialist aggression, and considers Abyssinia's fight as part of the fight of all exploited nations for freedom. The Congress condemns the Great Powers and the League of Nations for their policy in regard to the Italo-Abyssinian War."[198] Nehru's presidencies (1936–7), together with those of Bose (1938–9), coincided with the Second Italo-Ethiopian War, Hitler's remilitarization of the Rhineland, the Spanish Civil War, the Second Sino-Japanese War, the Austro-German Anschluss, and the Munich Agreement.[199] In short, Nehru and Bose presided over the Congress amid the denouement of interwar fascism.

At the same time, British prime ministers Stanley Baldwin and Neville Chamberlain placated fascist expansionism. For Indian anti-imperialists, and Dutt in particular, this appeasement-driven foreign policy belied the similarities between fascism and liberal-imperialism:

> The National Government and the imperialist powers on the League have in fact continuously pressed forward a line for agreement with Italy by the joint spoliation of Abyssinia. To support the National Government, which has continuously supported German fascism, which has declared its sympathy for Italian fascist overseas expansion, which is seeking to carve up Abyssinia, means to fail to fight for Abyssinia and to assist the world fascist offensive.[200]

Only weeks after the fall of Addis Ababa, the fascist-imperialist war spread to Spain. Convinced it would eventually reach India, the Congress intervened. Nehru, Bose, and others were determined that "Abyssinia will not have suffered in vain."[201]

We English Do Keep Our Word

On March 15, 1941, during the British assault on Keren, the 5th Indian Division of the British-Indian Army marched on Fort Dologoroduc in Italian Eritrea. As Mahrattas, Frontier Force Sikhs, Dogras, and the 2nd West Yorkshires advanced, the loudspeaker unit of George Steer broadcasted anti-Italian propaganda in Tigrinya, an Afro-Asiatic language spoken by ethnic Tigray-Tigrinya in Northern Eritrea. Later that night, Steer changed course. He instructed his unit to play Italian records—Peace, Peace, My God! and Your Little Hands Are Frozen,[202] among them—until a British artillery unit "told them to shut up."[203] The following morning, more than sixty Italian soldiers surrendered.[204]

George Steer was in Addis Ababa during the Second Italo-Ethiopian War. He was one of the few white Britons to grasp the importance of the conflict. "Ethiopia," he warned, "is nearer to Europe than they think."[205] A keen anti-fascist, Steer criticized Italian imperialism, the League of Nations, and Anglo-French Isolationism: "But of the many that I saw dead or dying, there is not one of them whose blood does not lie on the head of Mussolini. He is the deliberate murderer of all of them. . . . Let us [Britain and France] give him a loan and bring him back into the European circle."[206] Steer married his first wife, Margarita de Herrero, in the grounds of the British Legation during the May Days of 1936 (after Haile Selassie had fled but before Italian forces had arrived in Addis Ababa).[207] Less than one year later, Margarita Steer died in childbirth while George reported on the Spanish Civil War in Bilbao.

In 1939, Steer married Esme Barton—the youngest daughter of Sydney Barton, the former British minister in Addis Ababa. Exiled emperor Haile Selassie attended the ceremony, and was named godfather of their son. In November, the *Daily Telegraph* dispatched Steer to report on the Winter War in Finland. After the outbreak of the Second World War, he joined the British Army, where he led his Ethiopian Forward Propaganda Unit during the East African Campaign. After the liberation of Addis Ababa, Steer's unit was rerouted to Bengal (and later Burma) to break the morale of the Japanese Army, part of which included the Indian National Army led by Subhas Bose. Steer died in 1944, after a driving accident in Bengal.[208]

Steer reported on fascism for nearly a decade. He disseminated the uncomfortable truth of Italo-German expansionism and warned the British public that it would soon engulf Europe. Most famously, Steer publicized fascist atrocities. In Ethiopia, he reported that the Royal Italian Army poisoned civilians with mustard gas, destroyed Red Cross ambulances, and used aerial bombing as a terror tactic. England, however, "saw Ethiopia as a series of submissions, non-resistance, ceremonial occupations, roadbuilding and Italian propaganda flickering dully across sham-pacific newsreels."[209]

Less than a year after the fall of Addis Ababa, Steer reported on the German bombing of Guernica. His account captivated English audiences. *The Times* reprinted his column every day for more than a week. Across Europe, outrage abounded. Indignation in Spain, indifference in Ethiopia—this, Indian anti-imperialists discovered, was the unconscious imperialism of white Britain. Many in Europe believed that the bombing of Guernica heralded an age of aerial destruction. Dutt, Nehru, and Indian anti-imperialists disagreed. Guernica, they argued, radicalized, rather than inaugurated, colonial violence. It perfected the terror bombing that destroyed Ethiopia, and "brought the brutality of colonial warfare home to white people."[210]

Seen from the outside-in, the Second Italo-Ethiopian War exhibited the similarities between fascism and liberal-imperialism. Invoking the New Imperialist covenant, the governments of Italy and Great Britain negotiated the fate of Ethiopia. As with the Scramble, Africa remained a continent to be partitioned in the interest of preserving European peace. Even many within the British Left—a purported anti-fascist and anti-imperialist bulwark—ignored the conflict. Frustrated, Indian anti-imperialists condemned not only Italian fascism but also British nonintervention and the League of Nations. From their perspective, the Second Italo-Ethiopian War culminated in the Scramble for Africa. Within Europe, fascism and liberal-imperialism differed in significant ways; outside of Europe, however, they appeared remarkably similar. "The same dream runs through them all," Dutt argued, "yet they cannot all be fulfilled. At the most, only one can be fulfilled at the expense of the remainder. Only one imperialism can achieve world hegemony at the expense of every other. And the path to this fulfillment of one world imperialist domination must lie through oceans of blood."[211]

Just before he left Ethiopia, George Steer bid farewell to his friend Lij Andarge Masai:

> He seemed doubtful of the future, but I reassured him. "After all," I said, "we may have been slow, but we English do keep our word. We have solemnly signed a Covenant which *guarantees* to you your independence and territorial integrity. We have said many times that we stand by our signature, and that we will uphold the Covenant and its entirety.
>
> Lij Andarge really believed what I said."[212]

Notes

1 Haile Selassie, "The Lion is Freed," *Time* magazine, September 8, 1975.
2 Rabindranath Tagore, "108," in *The English Writings of Rabindranath Tagore: Volume One: Poems*, ed. Sisir Kumar Das (New Delhi: Sahitya Akademi, 1994), 382. Tagore's poetry is in the public domain.

3 Cripps formed the Socialist League after the Independent Labour Party split from the Labour Party in 1932.

4 R. Palme Dutt, *Decisive Days Ahead* (London: Communist Party of Great Britain, 1935), 19.

5 Similarly, Fenner Brockway, general secretary of the Independent Labour Party and a member of the League Against Imperialism, contended in *The New Statesman* that Ethiopia was doomed: "One result of the present crisis can be prophesied safely: whether there is war or not, Abyssinia will lose its independence." Dutt, *Decisive Days Ahead*, 19.

6 Born to a Bengali father and Swedish mother, Dutt developed an early interest in revolutionary politics. Educated at Balliol College, Oxford, he protested Britain's entry into the First World War and was imprisoned for refusing the draft (1916). In 1920, under direction from the Comintern, Dutt co-founded the Communist Party of Great Britain by merging several smaller organizations, including the British Socialist Party, the Socialist Labour Party, and the National Guilds League. John Callaghan, *Rajani Palme Dutt: A Study in British Stalinism* (London: Lawrence & Wishart, 1993), 81–140.

7 There is considerable debate over the British Left's response to the Second Italo-Ethiopian War. For an overview, see: Stephen Howe, *Anticolonialism in British Politics: The Left and the End of Empire, 1918–1964* (Oxford: Oxford University Press, 1993), 100–3; Michele Louro, *Comrades Against Imperialism: Nehru, India, and Interwar Internationalism* (Cambridge: Cambridge University Press, 2018), 204; Priyamvada Gopal, *Insurgent Empire: Anti-Colonial Resistance and British Dissent* (London: Verso, 2019), 333–4.

8 Dutt, *Decisive Days Ahead*, 18–19. In Europe during the interwar era, the terms "Abyssinia" and "Ethiopia" were used interchangeably. Additionally, I use the term "British left" to mean white, politically active liberals, Marxists, socialists, anarchists, and any other individuals left of center. It is important to note, that the British Left encompassed a variety of individuals with myriad ideological differences. As Barbara Bush has argued: "We must also distinguish between white anti-imperialists, associated mainly with the Marxist left, and liberal and reformist critics of colonialism . . . . Anti-imperialists opposed imperialism *per se* in contrast to critics of colonialism who directed their energies to reforming rather than abolishing colonial rule. However, white supporters of black causes, liberal of left, were not personally 'in resistance' to racial and colonial oppression. This is reflected in the differing content and language of white and black oppositional discourses." Barbara Bush, *Imperialism, Race and Resistance: Africa and Britain, 1919–1945* (London: Routledge, 1999), 16.

9 Many leftists joined pan-Africanists, Indian students, the (moribund) League Against Imperialism, and anti-colonialists such as Amy Ashwood Garvey, C. L. R. James, and George Padmore in protesting Italian aggression. However, while "the Italian

invasion of Ethiopia created an opening for black intellectuals to engage with a range of white sympathizers . . . it [ultimately] exacerbated the fissures between them, engendering new attempts at organizing people of African descent autonomously." Marc Matera, *Black London: The Imperial Metropolis and Decolonization in the Twentieth Century* (Oakland: University of California Press, 2015), 16.

10 Rajani Palme Dutt, "Notes of the Month," in *Labour Monthly*, October 1, 1935, 17. First seen in Bush, *Imperialism, Race and Resistance*, 240–1.

11 Another notable exception was Sylvia Pankhurst. For more than three decades, Pankhurst had led the struggle against patriarchal chauvinism. Fearing that the British Left would soon forget Ethiopia, she established a newspaper, the *New Times and Ethiopia News,* to "keep the question of Ethiopia alive." The first issue went to press on May 5, 1936—the same day the Royal Italian Army entered Addis Ababa. Richard Pankhurst, "Sylvia and New Times and Ethiopia News," in *Sylvia Pankhurst: From Artist to Anti-Fascist*, ed. Ian Bullock and Richard Pankhurst (New York: St. Martin's Press, 1992), 154. See also Katherine Connelly, *Sylvia Pankhurst: Suffragette, Socialist and Scourge of Empire* (London: Pluto Press, 2013), 129. Additionally, according to Barbara Bush, the National Council of Civil Liberties—whose members included Ronald Kidd, Vera Brittain, and E. M. Forster—developed a "more consistently radical approach to race and colonial problems, which centred on the defence of the civil rights of blacks in Britain and the colonies." Bush, *Imperialism, Race and Resistance*, 241.

12 There has been substantial historiographical debate over the term "New Imperialism." Scholars "have disagreed about the precise definition of this term, its explanatory value, and even the boundaries of the period to which it should be applied." Bradley Deane, *Masculinity and the New Imperialism: Rewriting Manhood in British Popular Literature, 1870–1914* (Cambridge: Cambridge University Press, 2014), 9. See also Peter Cain and A. G. Hopkins, *British Imperialism: 1688–2000* (London: Routledge, 1993); Michael Hardt and Antonio Negri, *Empire* (Harvard: Harvard University Press, 2001); Roger Louis, *The Ends of British Imperialism* (London: Bloomsbury Academic, 2006); John MacKenzie, *Propaganda and Empire: The Manipulation of British Public Opinion, 1880–1960* (Manchester: Manchester University Press, 2017).

13 Dutt, *Decisive Days Ahead*, 22–3.

14 Bush, *Imperialism, Race and Resistance*, 241.

15 To be sure, other factors played a significant role, particularly the geographical proximity of Spain to England and the relative celerity with which Italy conquered Ethiopia. Nevertheless, "British public opinion seemed thoroughly devoted to the League and to the concept of collective security." G. Bruce Strang, "Introduction," in *Collision of Empires: Italy's Invasion of Ethiopia and its International Impact*, ed. Bruce Strang (London: Routledge, 2013), 4.

16 Philip Morgan, *Italian Fascism, 1919-1945* (Basingstoke: Macmillan, 1995);
Louise Young, *Japan's Total Empire: Manchuria and the Culture of Wartime
Imperialism* (Berkeley: University of California Press, 1999); Ian Kershaw,
Hitler: 1936-1945, Nemesis (London: W.W. Norton & Company, 2001); R. M.
Salerno, *Vital Crossroads: Mediterranean Origins of the Second World War,
1935-1940* (Ithaca: Cornell University Press, 2002); Richard Bosworth, *Mussolini*
(London: Bloomsbury Academic, 2010); Shelley Baranowski, *Nazi Empire:
German Colonialism and Imperialism from Bismarck to Hitler* (Cambridge:
Cambridge University Press, 2011); Mark Mazower, *Hitler's Empire: Nazi Rule in
Occupied Europe* (London: Penguin UK, 2013); Patrick Bernhard, "Borrowing
from Mussolini: Nazi Germany's Colonial Aspirations in the Shadow of Italian
Expansionism," *The Journal of Imperial and Commonwealth History* 41, no. 4
(2013): 617–43; Robert Mallet, *Mussolini in Ethiopia, 1919-1935: The Origins of
Fascist Italy's African War* (Cambridge: Cambridge University Press, 2015); Patrick
Bernhard, "Hitler's Africa in the East: Italian Colonialism as a Model for German
Planning in Eastern Europe," *Journal of Contemporary History* 51, no. 1 (2016):
61–90; Matthew Hefler, "'In the Way': Intelligence, Eden, and British Foreign
Policy Towards Italy, 1937–38," *Intelligence and National Security* 33, no. 6 (2018):
875–93; Roy Douglas, "Chamberlain and Appeasement," in *The Fascist Challenge
and the Policy of Appeasement* (London: Routledge, 2021); M. Gonçalves, "The
Scramble for Africa Reloaded? Portugal, European Colonial Claims and the
Distribution of Colonies in the 1930s," *Contemporary European History* 30, no. 1
(2021): 2–15.

17 Leon Trotsky, *The Permanent Revolution and Results and Prospects* (Delhi: Aakar
Books, 1919), xxxii. See also Robert Paxton, *The Anatomy of Fascism* (New York:
Vintage Books, 2005), 148. Paxton contends that fascist regimes "had to produce
an impression of driving momentum . . . in order to fulfill these promises. They
could not survive without that headlong, inebriating rush forward." Paxton,
Paxton, *The Anatomy of Fascism*, 148.

18 Steven Morewood, "This Silly African Business: The Military Dimension of
Britain's Response to the Abyssinian Crisis," in *Collision of Empires*, 75.

19 The war itself, as Kasper Braskén has argued, "should not be downplayed as an
old style 'colonial war,' and in fact represented the first fascist, total war." Kasper
Braskén, "'Whether Black or White—United in the Fight!' Connecting the
Resistance against Colonialism, Racism, and Fascism in the European Metropoles,
1926-1936," *Twentieth Century Communism* 18 (2020): 141.

20 Like the term "fascism," "New Imperialism" remains somewhat nebulous, and is
often used in a beguiling manner. In this chapter, I use the term to refer primarily
to the Scramble for Africa (1884-1914), during which European states "began the
process of recognizing each other's claims to a continent not their own, drawing

up maps delineating which power would hold sway where, and establishing the rules to determine how the scramble would take place." Myles Osborne and Susan Kingsley Kent, *Africans and Britons in the Age of Empires, 1660–1980* (London: Routledge, 2015), 76. It is important to note that there are broader cultural, social, and political dimensions to the New Imperialist phenomenon: "There was much that was new about the New Imperialism, that rapid spasm of expansion that extended European control over almost all of African and significant portions of the Eastern Mediterranean, Southeast Asia, and Pacific territories in the final quarter of the nineteenth century. It encompassed new forms of control, new ideologies, new technologies, new state structures, new cultural elements, and new players in the game of empire. But in the end, what was most new about the New Imperialism was that it involved newly unified European states, that its practitioners justified their action through explicitly references to racial ideology, that it occurred far more rapidly and over a broader area than previous phases of imperialism had, and that it witnessed the widespread imposition of political, economic, and cultural domination over that territory." Sascha Auerbach, "The New Imperialism," in *The Fin-de-Siècle World,* ed. Michael Saler (New York: Routledge, 2015), 335.

21 This analytical lens expands upon the arguments of Peter Cain and A. G. Hopkins. In *British Imperialism,* they contended that "The 1930s were a period of renascent imperialism in Africa, as they were in South American and China. The 'imperial problem,' as defined by contemporaries, was particularly acute in the case of Africa because the continent had been divided and parts of it reassigned comparatively recently. The 'problem' itself was not, as hindsight might misleadingly suggest, how to deal with nationalism, but how to accommodate the 'have-not' nations without weakening the empire. The 'have-nots,' in the terminology of the day, were those deprived, not of food, but of colonies, and referred principally to Germany, Japan and (since demand for other people's territory was readily expandable) to Italy." Cain and Hopkins, *British Imperialism,* 586. See also: Bush, *Imperialism, Race and Resistance,* 228–70; Mallet, *Mussolini in Ethiopia,* 94–123; Morgan, *Italian Fascism,* 131–45.

22 In 1889, the newly coronated Menelik and Count Pietro Antonelli of Italy signed the Treaty of Wuchale, which recognized Menelik's sovereignty in exchange for coastal territory which became Italy's first official colony, Eritrea. Controversy, however, soon followed. The Amharic version of the treaty granted Ethiopia considerable sovereignty, as well as the option to conduct foreign affairs through the Italian government. By contrast, the Italian version, circulated to major powers across Europe, declared that Ethiopia was required to conduct all foreign affairs through Rome. Claiming he had been deceived, Menelik declared the treaty invalid. In response, the Italian government, led by the aggressive and expansionist

Francesco Crispi, ordered Italian troops to occupy Northern Ethiopia, including much of the Tigray. With little recourse, Menelik declared a general mobilization and set out to confront the Italian army. Paulos Milkias, Getachew Metaferia, *The Battle of Adwa: Reflections on Ethiopia's Historic Victory Against European Colonialism* (New York: Algora Publishers, 2005), 43–9.

23 General Baratieri preferred a partial withdrawal but was overruled by the Italian government.

24 Harold Marcus, *A History of Ethiopia* (Berkeley: University of California Press, 1994), 99.

25 The Italian casualty-rate at Adowa was higher than any other major European battle in the nineteenth century. Still, Menelik II's victory "was attributed to the hostile Ethiopian terrain. The centuries of independent statehood, intensely proud nationalism, fighting skill, numerical superiority, and close matching of firepower of Ethiopians with that of Italians was simply ignored." See Teshale Tibebu, "The 'Anomaly' and 'Paradox' of Africa," *Journal of Black Studies* 26, no. 4 (1996): 415.

26 King Victor Emmanuel II of Italy appointed Mussolini prime minister in October 1922. Morgan, *Italian Fascism*, 59–75.

27 Shortly thereafter, French Minister of Foreign Affairs Pierre Laval met with Mussolini in Rome. On January 7, 1935, they signed the Franco-Italian Agreement, which consigned a portion of French Somaliland to Italy, and tacitly accepted Mussolini's expansionist aims in Ethiopia. In return, Laval hoped for Italian support against Nazi expansionism.

28 Harold Marcus has contended that the League "was working against Ethiopia's interests. . . .The council's major powers tried to force humiliating concessions on Ethiopia so that an appeased Italy might then serve the needs of continental politics. Neither France nor Britain understood that to accommodate Mussolini beyond a certain point would destroy the league's credibility, the plausibility of collective security, and the European balance of power." Marcus, *A History of Ethiopia*, 140–1.

29 Rosaria Quartararo, "Imperial Defence in the Mediterranean on the Eve of the Ethiopian Crisis (July-October 1935)," *The Historical Journal* 20, no. 1 (1977): 220.

30 Marcus, *A History of Ethiopia*, 116–29.

31 Susan Pedersen, *The Guardians: The League of Nations and the Crisis of Empire* (Oxford: Oxford University Press, 2015), 5. Revisionist support for the League has since criticized its architects, rather than its administrators, for the failure of collective security. As Susan Pedersen has argued, "Great powers, like other states, understandably pursue their own interests; if they found that they could not do so through the mechanisms offered by the League, those mechanisms—and not the great powers—were at fault. International relations is the art of making great power interests and global stability coincide: if the League made that coincidence

more difficult, it deserved the opprobrium heaped upon it." Susan Pedersen, "Back to the League of Nations," *The American Historical Review* 112, no. 4 (2007): 1116.

32 Prior to the Second Italo-Ethiopian War, Mussolini was perhaps the most vocal opponent of Nazi expansionism. In response, many within the British government sought to formalize a grand anti-Nazi alliance with Italy and France. In April 1935, Mussolini, French prime minister Pierre Laval, and British prime minister Ramsay MacDonald formalized this ambition at Stresa, Italy. Though short-lived—and as some historians have contended, apocryphal—the Stresa Front sought to ensure Austrian independence, enforce German compliance with the Treaty of Versailles, and revivify the "Spirit of Locarno." During negotiations, Mussolini insisted that Laval and MacDonald ignore the Abyssinian Crisis and, afterward, contended that their silence constituted a tacit endorsement of Italian imperial sovereignty in the Horn of Africa. Two months later, Mussolini and the Royal Italian Army invaded Ethiopia. R. J. Q. Adams, *British Politics and Foreign Policy in the Age of Appeasement, 1935–39* (Stanford: Stanford University Press, 1993), 21.

33 Robert Mallet, "Fascist Foreign Policy and Official Italian Views of Anthony Eden in the 1930s," *The Historical Journal* 43, no. 1 (2000): 158.

34 Cristiano Ristuccia has contended that oil sanctions, though perhaps not decisive, would nevertheless have complicated Mussolini's decision to invade Ethiopia: "In the 1935 the League had more than a fair chance of forcing Italy to back down by means of a commercial embargo. In particular, an embargo imposed on oil products, although having a negligible impact on the military operations in Ethiopia, could have had a substantial effect on road transport and indirectly on industrial production." Cristiano Andrea Ristuccia, "The 1935 Sanctions against Italy: Would Coal and Oil Have Made a Difference?" *European Review of Economic History* 4, no. 1 (2000): 86.

35 "A Corridor for Camels," *The Times*, December 16, 1935, 15.

36 Many critics of the Hoare-Laval Pact contended that the National Government had betrayed its pledge—made during the 1935 General Election—for collective security through the League of Nations. Peter Neville, *Hitler and Appeasement: The British Attempt to Prevent the Second World War* (London: Hambledon Continuum, 2006), 52.

37 John Munro, *The Anticolonial Front: The African American Freedom Struggle and Global Decolonisation, 1945–1960* (Cambridge: Cambridge University Press, 2017), 15–75.

38 Liberia maintained close diplomatic ties with the United States.

39 Joseph Fronczak, "Local People's Global Politics: A Transnational History of the Hands Off Ethiopia Movement of 1935," *Diplomatic History* 39, no. 2 (2015): 245–53.

40 Neelam Srivastava, *Italian Colonialism and Resistance to Empire, 1930–1970* (London: Palgrave Macmillan, 2018), 67. Srivastava goes on to argue that the

"outrage felt by black communities all over the world, from Harlem to London, from Port of Spain to Accra, was fueled both by the act of the invasion itself and by what was perceived to be the betrayal of a black nation by its white so-called allies in the League of Nations. The League's failure to uphold sanctions against Italy, including the Soviet Union's continued sale of oil to the country, was deemed almost as culpable and despicable as Mussolini's declaration that Ethiopia represented for Italy its much-deserved 'place in the sun.' The invasion contributed much to strengthen support for anti-colonial movements both within the metropole and within the colonies, and it also played a key role in the development of Pan-Africanism. It was around the time of the Ethiopian war that many diasporic blacks began to identify explicitly as 'Africans,' though the articulation of Ethiopia as a black homeland had ancestral roots in black liberationist and religious movements." Srivastava, *Italian Colonialism and Resistance to Empire*, 67.

41 Haile Selassie, "The Emperor to the League: Full Text of the Emperor of Ethiopia's Great Speech," *New Times and Ethiopia News*, July 11, 1936, 2.

42 Selassie, "The Lion is Freed." Selassie was later named *Time*'s "Man of the Year."

43 Minkah Makalani, *In the Cause of Freedom: Radical Black Internationalism from Harlem to London: 1917-1939* (Chapel Hill: University of North Carolina Press, 2011), 3-22.

44 Matera, *Black London*, 2. Similarly, Robert Hill has contended that "the intense feeling of racial solidarity that Italian aggression against Ethiopia aroused among blacks throughout the world was extraordinary." Marcus Garvey and Robert Hill, *The Marcus Garvey and Universal Negro Improvement Association Papers*, vol. 10 (Berkeley: University of California Press, 2006), c.

45 Interestingly, Nazi Germany supplied the Ethiopian Empire with more than 15,000 rifles. Hitler hoped to frustrate the Italian invasion, giving him an opening to invade Austria. After the collapse of the Stresa Front, however, Hitler and Mussolini mended their relationship and, in due course, formed the Rome-Berlin Axis (1936). Zachary Shore, *What Hitler Knew: The Battle for Information in Nazi Foreign Policy* (Oxford: Oxford University Press, 2005), 70-1.

46 Makalani, *In the Cause of Freedom*, 7. See also Susan Pennybacker, *From Scottsboro to Munich: Race and Politics Culture in 1930s Britain* (Princeton: Princeton University Press, 2009); Cathy Bergin, ed., *African American Anti-Colonial Thought: 1917-1937* (Edinburgh: Edinburgh University Press, 2016); Sarah Dunstan, "The Capital of Race Capitals: Toward a Connective Cartography of Black Internationalisms," *Journal of the History of Ideas* 82, no. 4 (2021): 637-60.

47 George Padmore, "Ethiopia and World Politics," *Crisis Magazine*, May 1935, 138.

48 Across Africa and Asia, Europe's great powers disputed claims, contested boundaries, and even waged proxy wars. They would not, however, risk a second

world war to defend Ethiopian sovereignty. As Elisabetta Tollardo has argued, "While the Great Powers considered giving up an uncivilized African state preferable to souring relations with Italy, they still had to find a way to conciliate such a clear violation of the Covenant with the existence of the League." Elisabetta Tollardo, *Fascist Italy and the League of Nations 1922–1935* (London: Palgrave Macmillan, 2016), 49.

49 Black and Asian radicals "made pivotal connections between anti- fascism and the struggles against colonialism and racism. . . . For many anti-imperialist activists both in Europe and in the colonies it became a necessity to link analyses of fascism with those of imperialism. From an anti-imperialist perspective fascism simply meant the most brutal form of imperialism." Braskén, "Whether Black or White— United in the Fight!" 12.

50 In addition to Hill and Makalani, see Jonathan Schneer, *London 1900: The Imperial Metropolis* (New Haven: Yale Nota Bene, 2001); Brent Hayes Edwards, *The Practice of Diaspora: Literature, Translation and the Rise of Black Nationalism* (Cambridge: Harvard University Press, 2003); James Lorand Matory, *Black Atlantic Religion Tradition, Transnationalism, and Matriarchy in the Afro-Brazilian Candomblé* (Princeton: Princeton University Press, 2005); Kevin Grant, Philippa Levine, and Frank Trentmann, *Beyond Sovereignty: Britain, Empire, and Transnationalism, C. 1880–1950* (Houndmills, Basingstoke, Hampshire: Palgrave Macmillan, 2007); Philippa Levine, *The British Empire: Sunrise to Sunset* (Harlow, England: Pearson Longman, 2007); Catherine Lynette Innes, *A History of Black and Asian Writing in Britain: 1700–2000* (Cambridge: Cambridge University Press, 2008); Marilyn Lake, and Henry Reynolds, *Drawing the Global Colour Line: White Men's Countries and the Question of Racial Equality* (Carlton: Melbourne University Publications, 2008); Elleke Boehmer, *Empire, the National, and the Postcolonial: 1890–1920: Resistance in Interaction* (Oxford: Oxford University Press, 2010); Joseph Calvitt Clarke, *Alliance of Colored Peoples: Ethiopia and Japan Before World War II* (Woodbridge, Suffolk: James Currey, 2011); Kennetta Hammond Perry, "Black Britain and the Politics of Race in the 20th Century," *History Compass* 12, no. 8 (2014): 651–63.

51 Matera, *Black London*, 1.

52 Arlena Buelli, "The Hands Off Ethiopia Campaign, Racial Solidarities and Intercolonial Antifascism in South Asia (1935–36)," *Journal of Global History* (2022): 4. https://www.cambridge.org/core/journals/journal-of-global-history /article/hands-off-ethiopia-campaign-racial-solidarities-and-intercolonial -antifascism-in-south-asia-193536/0EF2D18F37E18BE79AF61618E2771A14.

53 Morewood, "This Silly African Business," 73.

54 During the Great Depression, the Italian economy did not perform as well as Mussolini claimed. These struggles partly motivated his decision to invade Ethiopia. Morgan, *Italian Fascism*, 107–44.

55 Giuseppe Flora, "Review: Gandhi in Italy," *East and West* 38, no. 1 (1988): 336.

56 Gandhi visited at the request of Luigi Scarpa, the ex-Italian consul in India.

57 Romain Hays, *Subhas Chandra Bose in Nazi Germany* (New York: Columbia University Press, 2011), 9.

58 Ibid.

59 Ibid.

60 Ibid.

61 Mohandas K. Gandhi, "Letter to Romain Rolland," December 20, 1931, in *The Collected Works of Mahatma Gandhi* (CWMG), vol. 48 (New Delhi: Publications Division Government of India, 1999), 429.

62 David James Fisher, *Romain Rolland and the Politics of Intellectual Engagement* (London: Transaction Publishers, 1988), 135.

63 Ibid.

64 Gandhi, "Cable to Croft," December 17, 1931, in *CWMG,* vol. 48, 426.

65 Peter Gonsalves, "The Mahatma, Il Duce and the Crucifix: Gandhi's Brief Encounter with Mussolini and its Consequences," *Salesianum* 74 (2012): 719.

66 Ibid., 715.

67 Ibid.

68 Tagore had visited Italy the year prior, but fell ill and returned to India before he could meet Mussolini.

69 Tapati Das Gupta, *Social Thought of Rabindranath Tagore: A Historical Analysis* (New Delhi: Abhinav Publications, 1993), 80.

70 S. Radhakrishnan, *Rabindranath Tagore: A Centenary, Volumes 1861–1961* (New Delhi: Sahitya Akademi, 1992), 140.

71 Quoted in Das Gupta, *Social Thought of Rabindranath Tagore,* 80.

72 Das Gupta, *Social Thought of Rabindranath Tagore,* 80.

73 Quoted in Krishna Dutt and Andrew Robinson, *Rabindranath Tagore: The Myriad-Minded Man* (London: Tauris Parke Paperbacks, 1995), 269–70.

74 In 1930, Tagore wrote a letter thanking Mussolini for "the lavish generosity you showed to me in your hospitality when I was your guest in Italy." Tagore, however, did not send the letter. Tagore, *Selected Letters,* 394.

75 Rabindranath Tagore to Romain Roland, July 13, 1926, in *Selected Letters,* 329.

76 In a letter to Gandhi, Tagore argued that nonviolence was a "force which is not necessarily moral in itself," and, in effect, "[could] be used against truth as well as for it." Rabindranath Tagore to Mohandas K. Gandhi, April 19, 1919, in *The Mahatma and the Poet: Letters and Debates Between Gandhi and Tagore, 1915–1941* (New Delhi: National Book Trust, 1997), 49. Similarly, Pankaj Mishra has contended that Tagore harbored "serious differences with Gandhi over what he saw as the xenophobic aspect of the anti-colonial movement." Pankaj Mishra, *From the Ruins of Empire: The Intellectuals Who Remade Asia* (New York: Farrar, Straus and Giroux, 2012), 221.

77 Gandhi, "The Greatest Force," October 12, 1935, in *CWMG*, vol. 62, 28.

78 Judith Brown, *Gandhi: Prisoner of Hope* (New Haven: Yale University Press, 1989), 320. In a letter written to Nehru, Gandhi confessed that "you have undoubtedly a much greater grasp of the situation [Ethiopia] . . . than I can ever hope to have." Gandhi, "Letter to Jawaharlal Nehru," October 17, 1935, in *CWMG*, vol. 62, 39.

79 Tagore travelled to more than thirty countries on five different continents. His work was beloved in Europe, Asia, South America, and Africa.

80 Quoted in Mishra, *From the Ruins of Empire*, 241. See also Stephen N. Hay, "Rabindranath Tagore in America," *American Quarterly* 14, no. 3 (1962): 439–63. In a similar episode at Carnegie Hall, Tagore "claimed that Americans ignored Britain's domination of India, and worried about Japan only because the latter 'was able to prove she would make herself as obnoxious as you can.' It was his final message to the West, greeted, according to the *New York Times*, by 'considerable laughter and hand-clapping.'" See Mishra, *From the Ruins of Empire*, 245.

81 Rajendra Verma, *Rabindranath Tagore: Prophet Against Totalitarianism* (New York: Asia Pub. House, 1964), 48.

82 Ibid.

83 Rabindranath Tagore, "107," in *The English Writings of Rabindranath Tagore: Volume One: Poems*, 381.

84 Jawaharlal Nehru, "Presidential Address: Lahore Congress Session" in *The Selected Works of Jawaharlal Nehru*, vol. 4, *First Series*, 195.

85 Quoted in Anton Pelinka and Renée Schell, *Democracy Indian Style: Subhas Chandra Bose and the Creation of India's Political Culture* (New Brunswick: Transaction Publishers, 2003), 91.

86 In Bombay, leftists circulated the anti-colonial pamphlet *Gandhi and Lenin*; in Bengal, Muzaffar Ahmed founded *Navayug* and *Langal*; and in Madras, M. Singaravelu launched the *Labour-Kisan Gazette*. Bipin Chandra, *India's Struggle for Independence: 1857–1947* (New Delhi: Penguin Books India, 1989), 297.

87 Joseph Stalin, "Speech Delivered by J.V. Stalin at a Meeting of Voters of the Stalin Electoral District, Moscow: February 9, 1946," in *Pamphlet Collection: J. Stalin*, trans. The Wilson Center: Digital Archive (Moscow: Foreign Languages Publishing House, 1950), 24–5.

88 Nina Tumarkin, *The Living and the Dead: The Rise and Fall of the Cult of World War II in Russia* (New York: Basic Books, 1994); Nurit Schleifman, *Russia at a Crossroads: History, Memory and Political Practice* (London: Frank Cass, 1998); Tim Rees, and Andrew Thorpe, *International Communism and the Communist International, 1919–1943* (Manchester: Manchester University Press, 1999); Teddy Uldricks, "War, Politics and Memory: Russian Historians Reevaluate the Origins of World War II," *History and Memory* 21, no. 2 (2009): 60–82; Silvio Pons, and

Allan Cameron, *The Global Revolution: A History of International Communism 1917–1991* (Oxford: Oxford University Press, 2014).

89 Rajani Palme Dutt, "On the Character of the Second World War," *People's Age* (Bombay), May 5, 1946.

90 Interestingly, Dutt never mentioned Stalin's ambivalence toward the Second Italo-Ethiopian War. Bernard Bayerlein, "Addis Ababa, Rio De Janeiro and Moscow 1935," in *The Double Failure of Comintern Anti-Fascism and Anti-Colonialism* (London: Routledge, 2020).

91 Duncan Hallas, "The Shyster Lawyer," *Socialist Review* 167 (1993): 30.

92 Callaghan, *Rajani Palme Dutt*, 8. In 1924, Dutt married Estonian Bolshevik Salme Murrik, with whom he spent the next twelve years in Brussels.

93 In his analysis of the Indian campaign for independence, Dutt often criticized Gandhi. In *Indian Politics,* he contended that "The existing ideology of 'non-violence,' which is still made a compulsory part of the Congress creed, is . . . at variance with the realities of the struggle and less and less corresponds to the outlook of large sections of the national movement. Many prominent members of the Congress, who have formally to subscribe to this dogma as the condition of their participation in its mass activities, to-day privately declare their disbelief in it." R. Palme Dutt and Ben Bradley, *Indian Politics: The Anti-Imperialist People's Front: Towards Trade Union Unity* (London: Publisher not identified, 193–), 9.

94 Callaghan, *Rajani Palme Dutt*, 104. During the Meerut Conspiracy Case, colonial officials arrested and convicted thirty-three trade unionists.

95 John Callaghan, "Dutt, (Rajani) Palme (1896–1974), Political Leader," *Oxford Dictionary of National Biography*, September 23, 2004; Accessed October 14, 2019.

96 As Stanley Payne has argued that Soviet theory "held that after fascism appeared as the instrument of finance capital, all other forces 'serving' capitalism were also 'objectively fascist.' This included not merely all right authoritarian forces and regimes but also, most prominently and insidiously, social democrats who 'collaborated' with capitalist forces in democratic systems. Thus as early as 1924 Socialists became 'social fascists.'" Stanley Payne, *A History of Fascism: 1914–1945* (Madison: University of Wisconsin Press, 1995), 443.

97 Rajani Palme Dutt, *The Coming War* (London: Communist Party of Great Britain, 1929), 3.

98 Julian Jackson, *The Popular Front in France: Defending Democracy, 1934–1938* (Cambridge: Cambridge University Press, 1988), 36–7.

99 Nicholas Owen, *The British Left and India: Metropolitan Anti-Imperialism, 1885–1947* (Oxford: Oxford University Press, 2007), 240–65.

100 Stuart Macintyre, *Science & Society* 61, no. 1 (1997): 147. In his review of Callaghan's biography, Macintyre draws attention to the opening epigram: "The

Ghoshes are high caste, the Boses are generous, the Mitras are cunning, But the Dutts are scoundrels."

101   Rajani Palme Dutt, "Speech Made by RPD During the 'Colonial Struggle for Liberation,' at the Memorial Hall, Farringdon St. on December 2, 1937," *Rajani Palme Dutt, Vice-Chairman, Communist Party of Great Britain: Scotland Yard Reports, Activities and Publications*, British Library (Hereafter BL), India Office Records and Private Papers, L/PJ/12/30, File 455(c)21.

102   R. Palme Dutt, *World Politics: 1918–1936* (New York: Random House, 1936), 204.

103   There were, of course, exceptions; nevertheless, as Peter Neville has argued, "The other factor in British government calculations was the state of British public opinion, which in 1935 was strongly pro-League and anti-war." Neville, 52. The approach of the Dominions, meanwhile, "was reactive and piecemeal." W. Neville Sloane, "The Paradox of Peaceful Coexistence: British Dominions' Response to the Italo-Abyssinian Crisis 1935–1936," in *Collision of Empire*, 185.

104   "Debate in British House of Commons on Public order Bill, November 16, 1936," Carnegie Endowment for International Peace (1937): 558.

105   Evelyn Waugh, *Waugh in Abyssinia* (London: Longmans, Green & Co, 1936), 40.

106   In *Indo-Ethiopian Relations for Centuries*, I. M. Muthanna contends: "The Indian firm of Muhamad Ali & Co. in Addis Ababa was short of food and it was closed subsequently in 1936. An Arab trader, a Hindu and a Somali were killed in Jigjiga during the troubles there in 1936. Wazir Ali Baig, an old Indian Resident in Ethiopia was expelled by the Italians." Wazir Ali said, "I have lived twenty-seven years in Ethiopia. During the World War I, I was the correspondent for Reuter and also sent weekly despatches to the Bombay Chronicle and the Hindustan Times in India." I. M. Muthanna, *Indo-Ethiopian Relations for Centuries* (Addis Ababa: Artistic Print, 1961), 141. Wazir Ali Baig also served as a correspondent for Sylvia Pankhurst's *New Times and Ethiopia News*: "Pankhurst's special correspondent was Wazir Ali Baig, originally from the Punjab, and thus a British colonial subject, who had lived in Ethiopia for more than 27 years. He seems to have been a member of the Indian trading community that did business in Ethiopia until the arrival of the Italians. When Italy invaded, he seems to have taken refuge in Djibouti (French colonial territory), from where he wrote most of his dispatches to Pankhurst. He acted as special correspondent for NTEN from 1936 until 1941, the year of his death from illness. He also happened to be Waugh's informant in Addis Ababa; in Waugh in Abyssinia, Waugh describes him as 'an imposing old rascal with the figure of a metropolitan policeman and the manner of a butler. He wrote and spoke nearly perfect English' and 'had a natural flair for sensational journalism,' which he supplied to most of the American and British correspondents in Addis during the war." Srivastava, *Italian Colonialism and Resistances to Empire*, 178.

107 "Statement Issued from the Foreign Dept. of the AICC on Abyssinian Indians: Information from a Letter from Shri Gulabchand Talakchand, Member of the Indian Association, Addis Ababa," *All India Congress Committee—Foreign Department Newsletter*, The Nehru Memorial Museum and Library (hereafter NMML), AICC Newsletters, 26/FD-31/1147/1939.

108 Ibid.

109 Ibid.

110 R. Palme Dutt, *Fascism and Social Revolution* (New York: International Publishers, 1934), 213.

111 Subhas Bose, "The Secret of Abyssinia and Its Lesson," in *Subhas Bose: Letters, Articles, Speeches and Statements, 1933–1937*, ed. Sisir Kumar Bose and Sugata Bose (Calcutta: Netaji Research Bureau, 1994), 327.

112 Ibid., 328.

113 Ibid., 327.

114 Tewodros's letter urged Queen Victoria to send military assistance. Internal opposition to his authority "had started as early as 1855. In the subsequent decade, Tewodros was to spend most of his time moving in haste from one province to another, faced with a fresh outbreak of rebellion before he had succeeded in putting down the previous one." Bahru Zewde, *A History of Modern Ethiopia, 1855–1991* (Columbus: Ohio State University, 2002), 43.

115 Marcus, *A History of Ethiopia*, 48–62.

116 Bose, "The Secret of Abyssinia and Its Lesson," 327.

117 *Agreement Between France, Russia, Great Britain, and Italy, Signed at London, April 26, 1915* (London: His Majesty's Stationary Office, 1920), 6.

118 Bose, "The Secret of Abyssinia and Its Lesson," 329.

119 Dutt, *World Politics*, 12.

120 Ibid., 243.

121 In Italy, this impulse manifested primarily through the revivification of the Roman Empire. Mussolini "garbed his movement in Roman imperial symbols, claimed descent from Garibaldi, wove fascist rituals into the young nation's memorial days, and acquired the sacred blessing of Italy's church. He called for the rebirth of Rome and the fulfillment of Italy's thwarted drive for dignity and power." Michael Mann, *Fascists* (Cambridge: Cambridge University Press, 2004), 131.

122 Ruth Ben-Ghiat, and Mial Fuller, eds., *Italian Colonialism* (New York: Palgrave Macmillan, 2005).

123 Quoted in Ian Campbell, *The Addis Ababa Massacre: Italy's National Shame* (Oxford: Oxford University Press, 2017), 21.

124 Dutt, *Decisive Days*, 16.

125 Strang, "Introduction," 3.

126 "Britain and the League: Sir S. Hoare's Speech, the Full Text," *The Times*, September 12, 1935, 7.

127 Adams, *British Politics and Foreign Policy*, 24.

128 Ibid.

129 As Ian Spears has argued, "Britain and France judged Ethiopia to be insufficiently 'vital' to challenge the Italian incursion or to uphold their pledges to the League." Spears, 48.

130 Dutt, *Decisive Days Ahead*, 21.

131 As Morewood has argued, "The intent was only to use force as a last resort lest Mussolini turned into a mad dog and went on the rampage attacking British interests." Morewood, "This Silly African Business," 75.

132 Morewood, "This Silly African Business," 80. Similarly, Bush has contended that "The new imperialist scramble of the 'have nots' was an ugly harbinger of war and revealed the more naked economic basis of imperial expansion. The primary concern of the British Government was the defence of empire. Cain and Hopkins (1993) thus see the 1930s as a period when the 'imperial problem' became acutely mirrored in a renascent imperialism in Africa, South America, and China. Where Africa was concerned, they argue, the problem was not so much African nationalism, but how to accommodate the 'have not' nations and the increasing intervention of the 'anti-colonial' US without weakening the empire." Bush, *Imperialism, Race and Resistance*, 256.

133 Ibid., 82.

134 Dutt, *World Politics*, 245.

135 Ibid.

136 According to Morewood, this fleet could "easily have bombarded the vulnerable Italian coast including the feeder port of Naples, enforced a crippling blockade against a country reliant on sea imports, exercised contraband control and rendered an oil embargo effective by preventing all Massawa-bound tankers from reaching their destinations in Eritrea. The most telling potential measure of all— denying the Suez Canal to Italian troop and supply ships—never received serious consideration." Morewood, "This Silly African Business," 73.

137 Bose, "The Secret of Abyssinia and Its Lesson," 328.

138 Ibid.

139 Morewood, "This Silly African Business," 75.

140 Ristuccia, "The 1935 Sanctions Against Italy," 86.

141 Quoted in: Gaynor Johnson, "Philip Noel-Baker, the League of Nations and the Abyssinian Crisis, 1935–1936," in *Collision of Empires*, 59.

142 Dutt, *World Politics*, 136.

143 Susan Pedersen has contended that the League "was founded upon and remained devoted to the principle of state sovereignty; indeed, insofar as these ideals led

politicians to play to the stands or alienated the great powers, they may have been counterproductive." Pedersen, "Back to the League of Nations."

144 Although envisioned as an arbiter of world peace, the League "was a product of empire." Mark Mazower, *No Enchanted Palace: The End of Empire and the Ideological Origins of the United Nations* (Princeton: Princeton University Press, 2009), 17.

145 Azaj Warqneh C. Martin, "Nero Fiddled While Rome Burned," *New Times and Ethiopian News*, May 23, 1936. According to Richard Pankhurst, Martin "had been taken as a child to India by members of the 1867–8 Napier expedition against Emperor Tewodros of Ethiopia. Assumed, incorrectly, to be an orphan, young Workneh had been re-christened, and given the name and surname of two British officers who provided for his upkeep. Having later followed a distinguished medical career, he was known in Britain as Dr. Charles Workneh Martin." Richard Pankhurst, *Sylvia Pankhurst: Counsel for Ethiopia: A Biographical Essay on Ethiopian Anti-Fascist and Anti-Colonialist History* (Hollywood: Tsehai Publishers, 2003), 9.

146 Jessi Gilchrist, "'Clouds of Mutual Suspicion:' Neville Chamberlain and Appeasement in the Mediterranean," *The International History Review* (2021): 1–18.

147 Ristuccia, "The 1935 Sanctions Against Italy," 86.

148 Ibid.

149 Pedersen, *The Guardians*, 289–393. See also: Martin Ceadel, *Semi-Detached Idealists: The British Peace Movement and International Relations, 1854–1945* (Oxford: Oxford University Press, 2000); Talbot Imlay, *Facing the Second World War: Strategy, Politics, and Economics in Britain and France, 1938–1940* (Oxford: Oxford University Press, 2003); David Edgerton, *Warfare State: Britain, 1920–1970* (Cambridge: Cambridge University Press, 2006); Bruce Strang, "The Worst of All Worlds: Oil Sanctions and Italy's Invasion of Abyssinia, 1935–1936," *Diplomacy & Statecraft* 19, no. 2 (2008): 210–35; Joseph Maiolo, *Cry Havoc: How the Arms Race Drove the World To War, 1931–1941* (New York: Basic Books, 2010); Helen McCarthy, *The British People and the League of Nations: Democracy, Citizenship, and Internationalism, 1918–1945* (Manchester: Manchester University Press, 2013).

150 Imlay, *Facing the Second World War*, 186–242.

151 Morewood, "This Silly African Business," 77.

152 Edgerton, *Warfare State: Britain*, 15–58.

153 A. J. P. Taylor, *The Origins of the Second World War* (New York: Simon & Schuster, 1961), 90. First seen in Morewood, "This Silly African Business," 74.

154 Dutt, *World Politics*, 179.

155 Cain and Hopkins, *British Imperialism*, 587.

156 Mallet, *Mussolini in Ethiopia*, 154–86. See also R. M. Salerno, "Britain, France and the Emerging Italian Threat, 1935–38," in *Anglo-French Defence Relations Between*

the Wars, ed. Martin Alexander and William Philpott (London: Palgrave Macmillan), 72–8; Strang, "Worst of All Worlds," 210–14; Andrew Holt, "'No More Hoares to Paris'; British Foreign Policy Making and the Abyssinian Crisis, 1935," *Review of International Studies* 37, no. 3 (2011): 1388–90; Manolis Koumas, "Patterns of the Future? British Mediterranean Strategy and the Choice Between Alexandria and Cyprus, 1935–8," *The International History Review* 33, no. 3 (2011): 489–95.

157 Daniel Hucker, *Public Opinion and the End of Appeasement in Britain and France* (New York: Routledge, 2011), 23–50.

158 Caedel, 328.

159 Robbie Shilliam, "Ethiopianism, Englishness, Britishness: Struggles Over Imperial Belonging," *Citizenship Studies* 20, no. 2 (2016): 243–9.

160 Quoted in: Adams, *British Politics and Foreign Policy*, 25.

161 Arthur Herman, *Gandhi & Churchill: The Epic Rivalry That Destroyed an Empire and Forged Our Age* (New York: Bantam Books, 2009), 418–19.

162 Quoted in William Manchester, *The Last Lion: Winston Spencer Churchill: Alone, 1932–1940* (New York: Bantam Books, 1988), 161.

163 "Britain and the League: Sir S. Hoare's Speech," 7.

164 Ibid.

165 Bose, "The Secret of Abyssinia and Its Lesson," 327.

166 Campbell, *The Addis Ababa Massacre*, 29–48. As Kapser Braskén has contended, "Mussolini's thinking was determined by Social Darwinism and his millenarian belief that it was Italy's destiny to rule over inferior peoples. When comparing Nazism and Italian Fascism it has rightly been concluded that anti-Semitism never played a central role in Italian fascism. This does not however mean that Italian fascism was free from either biological or cultural racism . . . . Once in power in Ethiopia the Italians enforced fierce segregation between the white Italian population and the Ethiopians. If Mussolini's social Darwinism is taken into consideration, Italy's war connections both to European colonialism and radical racial theories in particular become clear." Braskén, "Whether Black or White— United in the Fight!" 140–1.

167 Priya Satia, *Spies in Arabia: The Great War and the Cultural Foundations of Britain's Covert Empire in the Middle East* (Oxford: Oxford University Press, 2008), 7. For scholarship examining the Northwest Frontier, see Elisabeth Leake, *The Defiant Border: The Afghan-Pakistan Borderlands in the Era of Decolonization* (Cambridge: Cambridge University Press, 2017), 20–65.

168 Makalani, *In the Cause of Freedom*, 7. Similarly, Ian Spears has contended Ethiopia's isolation "was a demonstration of the double standard that Europe applied to non-European states." Spears, 33.

169 George Fitz-Hardinge Berkeley, *The Campaign of Adowa and the Rise of Menelik* (Westminster: Archibald Constable & Co., 1902), 61.

170 James D. Young, *Socialism Since 1889: A Biographical History* (New York: Rowman & Littlefield, 1988), 155.

171 Norman Maclean Leys, *Kenya* (London: L. & Virginia Woolf at the Hogarth Press, 1925), 334. First seen in Young, *Socialism Since 1889,* 155.

172 As Minkah Makalani has argued, "black and Asian radicals were engaged in parallel debates about race and nation within Marxism. And black radicals entered the theoretical breach opened by Asian radicals to raise the importance of race in socialist thought. Bringing Asian radicals into a history of early-twentieth-century radical black internationalism alters the standard narrative arc of accounts by allowing black radicals in communist parties in England, France, and the United States a history outside the white Left." Makalani, 5.

173 Young, *Socialism Since 1889,* 155.

174 Bush, *Imperialism, Race and Resistance,* 241. Similarly, Marc Matera has contended that "as fears of military escalation mounted . . . attention to Ethiopia's plight abated." Matera, *Black London,* 75.

175 Mary Davis, *Sylvia Pankhurst: A Life in Radical Politics* (Sterling, VA: Pluto Press, 1999), 97. Part of this ambivalence was the looming German threat. As Martin Caedel has argued, "When the National Government, by failing even to introduce an oil embargo, tacitly allowed Mussolini to crush Abyssinia, there was nothing approaching the outcry there had been over the Hoare-Laval pact." Caedel, 328.

176 Bush, *Imperialism, Race and Resistance,* 241.

177 Ibid., 240–1.

178 Dutt, *Decisive Days Ahead,* 18–19.

179 Ibid., 18.

180 Ibid.

181 Quoted in Stephen Dorril, *Blackshirt: Sir Oswald Mosley and British Fascism* (London: Viking, 2006), 352.

182 Bush, *Imperialism, Race and Resistance,* 257.

183 Dutt, *World Politics,* 325.

184 Quoted in *Waugh,* 48. While this expression captured the atmosphere at Geneva, as well as the indifference of the Left, it "was wildly unlike London. There the editorial and managerial chairs of newspapers and publishing offices seemed to be peopled exclusively by a race of anthropoids who saw, heard and spoke no other subject. Few of them, it is true, could find that country on the map or had the faintest conception of its character." *Waugh,* 48.

185 George Steer, *Caesar in Abyssinia* (Boston: Little, Brown and Company, 1937), 371.

186 Bereket Habte Selassie, *Emperor Haile Selassie* (Athens, OH: Ohio University Press, 2014), 195. Bereket Habte Selassie was a state official who held several important positions in Haile Selassie's government.

187   Hugh Thomas, *The Spanish Civil War: Revised Edition* (New York: Random House Publishing, 2013), 352.

188   Haile Selassie, "A Message from the Ethiopian Emperor," *New Times and Ethiopian News*, May 9, 1936.

189   Peter Neville, *Mussolini* (London: Routledge, 2004), 135.

190   Jawaharlal Nehru, *Glimpses of World History* (New York: John Day Company, 1942), 958.

191   There is considerable debate over whether the militarist regime of Francisco Franco was fascist. I address this question in Chapter 2.

192   Quoted in Richard Pankhurst, 25. A few years later, in 1938, C. L. R. James contended: "Sir Stafford Cripps has the typical vice of many European Socialists, even revolutionaries. He conceives Africans as essentially passive recipients of freedom given to them by Europeans." C. L. R. James, "Sir Stafford Cripps and 'Trusteeship,'" *International African Opinion* 1, no. 3 (1938).

193   Emmanuel Abrahams, "Ethiopia," *The Keys: Published Quarterly by the League of Colored Peoples*, 5, no. 3 (1938).

194   Rabindranath Tagore, "Message to World Peace Congress," in *The English Writings of Rabindranath Tagore: Volume Three; A Miscellany*, 813.

195   As Arlena Buelli has argued, "This South Asian support for antiracist and anticolonial causes promoted by Africans and people of African descent was not confined to the two years of invasion itself. On the contrary, recent historiography has demonstrated that it followed from decades of growing mutual interest, intellectual exchange and political collaboration. In fact, the increasing mobility and interconnectedness characterizing the interwar years brought otherwise distant actors who already shared experiences of subordination and exploitation into contact." Buelli, 2.

196   Louro, *Comrades Against Imperialism*, 204.

197   For Nehru, the Second Italo-Ethiopian War "prompted a stronger recognition of the connection between Indian and African struggles, while at the same time it strengthened [his] conceptualization of fascism as one and the same with imperialism." Louro, *Comrades Against Imperialism*, 205.

198   Nehru, "Presidential Address at Faizpur," in *Toward Freedom: The Autobiography of Jawaharlal Nehru* (New York: The John Day Company, 1941), 415.

199   Bose did not complete his second term as Congress president. I address this controversy in Chapter 3.

200   Dutt, *Decisive Days Ahead*, 17–18.

201   Bose, "The Secret of Abyssinia and Its Lesson," 325.

202   Nicholas Rankin, *Telegram from Guernica: The Extraordinary Life of George Steer: Reporter, Adventurer and Soldier* (London: Faber and Faber), 287.

203   Ibid.

204 On April 6, 1941, Indian, British Commonwealth, Free French, Free Belgian, and
     Ethiopian forces liberated Addis Ababa. One month later, on May 5, Emperor
     Selassie reentered the Ethiopian capital. He remained in power for nearly thirty-
     three years.

205 Steer, *Caesar in Abyssinia*, 9.

206 Ibid., 393.

207 Rankin, *Telegram from Guernica*, 100.

208 Ibid., 237–327.

209 Steer, *Caesar in Abyssinia*, 143.

210 Rankin, *Telegram from Guernica*, 5.

211 Dutt, *World Politics,* 348.

212 Steer, *Caesar in Abyssinia*, 407.

2

"All the Best Matadors Were Fascists"[1]

India and the Spanish Civil War

They pray for success;
for they must raise weeping and wailing
in their wake, sever ties of love,
plant flags on the ashes of desolated homes,
devastate the centres of culture
and shrines of beauty,
mark red with blood their trail
across green meadows and populous markets
and so they march to the temple of Buddha, the compassionate,
to claim his blessings,
while loud beats the drum rat-a-tat
and earth trembles

—Rabindranath Tagore[2]

Late one night in 1938, Jawaharlal Nehru—leader of the INC and the first prime minister of independent India—awoke to the spectacular thunder of German, Italian, and Spanish planes roaring above him.[3] Rushing to his balcony, Nehru watched as fascist bombs consumed Barcelona's coastline.[4] "There I remained," he later reflected, "There I saw much else that impressed me powerfully; and there, in the midst of want and destruction and impending disaster, I felt more at peace with myself than anywhere else in Europe. There was a light there, the light of courage and determination and of doing something worth while."[5] Spain captivated Nehru. He believed that the light guiding Republican Spain animated his own war against British fascism. Indeed, for Nehru, the Spanish Civil War—in addition to a sectarian political conflict and a Western ideological struggle—was also part of a global war between self-determination and fascist imperialism. Seen through this lens, the Congress and the Republic fought for the same independence.[6] "We watch this struggle," Nehru argued, "not merely with the sympathy of friendly outsiders, but with the painful anxiety of those who are themselves involved in it."[7]

More than twenty thousand books have been written about the Spanish Civil War—a "literary epitaph that puts it on par with the Second World War."[8] Much of this scholarship has examined the Anglo-French policy of nonintervention.[9] British prime ministers Stanley Baldwin and Neville Chamberlain faced the difficult decision of supporting either fascism or communism (as many in England understood it). With little recourse, they tried desperately to contain the conflict. For Indian anti-fascists, debates over intervention resembled a colonial contest between Europe's great powers. Fascism, Nehru contended, had radicalized imperial ideologies. With much of Africa and Asia colonized (particularly after the Second Italo-Ethiopian War), fascist nation-states turned their rapine gaze inward, to Europe. The Spanish Civil War, Nehru argued, was not simply a struggle between fascism and communism, with Britain as a beleaguered spectator, but rather an imperial transaction shaped by satisfied (Britain and France) and unsatisfied (Germany and Italy) powers.

The constitution of the Second Spanish Republic guaranteed the right of autonomy, or devolution, to all regions.[10] For Nehru, it represented a commitment to self-determination and the repudiation of Spain's violent imperial past (he conspicuously ignored Spain's colonial presence in North Africa). By contrast, General Franco and the Nationalists venerated the Spanish Empire and—much like Italian fascists—sought to resurrect *el imperio donde nunca se pone el sol* (the empire on which the sun never sets).[11] Nehru maintained that, rather than defend a democratically elected and internationally recognized government, Whitehall instinctively supported the imperialist Franco. Even as fascist Italy and Nazi Germany intervened in support of the Nationalists, the British government remained committed to nonintervention. It acquiesced, or tacitly supported, fascism's colonization of Spain.

Seen from India, the Spanish Civil War pitted Europe's great powers against the self-determination of the Spanish people (aided by the International Brigades and, eventually, the Soviet Union).[12] Whether through intervention or nonintervention, fascist and imperialist nation-states betrayed the Second Spanish Republic. In this chapter, I contend that seen from the outside-in the Spanish Civil War, in addition to a struggle between republicanism and militarism (perhaps fascism), was also a war between self-determination and Europe's satisfied and unsatisfied imperial powers. Imperial nation-states, and Britain in particular, had long repudiated the self-determination of nations around the world. Rather than risk its empire in an intra-imperialist war, the British government forsook the self-determination of the Spanish people. In Spain, as in Ethiopia, the paramountcy of empire informed British isolationism. Nehru and other anti-colonialists contended that British economic, military, and cultural dependence on India bound Britain to isolationism, and thus fascism.

Caesarism at the Door

The Spanish Civil War erupted in July 1936 when army officers led by General José Sanjurjo issued a *pronunciamiento* condemning the Second Spanish Republic.[13] The Nationalists—monarchists, *Falangists,* Carlists, and conservatives, among them—united under a banner of anti-communist, pro-Catholic, autocracy.[14] The politically multifarious Republic initially espoused democratic self-determination, but with the advent of Soviet intervention increasingly promulgated a Marxist people's republic.[15] Spain's byzantine web of alliances often bewildered foreign observers. For Britons, in particular, it bedeviled their antiquated, largely imagined, understanding of *el Imperio Español.* Indeed, across England, Spain remained an "exotic country, the land of the Inquisition, the subject of adventure stories and historical novels with titles like *Spanish Love, Spanish Bayonet,* and *Spanish Dancer."*[16] Spain, Raymond Lacoste argued, was "like Africa in Europe."[17]

Many Britons disentangled the Spanish imbroglio by mischaracterizing it as a struggle between fascism (the Nationalists) and communism (the Republic).[18] Shortly after Sanjurjo's *pronunciamiento,* Prime Minister Stanley Baldwin allegedly told a colleague: "We English hate fascism, but we loathe bolshevism as much. So, if there is somewhere where fascists and Bolsheviks can kill each other off, so much the better."[19] In an effort to circumscribe the conflict, Baldwin, together with French prime minister Léon Blum, created a nonintervention committee to discourage foreign involvement.[20] Attendees "piously condemned intervention but resisted the creation of any effective means of preventing it."[21] Germany and Italy lent considerable support to the Nationalists, while the Soviet Union aided the Republic.[22]

Around the world, the Spanish Civil War developed into a lightning rod—both a romanticized bulwark against a revolutionary ideology (fascism or communism) and the dreaded spark from which a global war might erupt. It was at once a class war, political war, religious war, a Western ideological war, and a global revolutionary war.[23] In India, the outbreak of the Spanish Civil War "shook [Jawaharlal] Nehru to the inner depths of his being."[24] Together with other anti-colonialists, he sought to organize an "Aid Spain campaign" that would provide financial and material support to the Republic. Nehru, however, presided over a fractious Indian National Congress.[25] After the February 1936 death of his wife, he had hoped to preoccupy himself with Congress affairs. Yet frustration with Gandhian nonviolence had begun to disaffect the Congress campaign for independence. For years, a younger generation of anti-colonialists had privately opposed Gandhian spirituality, yet still believed in the efficacy of civil disobedience.[26] By 1936, this faith had largely eroded. Gandhi's tendency "to unilaterally call off a movement, his compromises at the moments of the movement's greatest strengths, had disillusioned too many. They had already been looking at other forms of political movement and left-wing, or more specifically socialist, ideas, Marxian or other, were beginning to make an impact."[27]

It can be tempting to depict the Lucknow meeting of the INC (1936) as the provenance of Gandhi's political marginalization. In March, Subhas Bose implored Nehru to challenge Gandhian dominance of the Congress, convinced that the Mahatma would "never take a stand which will alienate you."[28] Nehru had long expressed frustration with Gandhi—over his suspension of civil disobedience in the aftermath of Chauri Chaura, in debates over dominion status in 1928, after the Gandhi-Irwin Pact in 1931, during his fast protesting separate electorates for untouchables in 1932, and again in 1934 upon the suspension of civil disobedience.[29] Nehru, however, understood the paramountcy of Congress unity, and only wavered in his commitment to Gandhi.[30] "Nehru has the brains," Lord Linlithgow explained to Frances Gunther, "but Gandhi has the people; if they can be separated, we are safe."[31]

As the Congress splintered, Nehru increasingly became the solution. His stature among the Left (at least until 1939) and his stubborn loyalty to Gandhi made him the only acceptable leader to both leftists and traditionalists: "The right's great respect—and need—for Gandhi, the left's for Nehru, Nehru's unwillingness to take steps that might bring about an open conflict with Gandhi, and Gandhi's intermediary role became the basis of Congress's functional unity."[32] Nehru was perhaps the only figure around which the Congress could unite.[33] Some even cast him as the Indian Mussolini—a dynamic figure that appealed to both Nationalists and socialists. "I shall put it in Hegelian terms," one correspondent wrote to Nehru in 1936, "Capitalism is the thesis, Socialism is the antithesis and Fascism the synthesis."[34]

Nehru abhorred fascism and its cult of personality and often discouraged followers from seeing him as the savior of India.[35] In his now-famous article, "Rashtrapati" (Leader of the Nation), Nehru—writing under the pseudonym Chanakya—cautioned that "a little twist and Jawaharlal might turn dictator . . . he has all the makings of a dictator in him—vast popularity, a strong will directed to a well defined purpose, energy, pride, organisational capacity, ability, hardness, and with all his love of the crowd, an intolerance of others and a certain contempt for the weak and inefficient."[36] Written in 1937, "Rashtrapati" largely reflected Nehru's institutional fatigue. After two years as Congress president (1936–7), he feared a third term would encourage the notion that only he could lead India to independence. "In this revolutionary epoch," he warned, "Caesarism is always at the door, and is it not possible that Jawaharlal might fancy himself as a Caesar?"[37]

Presiding over an increasingly divided Congress, facing unrealistic expectations in domestic politics, disillusioned with Gandhian ideology, and mourning the death of his wife, Nehru considered resigning as Congress president.[38] "Again and again," he wrote in his autobiography, "I considered this question of resignation. I found it difficult to work smoothly with my own colleagues in the Congress executive, and it became clear to me that they viewed my activities with apprehension. . . . I decided to finally resign and I informed Gandhiji of my decision."[39] Before Nehru could retire, however, the outbreak of the Spanish Civil War compelled him to stay:

> Soon afterwards a far-away occurrence, unconnected with India, affected me greatly and made me change my decision. This was the news of General Franco's revolt in Spain. I saw this rising, with its background of German and Italian assistance, developing into a European or even a world conflict. India was bound to be drawn into this and I could not afford to weaken our organization and create an internal crisis by resigning just when it was essential for us to pull together.[40]

Nehru believed that the Congress-led campaign for independence encompassed not only Europe's empires but any nation bereft of self-determination.[41] "It has long been recognized," he argued in the *National Herald*, "that the struggle in Spain has a vital significance for all those who care for freedom. It is thus intimately related to our own struggle for freedom."[42] Seen from the outside-in, the Second Spanish Republic and the INC struggled against an interrelated oppression. "Fascism," Nehru argued, "cannot be separated from empire."[43]

Europe's Blood Brothers

In July 1938, after touring what remained of the Second Spanish Republic, Nehru travelled to London, where he met Lord Linlithgow, the viceroy of India. Following the passage of the Government of India Act (1935)—which Nehru decried as a "charter of slavery"[44]—the Congress triumphed in provincial elections (forming majorities in eight of eleven provinces).[45] In response, Linlithgow requested a meeting with both Nehru and Gandhi. Nehru initially refused out of solidarity with political prisoners on a hunger strike at the Kālā Pānī (Cellular Jail) in the Andaman Islands.[46] After several weeks, however, Gandhi interceded and the strike concluded, freeing Nehru to meet with the viceroy. During their brief meeting, Nehru proclaimed that he "gave England at the outside ten years before India [became] independent."[47] Afterward, a "nonplussed"[48] Linlithgow recorded his impression of the anti-colonial leader:

> Mr. Jawaharlal Nehru lunched with me today. After a long account of his experiences in Spain he gave me his views about Russia. . . . This is the first time upon which I have met Mr. Nehru and I must confess myself profoundly disappointed (or ought I to say relieved!) by what I found. It appears to be quite impossible to bring Mr. Nehru to earth or to persuade him to face current problems in a practical fashion. Any fact or opinion which does not fit in to the scheme of his theories is at once brushed aside.[49]

Linlithgow, the pragmatic imperialist, could not fathom Nehru, a romantic anti-colonialist. "A wide gap separated us," Linlithgow told Nehru, "and we [will] look at each other across it."[50]

The chasm separating Linlithgow and Nehru extended to Spain. As viceroy, Linlithgow epitomized Britain's imperial ethos. Like many in the National Government, he interpreted international developments through the prism of colonialism. From this perspective, intervention—whether in support of Nationalist or Republican Spain—jeopardized the inviolability of empire. As Winston Churchill argued: "French partisanship for the Spanish communists, or British partisanship for the Spanish rebels, might injure profoundly the bonds which unite the British Empire and the French Republic."[51] Europe's satisfied powers sought the preservation of the imperial status quo. Whitehall, in particular, approached Spain with "Olympian detachment."[52]

Nehru, by contrast, considered intervention in Spain an ideological, if not moral, obligation. A socialist (broadly defined), Nehru rejected the nation-state paradigm—apotheosized, as it was, in this era of extreme ethnic nationalism.

He divided nations into colonizer and colonized regardless of their state. In Spain, Nehru identified not with ethnic Spaniards, but with the defense of self-determination.[53] In his presidential address to the Faizpur Congress (1937), Nehru contended that the Spanish Civil War was part of a global conflict between freedom and fascism-imperialism:

> In the world to-day these two great forces strive for mastery—those who labour for democratic and social freedom and those who wish to crush this freedom under imperialism and fascism.... And the struggle to-day is fiercest and clearest in Spain, and on the outcome of that depends war or peace in the world in the near future, fascist domination or the scotching of fascism and imperialism.[54]

Nehru believed that fascism had radicalized British imperialism. After the Scramble for Africa, Europe's great powers had colonized nearly all of Africa and Asia. During the Paris Peace Conference, the victorious Allied powers—primarily Britain and France—stripped or attenuated the imperial ambitions of the German and Italian empires. Nehru maintained that, in response, these unsatisfied imperial powers intensified Europe's colonial ethos. With Africa and Asia arrogated, they turned their covetous gaze inward, to Europe itself. "The real lesson of Spain," Nehru argued, "is that fascism and imperialism are blood brothers, marching in hand in hand. . . . We who stand for Spain must learn that lesson in all its implications and stand equally for the ending of fascism and empire and all that they signify." [55]

Seen from the outside-in, the Indian campaign for independence encompassed the Spanish Civil War (and vice-versa). Revolutionary forces in both India and Spain struggled against a foreign oppressor.[56] Victory in Spain was victory in India—victory against the forces of colonialism that had enslaved Afro-Eurasia.[57] At a demonstration in Trafalgar Square commemorating the second anniversary of the outbreak of the war, Nehru urged listeners to recognize the similarities between the Second Spanish Republic and the Congress-led campaign for independence: "The Government you have is a fascist government. Why? Because the British Empire is imperialist and that encloses fascism."[58] As Republican and Congress flags waved above him, Nehru urged listeners to "pull up the roots of fascism and imperialism."[59] For many anti-fascists, Spain represented the first instance of popular and international resistance against fascism. For Nehru, it was the first battle in a war that would culminate in Indian independence.

Together with the Congress, Nehru organized an Aid Spain campaign to support the Second Spanish Republic.[60] Foodstuffs and other materials were collected at Swaraj Bhawan; Congress ministries coordinated several All-India

Spain Day celebrations to promote awareness of the conflict; anti-colonialists across India publicly denounced the Anglo-French policy of nonintervention; Ram Manohar Lohia and the INC Foreign Department raised 50,000 rupees to send to the Republic; and the Congress sponsored a medical mission to Barcelona led by Dr. Madan Mohan Lal Atal, part of which included an ambulance with the placard: "Spain India Aid Committee: To the Courageous Spanish Democrats [from] the People of India and Ceylon."[61]

Around the world, Indian anti-colonialists—including Krishna Menon, Rajani Palme Dutt, S. K. Datta, Bhicoo Batlivala, Jayaprakash Narayan, Kamaladevi Chattopadhyay, and others—denounced General Franco and the Nationalists. From his home in Bengal, Rabindranath Tagore urged all Indians to support the Second Spanish Republic: "In Spain, world civilization is being menaced and trampled underfoot. International Fascism is pouring men and money in aid of the rebels. In Spain this inhuman recrudescence of obscurantism, of racial prejudice, of rapine and glorification of war must be given the final rebuff. Civilization must be saved from its being swamped by barbarism."[62] Interestingly, Tagore's condemnations of fascism sparked criticism from Nazi Germany. At the 1937 Nuremberg Rally, Joseph Goebbels branded Tagore a "world liberal," and reaffirmed the "well-known fact that Tagore was a Jew whose real name was Rabbi Nathan."[63] Of course, Goebbels never mentioned that as a student he had praised Tagore's poetry, describing *The Gardener* as "a wonderful collection of love songs."[64]

In London, the India League staged protest marches, organized food drives, and even sponsored benefit concerts. Performances exhibited South Asian dance and music—most frequently, Tagore's *Jana Gana Mana*—and often harmonized the sarod, sitar, or *israj* with the violin and clarinet.[65] Afterward, Krishna Menon, John Strachey, Sehri Saklatvala, Dr. Protool C. Bhandari, and other India League representatives urged audiences to donate food and money to the Aid Spain campaign.[66] "Let us remember," Menon argued during one such event, "that the struggle [the Spanish Civil War] entails many problems of which we must concern ourselves."[67] A close friend of Nehru and secretary of the India League, Menon implored all Indians to grasp "the necessity and the implication of the people of India taking their part in mobilizing material support for the Spanish Republic."[68]

During the war, supporters of the Republican government evacuated as many as 30,000 children to England, Mexico, the Soviet Union, and Western Europe.[69] Relief programs within these countries provided food, medical care, and shelter. In the Soviet Union, arriving children were greeted by thousands of waving handkerchiefs—part of a three-day welcoming ceremony featured in *Pravda.*[70] In London, Indira Nehru (later Indira Gandhi) urged Indian and English leftists to help rescue Spanish children. A student at Badminton in Bristol, Indira had attended a lecture detailing Republican efforts to feed and shelter thousands of orphans. The speaker's description profoundly affected her. "We were glad," she later wrote to her father, "that all that was possible was being done for their [the children's] safety and welfare. But this was only in the daytime. At night they woke up at the sound of bombs—the little ones cried and the older ones remembered the terrible scenes of war."[71] Indira addressed several Aid Spain rallies, urging audiences to contribute to various Republican relief funds. Badminton even adopted two Basque orphans.

As England and France clutched desperately to nonintervention, German and Italian intervention developed into a decisive Nationalist advantage.[72] The quintessence of pro-Franco foreign involvement occurred in April 1937, at Guernica. The German Condor Legion—Luftwaffe soldiers under the direction of Hugo Sperrle—bombed defenseless civilians in the Basque town of Guernica. Commemorated in Pablo Picasso's famous painting, the destruction of Guernica shocked the world. "The bombing of Guernica," Nehru argued, "an unfortified city, with incendiary bombs, the killing thereby of 800 civilians, and the destruction of a large part of the city came as a terrible shock to the peoples of the world."[73] Nehru contended that Europe's "blood brothers," fascism and imperialism, oppressed progressive forces in both Spain in India. He believed, moreover, that the Republican defense and the Indian independence movement were interrelated; both defied violent, exploitative, and racially motivated totalitarianisms. Nehru, consequently, argued that Indians acutely understood the tragedy of Guernica, because they themselves had experienced it.

During the Waziristan Campaign (1936–9), British colonial forces brutally quashed the Waziri and Mahsud tribesmen of Waziristan. Only months after the outbreak of the Spanish Civil War, local Waziri led by the Fakir of Ipi opened fire on British colonial forces in a valley just outside Bichhe Kashkai.[74] To reassert colonial hegemony, British forces bombed the Waziri.[75] How, Nehru argued, could English citizens condemn the bombing of Guernica while ignoring a similar tragedy in Afghanistan: "The Indian people cannot but note the difference when British citizens are bombed in Spain and when Indian people are bombed on the North West Frontier."[76] British bombing in Afghanistan, Nehru argued, evinced the similarities between fascism and liberal-imperialism. Innocents in both Guernica and Waziristan suffered, yet English popular opinion only denounced the former: "Perhaps if British people will think over this point they will realise why in India we cannot regard the British Government as a symbol of democracy and cannot become enthusiastic about fighting for it in a war for democracy against dictatorship."[77] The Spanish Civil War underscored the hypocrisy of British liberalism—democracy for some, dictatorship for others; a system, Nehru contended, that left England the "subject of ribald comment from the whole world."[78]

~

One week before the outbreak of the Spanish Civil War, British captain Cecil Bebb piloted a Dragon Rapide aircraft to the Canary Islands. After retrieving General Francisco Franco, Bebb flew to Spanish Morocco, so that the General could join the Spanish African Army in its preparations for the coup against the Second Spanish Republic. One of the organizers of this plot was Juan de la Cierva, the inventor of the autogyro and the founder of *La Cierva Autogiro Company*. In August, as Franco's armies swept through Southern Spain, de la Cierva informed an Italian diplomat in London that he had purchased all the available aircraft in England and was preparing to deliver them to Nationalist General Emilio Mola. "British authorities," de la Cierva later explained, had given him "every facility even though they knew only too well that the aircraft were destined for the Spanish rebels."[79]

Whether pragmatic or diabolical—and considerable debate exists—Anglo-French nonintervention in the Spanish Civil War "undoubtedly contributed . . . to the defeat of the Republic."[80] Empire played a critical role in British nonintervention. Shortly after Sanjurjo issued his *pronunciamiento*, the National Government reiterated that its "pivotal foreign policy goal remained the defence of its extensive imperial interests."[81] Mussolini's palingenetic imperial vision demanded the transformation of the Mediterranean into a "Roman Lake"— an ambition which threatened British sovereignty in Gibraltar, Egypt, and Mandatory Palestine, among other places.[82] To protect these interests, and secure a modus vivendi (however fleeting) with the Italian Empire, imperialists within the National Government espoused nonintervention in the Spanish Civil War.

Seen from the outside-in, British nonintervention in Spain exhibited the similarities between fascism and liberal-imperialism. In the decades after the Spanish-American and Riff Wars, the Spanish military elite internalized imperial ideologies, often conflating Marxists and separatists with Cuban or Berber anti-colonialists. During the Spanish Civil War, many Nationalists "interpreted their defence of 'Spain' as an *imperial* duty."[83] Adolf Hitler and Benito Mussolini instinctively sympathized with Franco's colonization of internal enemies. In due course, Europe's unsatisfied imperialists furnished military aid to Spain's unsatisfied imperialists (General Franco and the Nationalists).[84] At the same time, the governments of Britain and France espoused nonintervention. In Spain, as in Ethiopia, Europe's satisfied imperial powers forsook an internationally recognized government in order to forestall conflict with unsatisfied powers. "So we find," Nehru argued, "British imperialism inclining more and more toward the fascist Powers, though the language it uses, as is its old habit, is democratic in texture and pious in tone."[85] The Spanish Civil War pitted Europe's satisfied and unsatisfied imperialists against the self-determination of the Spanish people (supported by the International Brigades and the Soviet Union). Whether fascist or liberal-imperialist, Britain, France, Italy, and Germany negotiated the fate of Spain.

To be sure, this perspective discounts the political and intellectual plenitude of the Spanish Civil War. It was a distinctly Spanish conflict that reflected its nation's unique social, religious, political, economic, and cultural development.[86] Nehru, moreover, too often homogenized the multifarious National Government. Many within Whitehall sympathized with the Republic, yet also confronted additional considerations: French diffidence, a looming war with Nazi Germany, the etiolation of the League of Nations, and an anti-war public opinion.[87] Across England, "there was no ground-swell of public support to send British troops to Spain."[88] From the perspective of Baldwin or Chamberlain, the Spanish imbroglio, whether won by Nationalists or Republicans, would inevitably undermine Britain's international standing.[89] As an adviser to Anthony Eden explained: "An extreme right victory is likely to be embarrassing in respect of our foreign policy and interests, while an extreme left victory might be equally embarrassing, though in a different way, to any country which desires the maintenance of ordinary democratic government in those countries in which it still survives."[90] Embarrassed on both ends, many in Whitehall prioritized circumscription.

Materially, the Congress's Aid Spain campaign accomplished little. It provided marginal support to the Second Spanish Republic, failed to capture the imagination of the Indian public, and its Spain-India Committee, as Nehru later admitted, "only existed on paper."[91] Nevertheless, for India's colonial elite— the leaders of the Congress campaign for independence—the Spanish Civil War mattered. "Wrapped up with the fate of Spain," Nehru argued, "is the fate of Europe, and wrapped up with the fate of Europe is the fate of the world."[92] Although romantic, and frequently quixotic, Nehru's intervention in Spain promulgated the ideological similarities between fascism and liberal-imperialism. Seen from

India, Spain had been victimized by great-power imperialism. Compelled by an ecumenical (albeit elitist) anti-colonialism, Nehru believed it was his moral responsibility to organize protest marches and sponsor a medical mission. As satisfied and unsatisfied imperial powers negotiated the fate of weaker states, so, too, would the Congress defend the self-determination of subject nations, even if only symbolically. Nehru contended that India's intervention in the Spanish Civil War "compelled the world's attention,"[93] and in 1938, he demonstrated his commitment to this vision by visiting Barcelona.

An Uncanny Sense of Doom

In June 1938, Nehru, Krishna Menon, and Bhicco Batlivala flew from Marseilles to Barcelona.[94] No one was there to greet them. "For a while," Nehru later recounted, "we did not quite know what to do."[95] Eventually, the Indian delegation boarded a bus bound for the city. Along the way, Nehru watched as:

> Barcelona appeared in the distance, spread out along the sea coast and going right into the interior, clinging to the pretty hills that dotted the landscape. It had a gracious appearance as it lay basking in the sunshine. Full of years and experience she seemed, with the burden of long history behind her, and yet strong and vital, smiling a warm welcome, despite her present sorrow, to the stranger who approached her.[96]

The Indian delegation was shocked to see *La Rambla* filled with people, "laughing and gay, hurrying to their work or business."[97] Trams swarmed with locals; neighborhood shops filled *Eixample*'s octagonal blocks. Even concert houses remained open. Still, the devastation of war was unmistakable. Buildings lay in ruin, craters lined the streets, and air-raid sirens shattered the calm of night. Shops were scarcely supplied, and locals wore threadbare clothing. Although "the people laughed, as Spaniards will, their faces were grave and pinched, and sorrow hung in the air."[98] Nehru spent five nights in Barcelona: "Five nights to the accompaniment of aerial bombardment. Five days and nights, crowded with events, and impressions, the memory of which will endure."[99] After arriving at the Hotel Majestic, Nehru watched as Nationalist planes bombed Barcelona. Fifteen persons were killed.[100]

Spain nevertheless captivated its Indian interlopers. For nearly two years, Nehru had contended that the Spanish Republic fought against not only General Franco and the Nationalists but also Europe's satisfied and unsatisfied imperial powers. Working together, the governments of Britain, France, Italy, and Germany betrayed the self-determination of the Spanish people. "The imperialist and fascist on one side," Nehru argued, "the socialist and nationalist on the other."[101] To be sure, Nehru's ardent support of the Republic conditioned his experience of Barcelona. As the leader of the Congress's Aid Spain movement, he was predisposed to seeing the anti-imperialist virtues he had campaigned to defend. At the same time, the Republican government inveigled his political ambitions by "evoking the sense of a state visit and attaching great importance to the Indian delegation."[102]

Nehru expected chaos in Spain. When war broke out, the army largely sided with General Franco, leaving the Republic to construct a new army while also defending itself—a process exacerbated by the Anglo-French nonintervention agreement.[103] By 1938, the Republican army had stabilized, due in large part to Soviet intervention. Nehru thus toured an ordered bureaucracy.[104] He met several government officials, including Foreign Minister Julio Álvarez del Vayo.[105]

Nehru and del Vayo went on several long walks—a Gandhian custom—during which del Vayo outlined the Republic's manifold challenges.[106] "[Most] of their defeats and retirements," Nehru recounted in *Homage to Spain* "were due, apart of course from the great superiority of the enemy in air-craft and mechanical equipment and big guns, to inexperience of Republican generals in large-scale operations, and sometimes to deliberate sabotage on the part of the old officers who had been employed by the Republic."[107] One of the Republic's gravest challenge was malnutrition.[108] Before the war, Northern Spain depended on food shipments from England and France. In the name of nonintervention, Nehru contended, "these two countries had been consistently . . . following a policy of strangling the Republic and indirectly aiding Franco."[109] The Republic fed its army, several cities, and tens of thousands of refugees from Nationalist territory. An honored guest, Nehru ate only a small piece of bread for breakfast; subsequent meals were similarly meager. "If this was the lot of the favoured ones," Nehru later reflected, "what of the others?"[110]

Nehru also visited the International Brigades. Initially comprised of foreigners, the Brigades at the time of Nehru's visit had largely been systematized. Each was, by decree, at least 50 percent Spanish. Nehru met with the American and British Brigades—the latter named after the recently deceased Shapurji Saklatvala, an Indian communist and former Member of Parliament. British machine gunners put on a thrilling display with their maxim gun. Their intrepidity captivated Nehru: "There was nothing in the way of comfort, and yet . . . their spirits were infectious, and watching their enthusiasm and determination, it was difficult to conceive that the cause they served could ever lose."[111] The will to act against fascist imperialism appealed to Nehru. It was what he sought in India, particularly as he grew increasingly frustrated with Gandhian nonviolence. He even fantasized about joining the International Brigades: "Reluctantly I came away from these gallant men of the International Brigade, for something in me wanted to stay on this inhospitable looking hillside which sheltered so much human courage, so much of what was worthwhile in life."[112] The Brigades captured Nehru's imagination. He was, of course, committed to India; but Spain, with its movement, gravity, and zeal, profoundly affected him.[113]

Nehru's final meeting was unforgettable. He had heard much about "Spain's Modern Joan of Arc,"[114] La Passionaria (Dolores Ibárruri), and "was anxious to meet her." The Basque revolutionary captivated audiences with her indictments of General Franco and the Nationalists—most famously, her "¡No Pasarán!" (They shall not pass!) speech during the 1936 Siege of Madrid.[115] Over the course of the war, she became an international icon. The *Times of India* described her as "the most influential woman in the world today."[116] Nehru spoke with La Passionaria for over an hour:

> Her extraordinary vitality overwhelmed me and I felt that she was one of the most remarkable women I had met. . . . Impassioned words would pour out of her lips, tumbling over each other, her face would be lighted up by the fire within, and her fine eyes would sparkle and hold you. I heard her in a little room, only understanding part of what she was saying in Spanish, but the music of her language filled me, and her changing face and eyes were full of meaning. I understood then the power that she wielded over the Spanish masses.[117]

La Passionaria mesmerized Nehru. She represented "the common man and woman who had suffered and been exploited for ages and were now determined to be free."[118]

Nehru's experiences in Spain substantiated his conviction that the Spanish Civil War pitted freedom and self-determination against the forces of fascist imperialism.[119] At a reception hosted by a local branch of *Rassemblent Universel Pour la Paix,* he characterized Anglo-French nonintervention as a "tragedy."[120] Empire and democracy, he contended, were irreconcilable; "one must swallow the other."[121] The British government had long denied self-determination to subject nations within its empire. Now, imperialist avidity had turned inward to Europe. Great powers would decide the fate of the Second Spanish Republic, just as they had in Ethiopia, India, and elsewhere. A satisfied imperialist, the

National Government would not risk war, nor jeopardize its empire, to defend the self-determination of the Republic. Nehru contended that this commitment to nonintervention exhibited the entropy of British liberal principles. "Britain is in a corner," he explained, "and imperialism, when driven into a corner, always turns to fascism—it is inevitable."[122]

~

In addition to Nehru, Menon, and Batlivala, several more Indians participated in the Spanish Civil War. Gopal Mukund Huddar joined the Shapurji Saklatvala (British) battalion of the International Brigades under the name John Smith.[123] Captured by Nationalist forces, he was eventually released and celebrated in India as "the only Indian that fought against Franco."[124] In 1938, at a rally in Bombay honoring his return from Spain, Huddar contended that "The fight for democracy is in India just as it is in Spain. The very same British Imperialism which helps Franco and Mussolini in their attempt to destroy Spain is holding us down. We have to fight against it."[125] A former president of the Cambridge Union and member of the Indian Student's Organization visited Catalonia with two Indian students. The group reported stopping frequently to shield themselves from bombs dropped by Nationalist planes. Upon their return, they urged all Indians to send food and clothing to the Republic.[126]

Famed novelist Mulk Raj Anand also visited Spain. Like Nehru, Anand believed that the Spanish Civil War and the Indian campaign for independence were interrelated:

> It was not the hectic blaze of a transient emotion that made me come to Spain . . . [but] the growing realization that nothing we could do was enough to help the Spanish people in their struggle for existence. . . . As I sat from day to day writing a long novel about the peasants of my country while news of the Spanish war was coming in, I became conscious that the problem of the agrarian masses of India was not very unlike that which faced the Spanish peasants, since both these people are emerging from feudalism, since both have for centuries been oppressed by a capacious landlordism, since both are face to face with the brutal tyranny of an upper class anxious to secure its privileges and possessions even if that involves the virtual extermination of the vast masses of the people.[127]

Travelling along various fronts, Anand met dozens of popular front soldiers. Their fortitude humbled him. Still, Anand lamented a miasma of expectancy; he felt an "uncanny sense of doom"[128] had vitiated the Republic. Describing the famous *El Generalisimo* propaganda poster, in which a macabre Franco leads symbols of the military, capitalism, and the clergy, Anand wondered:

> What can they think, who see staring them in the face the incarnate symbol of devilishness—that vivid poster which shows the fascist general Death stalking the earth in tall boots with the deep-socketed fleshless skeleton of his head crowned with a tall German helmet, the train of his cloak borne by the servile lackeys . . . who follow like hateful little evil dwarfs behind?[129]

Like Nehru, Anand identified profound similarities between fascism and liberal-imperialism. "The menacing rise of fascism," he argued, "through the connivance, if not the active assistance, of the western 'democratic' rulers, had begun to disclose the corruption of the capitalist system to us, both in its imperialist and its fascist forms. And freedom, like peace, seemed indivisible."[130] Anand drafted part of his award-winning novel *Across the Black Waters* while in Spain. During the infamous May Days (1937)—often described as a "civil war within the Civil War,"[131] or an "urban rebellion directed against state power"[132]— Anand opposed anarchist and anti-Republican forces. This position sparked criticism from George Orwell, whose *Homage to Catalonia* famously decried Soviet influence over the Second Spanish Republic. Years later, Anand recalled the impassioned debates he shared with Orwell: "In the 30's, on my return from Spain, a whole year was occupied in verbal quarrels with George Orwell. . . . As he was with the Anarchists, and I with the Republicans, the debate remained inconclusive. Though we still remained friends. And it was fun."[133]

Upon returning to England, Anand urged all Indians to support the Republic. He contended that General Franco and the Nationalists—much like the Raj— would preside over a repressive and exploitative regime. Like Nehru, Anand believed Indians could not stand by while the injustices they fought for in South Asia took hold elsewhere. Indian independence, he argued, encompassed Spain, and resisted fascist imperialism around the world: "All of us were united, wherever we were, with thousands of others in the faith that we would have to defend world heritage from the attacks of the fascists."[134]

In 1937, poet and political activist Nancy Cunard circulated a questionnaire asking nearly two hundred British writers: "Are you for, or against, the legal government and people of Republican Spain? Are you for, or against, Franco and Fascism?"[135] A trenchant anti-fascist, Cunard decried the insouciance of Britain's intelligentsia. "The equivocal attitude," she argued, "the Ivory Tower, the paradoxical, the ironic detachment, will no longer do."[136] Of the nearly 150 writers that responded, more than 125 endorsed the Republic, including T. S. Elliot,

Sylvia Townsend-Warner, George Padmore, C. L. R. James, and Aldous Huxley. Samuel Becket's pithy ";UPTHEREPUBLIC!"[137] remains a source of considerable controversy; various scholars have interpreted it as either earnest or sardonic. Included among the writers of *Authors Take Sides* was Mulk Raj Anand. In an impassioned condemnation of General Franco and the Nationalists, he urged all Britons to support the Republic:

> ALL THE TRUTH OF MY BEING, all the intensity of passion of which I am capable urges me to tell you that I stand for the People of Republican Spain against Franco and Fascism; that I feel that in this tragic hour of Spain's destiny, in the moment of her utmost suffering, it is the duty of all of us to look into our consciousness and inquire whether we can sit still and see the flower of Spain's manhood sacrificed before the greed of a few who dream of power and feed their insatiable lust for glory and wealth on the blood of men, women and children.[138]

For Anand, Nehru, and Indian anti-colonialists around the world, the Spanish Civil War mattered. Seen from the outside-in, Europe's imperial powers negotiated the fate of an internationally recognized member-state of the League of Nations. In Spain, as in Ethiopia, the governments of Britain, France, Italy, and Germany betrayed a proud and historic nation. Such perfidy, Nehru contended, belied any difference between fascism and liberal-imperialism.

Frothy Sentiments and Pious Platitudes

Nehru's Aid Spain campaign did spark criticism. Many Indians sympathized with the Republic; they were, however, reluctant to devote critical resources to an unfamiliar foreign nation while many of their countrymen starved. "Apart from the improbability of the 'S.S. Nehru' ever reaching the shores of Republican Spain," N. K. Menon wrote to the *Times of India*:

> Can any sane man seriously suggest that India can afford to give away foodstuffs in charity, more particularly now when thousands of our men, women, and children in Bengal and the U.P. are dying of hunger and cold on account of the devastating floods? Or is it suggested that the misery and starvation of Indians are of so very long standing that they have become accustomed and reconciled to them as inevitable conditions of life?[139]

Others believed that the Spanish Republic had become a vehicle for Soviet manipulation. As in Europe, many Indians ignored (or were simply unaware of) the Republic's multifarious political composition and understood the

Spanish Civil War as a conflict between communism and fascism. Opposed to the former, many conservatives—like Baldwin, Chamberlain, and the National Government—advocated nonintervention: "Do the politics of Republican Spain," one anti-interventionist contended, "deserve our sympathy? It is sheer humbug to speak of the ideal of the Spanish 'Government' as democratic. It is as democratic as the autocratic government of Russia, and so little republican that the founders of the Republic have withdrawn their allegiance from it."[140]

Merchant Indians worried about the economic and political ramifications of Congress advocacy. More than two hundred Sindhi merchants lived in Spain's North African colonies (primarily in Morocco). Many feared that Nehru's anti-Nationalist rhetoric endangered their livelihood: "At present all these Indians are living, and their millions' worth property is in territory under General Franco's Government, and by passing such a one-sided [pro-Republican] resolution the Congress has certainly prejudiced their interests."[141] Citing both safety concerns and a precedent of Indian nonintervention, several business leaders implored Nehru and the Congress to suspend the Aid Spain campaign.

Subhas Bose also opposed Indian intervention in the Spanish Civil War. Like Nehru, Bose was an outstanding anti-imperialist. "Ours is a struggle," he argued in his presidential address to the Haripura Congress (1938), "not only against British imperialism, but against imperialism as well. . . . We are therefore, fighting not for the cause of India alone, but for humanity as well."[142] Bose was keenly aware of foreign affairs. Like many leftists within the Congress, he sought to further internationalize the Indian campaign for independence. Yet whereas Nehru interpreted international developments as a romantic, Bose did so as an uncompromising pragmatist. "Foreign policy," he wrote in a letter to Nehru, "is a realistic affair to be determined largely from the point of view of a nation's self interest. . . . Now, what is your foreign policy? Frothy sentiments and pious platitudes do not make a foreign policy. It is no use championing lost causes all the time."[143]

Bose sought to wrest concessions from the National Government by cultivating an alliance with its enemies. He often praised Mussolini, twice meeting with him in Italy (Nehru refused a similar request, citing, among other things, the Italian invasion of Ethiopia and the "difficulties in which Gandhi was placed by the Rome Interview of 1931"[144]). Bose's political pragmatism frequently led to allegations that he was a fascist or fascist sympathizer.[145] "Subhas Bose," a 1937 article in the *Chicago Tribune* alleged, "has been agitating for years to get Fascist support in India, but has been blocked by socialist views of the other nationalist leader Pandit Jawaharlal Nehru."[146] Debates over Bose (the subject of

Chapter 3) continue to this day and are largely beyond the scope of this chapter. At the very least, he believed that Indian independence required foreign aid and instinctively looked to Britain's adversaries. His ideology, V. S. Patil has argued, was that "of [British prime minister Winston] Churchill who said when Hitler invaded Russia: 'I would willingly shake hands with the devil himself if it meant saving my country.'"[147]

Though perhaps destined to clash, Nehru and Bose espoused socialism within the Congress.[148] Until the late 1930s, this vision assured their mutual support. "Among the front-rank of leaders of today," Bose wrote to Nehru before the Faizpur Congress (1936), "you are the only one whom we can look up to for leading the Congress in a progressive direction."[149] Like many leftists, Bose hoped Nehru would inculcate the Congress with Marxist-Leninist anti-imperialism. In February 1936, Bose visited Nehru in Lausanne, Switzerland, where Kamala Nehru was being treated for her tuberculosis. Discussing, among other things, Marxism, the Congress, and the Government of India Act, the pair agreed to further internationalize the campaign for independence.[150] This end, however, was pursued through different means.

Nehru publicly condemned fascism, whereas Bose sought to take advantage of the growing tension between Britain and the Rome-Berlin Axis. "One of Subhas's grievances against me," Nehru complained to Krishna Menon, "is his objection to the foreign policy I have sponsored . . . . He talks about the folly of my espousing lost causes [Spain, in particular] and of always condemning Germany and Italy. He calls himself a realist in foreign as well as internal politics. This realism of his leads to entirely different conclusions."[151] While Nehru contended that fascism and imperialism were blood brothers, Bose was averse to denouncing potential allies. He was single-minded in his pursuit of independence and, as a result, understood the Spanish Civil War almost exclusively through the lens of Indian independence.

Bose contended that the Spanish Civil War was a two-front, pan-European conflict between Italian and British naval superiority in the Mediterranean, and German and Anglo-French hegemony in Central Europe. "It would be puerile," Bose explained, "to think or suggest that Italy has plumped for Franco because of her sympathy for the latter's Fascist aims or her hatred of communism . . . . She is pouring out her blood and money for Franco primarily for strategic reasons."[152] With Spain under Italian influence, Mussolini would control Gibraltar—the gateway to the Mediterranean. In the event of war, he could "destroy Gibraltar and menace both the trade routes of Britain—the Mediterranean route and the Cape route. What is more, she could get over the blockade by using land routes over Spain in order to bring imports from the Atlantic side."[153] Bose supported Italian intervention in Spain insomuch as it weakened the British imperial colossus. After Italian victories in both Ethiopia and (presumably) Spain, Bose contended that Mussolini was a satisfied power. He was "far too shrewd a politician"[154] to risk another world war. Intervention in Spain, consequently, represented a judicious expansion of Italian influence. Mussolini, Bose argued, knew "fully well that none of the Big Powers is yet ready for an international war."[155]

Bose similarly contended that Hitler intervened in Spain to divide the Little Entente—the defensive alliance between Czechoslovakia, Romania, and Yugoslavia supported by France. If Hitler controlled Spain, then in the event of a world war he could "stab [France] in the back by cutting off her communications with North Africa, from where France always obtains large supplies of men and materials."[156] Bose believed that Germany intended to surround France and "make her agree to a Western Pact, giving Germany a free hand in Central and Eastern Europe."[157] Whereas, Mussolini could be appeased, Bose contended that Hitler possessed a rapacious appetite. Like Nehru, Bose argued that Hitler's intervention in Spain augured a much wider conflict: "Germany under Hitler is an incalculable factor . . . Nazi Germany has been dreaming dreams which can be fulfilled only through the arbitration of war."[158]

~

For decades, leftists in India quarreled with one another. Amid the rise of popular front politics (1935) and the election of Nehru as Congress resident (1936–7), many leftist organizations—including the Communist Party of India—collaborated with the Congress. Despite their ideological dissidence, this assemblage generally sought to support independence movements from around the world. Some, like Nehru, believed independence encompassed anti-fascist campaigns such as the Spanish Civil War. Supporting the Republic, they argued, promulgated Indian anti-imperialism on a global stage. In *Spain! Why?*, Nehru contended: "[B]y our giving food-stuffs to the Spanish people we compel the world's attention to our view-point. Thereby we begin to function in the international sphere and the voice of India begins to be heard in the councils of the nations."[159] Nehru subsumed fascism and anti-fascism into his anti-imperialist worldview. The Republic, he contended, fought for self-determination against satisfied and unsatisfied imperialists. From this perspective, Congress support of the Republic went beyond frothy sentiments and pious platitudes and challenged the hypocrisy of liberal-imperialism by exhibiting its similarities to fascism.

Others, like Bose, criticized the incongruousness of Nehruvian anti-imperialism. Devoted entirely to Indian independence, Bose did not contemplate the consanguinity between fascism and imperialism, merely the ways in which the former might help him dismantle the latter. Compared to Nehru, Bose's position was more logical, if not more implacable. He preferred a Nationalist victory because it would diminish Britain's global standing, and contended that denouncing Italy, Germany, and Francoist-Spain alienated potential allies in the campaign for independence. "In connection with our foreign policy," he argued during his presidential address at Haripura (1938), "the first suggestion that I have to make is that we should not be influenced by the internal politics of any country or the form of its State."[160]

Despite their occasional intransigency, Bose's contentions highlight the paradoxes of Nehruvian anti-fascism. Devoted to Gandhian nonviolence, Nehru urged Whitehall to violently combat fascist aggression. Additionally, if Britain successfully defended the Republic, it would only strengthen the British Empire. Finally, by exhorting British intervention in Spain, Nehru demanded the mobilization of the imperial war machine that had despoiled India. Only five months after the Francoist victory, Whitehall realized these demands when it declared war on Nazi Germany. Rather than support Britain, however, Nehru demanded a guarantee of independence in exchange for Congress support of the war effort.[161] Had Nehru acknowledged these and other contradictions, he might have "foreseen the inevitable conflicts coming ahead as the world descended into a war that would pit fascism against imperialism."[162] These incongruities, however, were "neither recognized nor deeply problematic for Nehru."[163] Nehru understood international developments through the prism of anti-imperialism. Analyzing British foreign policy in this way occasionally blinded him to its complexity.

Europe's Cuadrilla

In April 1939, General Franco and the Nationalists declared victory. In due course, the military dismantled what remained of the Second Spanish Republic. From its ashes, Spain emerged a fascist nation. Only eight years prior, as Europe descended into economic depression, Spain had embraced republicanism—the only country in Europe to do so. The Republic's promise, however, belied its fate.

In *Homage to Catalonia*, George Orwell describes a wall in Barbastro where he came upon:

> A poster dating from the previous year and announcing that "six handsome bulls" would be killed in the arena on such and such a date. How forlorn its faded colours looked! Where were the handsome bulls and the handsome bullfighters now? It appeared that even in Barcelona there were hardly any bullfights nowadays; for some reason all the best matadors were Fascists.[164]

Descriptions of bullfighting tend to distort the complexity of Iberian cultures, ethnicities, and languages.[165] Orwell's metaphor nevertheless captured the dynamism with which fascism overwhelmed Europe. Hitler and Mussolini decisively supported General Franco and the Nationalists. Like matadors, they slowly killed the Second Spanish Republic. The National Government, meanwhile, retreated into isolationism—a policy, as one Labour politician put it, of "malevolent neutrality."[166]

Indian understandings of the Spanish Civil War broaden Orwell's metaphor. Emerging from the ashes of the great war, fascism radicalized imperial ideologies. With exiguous "unclaimed" territory remaining in Africa and Asia, fascists turned their gaze inward, to Europe. In Spain, they supported concomitant unsatisfied imperialists—General Franco and the Nationalists—while satisfied imperialists clutched desperately at nonintervention. The National Government, in particular, would not risk its empire in a war to defend the self-determination of the Spanish nation. As in Ethiopia, the sanctity of empire bound Britain to fascism. Returning to Orwell's metaphor, in Spain, the matador traditionally performed as a cuadrilla, alongside banderilleros and picadors. Seen from the outside-in, if the Nationalists symbolized matadors, then unsatisfied imperialists represented the banderilleros, and satisfied imperialists the picadors. Together, this fascist-imperialist cuadrilla murdered democratic Spain.

There are limitations to this perspective. Many Indian anti-colonialists, but particularly Nehru, mischaracterized the politics of the Nationalists as well as the Republicans. The labels "'fascist' and 'communist' were inappropriate: this was a conflict framed not by the ideologies of twentieth-century Europe, but rather by Spanish history."[167] Additionally, Indian support of the Republic created ideological and intellectual paradoxes which Nehru largely ignored. Most notably, his "hawkish argument[s]"[168] in Spain contradicted his "advocacy of peace"[169] in India. Finally, Nehru's Aid Spain campaign substantiates subaltern criticisms that he prioritized European political developments over the suffering of India's impoverished masses.[170] In a report written for the AICC, General

Secretary J. B. Kripalani celebrated the ways in which the Aid Spain campaign demonstrated India's commitment to freedom and self-determination:

> We succeeded in presenting last year a visible token of our sympathy and association to the Spanish Popular Front. A medical ambulance unit is even at the present moment serving on Spanish Battlefields. . . . Spanish Democracy has, no doubt, been made aware of our whole-hearted association with it, but this knowledge is not confined to Spanish frontiers. The fact that the Indian National Congress has all along condemned the British National Government for its non-interventionist policy . . . has also served to sever India, in the eyes of the world, from the British connexion.[171]

Congress intervention in Spain nevertheless robbed Indians of critical foodstuffs. Every day, thousands of Indians starved, while many more were denied proper medical care. Nehru, moreover, frequently contended that the Spanish Civil War captured the imagination of ordinary Indians. The elite leftists of the Congress, however, hardly represented India. Most Indians knew nothing of Spain.[172] Nehru's Aid Spain campaign, consequently, contributed to Indian suffering while also deepening the chasm between the Congress and subaltern India.

Even so, when he visited Barcelona, Nehru represented the Congress; and at least internationally, the Congress was seen to represent India. Nehru "needed no 'entrance ticket' to the world stage by 1938."[173] Though self-aggrandizing, elitist, and largely symbolic, Nehru's Aid Spain campaign aided an ideological ally (Republican Spain), demonstrated India's independence from the British Empire, and exhibited the similarities between fascism and liberal-imperialism.

At least in Spain, perhaps not all the best matadors were fascist.

Notes

1 George Orwell, "Homage to Catalonia," in *Orwell in Spain: The Full Text of Homage to Catalonia with Associated Articles, Reviews and Letters*, ed. Peter Hobley Davison (London: Penguin, 2001), 40.

2 Rabindranath Tagore, "108," in *The English Writings of Rabindranath Tagore: Volume One: Poems,* ed. Sisir Kumar Das (New Delhi: Sahitya Akademi, 1994), 382. Tagore's poetry is in the public domain.

3 Portions of this article appear in: Michael Ortiz, "Spain! Why?: Jawaharlal Nehru, Non-Intervention, and the Spanish Civil War," *European History Quarterly* 49, no. 3 (2019): 445–66.

4 Javier Rodrigo, *Fascist Italy in the Spanish Civil War, 1936–1939* (New York: Taylor & Francis, 2021).

5 Jawaharlal Nehru, *Toward Freedom: The Autobiography of Jawaharlal Nehru* (New York: The John Day Company, 1941), 358.

6 William Kuracina, "Colonial India and External Affairs: Relating Indian Nationalism to Global Politics," *Journal of Asian and African Studies* 42, no. 6 (2007): 517–32; Michele Louro, *Comrades against Imperialism: Nehru, India, and Interwar Internationalism* (Cambridge: Cambridge University Press, 2018); Maria Framke, "Political Humanitarianism in the 1930s: Indian Aid for Republican Spain," *European Review of History* 23, nos. 1–2 (2016): 63–81.

7 Nehru, *Toward Freedom*, 416.

8 Paul Preston, *The Spanish Civil War; Reaction, Revolution, and Revenge* (New York: W. W. Norton, 2007), 2.

9 Some scholars have contended that British nonintervention in Spain emboldened fascist aggression in Austria, Czechoslovakia, and Poland. See Winston Churchill, *The Second World War, Volume 1: The Gathering Storm* (New York: Houghton Mifflin Company, 1948); L. B. Namier, *Diplomatic Prelude* (London: The Macmillan Press, 1948); John Wheeler-Bennett, *Munich: Prologue to Tragedy* (New York: Duell, Sloan and Peace, 1948). Others have argued that, devoid of suitable alternatives and committed to an ambitious rearmament program, British prime ministers Stanley Baldwin and Neville Chamberlain dexterously circumscribed a potential world war. See A. J. P. Taylor, *The Origins of the Second World War* (New York: Touchstone, 1961); W. Laird Kleine-Ahlbrandt, *The Policy of Simmering: A Study of British Policy During the Spanish Civil War, 1936–1939* (The Hague: M. Nijhoff, 1962); Martin Gilbert, *The Roots of Appeasement* (New York: New American Library, 1966); Keith Robbins, *Munich: 1938* (London: Cassell & Company, 1968); Donald Cameron Watt, *How War Came: Immediate Origins of the Second World War, 1938–1939* (London: Mandarin, 1989); Tom Buchanan, *Britain and the Spanish Civil War* (Cambridge, UK: Cambridge University Press, 1997). Still others have asserted that a decidedly anti-communist Whitehall supported General Franco and the Nationalists by willfully impeding French and Soviet support of the Republic. See Jill Edwards, *The British Government and the Spanish Civil War, 1936–1939* (London: Macmillan, 1979); Douglas Little, *Malevolent Neutrality: The United States, Great Britain, and the Origins of the Spanish Civil War* (Ithaca: Cornell University Press, 1985). Enrique Moradiellos, *La Perfidia de Albión: El Gobierno Británico y la Guerra Civil Española* (Madrid: Siglo Veintiuno Editores, 1996).

10 Henrique Monteagudo, "Spanish and Other Languages of Spain in the Second Republic," in *A Political History of Spanish: The Making of a Language*, ed. José Del Valle (Cambridge: Cambridge University Press, 2013), 106.

11 Hugh Thomas, *The Spanish Civil War* (New York: Harper and Brothers, 1961), 1–186; Gabriel Jackson, *The Spanish Republic and the Civil War, 1931–1939* (Princeton: Princeton University Press, 1965), 3–24; Michael Alpert, *A New International History of the Spanish Civil War* (London: Macmillan, 1994), 87–94; Filipe Ribeiro De Meneses, *Franco and the Spanish Civil War* (London: Routledge, 2001), 23–37; Andy Durgan, *The Spanish Civil War* (New York: Palgrave Macmillan, 2007), 105–29; Judith Keene, *Fighting for Franco: International Volunteers in Nationalist Spain during the Spanish Civil War, 1936–1939* (London: Leicester University Press, 2007), 18–44; Julián Casanova, *A Short History of the Spanish Civil War* (London: I.B. Tauris, 2013), 21–80; José E Álvarez, *The Spanish Foreign Legion in the Spanish Civil War, 1936* (Columbia, MI: University of Missouri Press, 2016), 1–27.

12 Jorge Marco, "Transnational Soldiers and Guerrilla Warfare from the Spanish Civil War to the Second World War," *War in History* 27, no. 3 (2020): 387–407; G. Tremlett, *The International Brigades: Fascism, Freedom and the Spanish Civil War* (London: Bloomsbury, 2020).

13 In August 1930, Niceto Alcalá Zamora, Miguel Maura, Fernando Sasiaín, and others formed a revolutionary committee to overthrow King Alfonso XIII and create a Spanish Republic—an act later deemed the Pact of San Sebastián. Although this coup d'état failed, its perpetrators won popular acclaim. The Pact of San Sebastián promised change, something conservatives, socialists, and even military leaders desired. In April 1931, republican candidates overwhelmingly won municipal elections. Days later, General José Sanjurjo y Sacanell informed King Alfonso that the military would no longer protect the monarchy. On April 14, 1931, King Alfonso fled (though did not abdicate), and reformers celebrated the birth of the Second Spanish Republic. The Republic's constitution extended suffrage to women, guaranteed freedom of speech, legalized divorce, and stripped nobility of privilege. In an era of obscurantism, Spain adopted the most progressive constitution in Europe. Though disillusioned with Primo de Rivera and the monarchy, conservatives nevertheless resisted the transformation of Spain. The Spanish Confederation of the Autonomous Right (CEDA)—a union of right and center-right parties led by José María Gil-Robles—won the 1933 elections. It then formed a coalition with the second largest political party, the Radical Republicans led by Alejandro Lerroux (one of the leaders of the Pact of San Sebastián). Together, Gil-Robles and Lerroux annulled many of the reforms guaranteed by the constitution. In response, opposition forces organized a general strike. Asturian miners occupied Oviedo, killing several government officials. After two weeks, the Spanish Army—led by General Francisco Franco—crushed the demonstration. The failure of reform radicalized the Spanish left, particularly the Spanish Socialist Workers Party led by Francisco Largo Caballero. Despite

considerable antagonisms, Caballero's socialists formed a popular front with anarchists, communists, and left-leaning republicans. Led by Manuel Azaña, the Spanish Popular Front defeated a conservative coalition of Carlists, CEDA, and monarchists in the 1936 election. Political polarization, violent clashes, and further radicalization followed. After the assassination of conservative leader José Calvo Sotelo, membership in José Antonio Primo de Rivera's fascist *La Falange* proliferated. Three days after Sotelo's funeral, on July 17, 1936, a cabal of army officers led by General Sanjurjo issued a *pronunciamiento* condemning the Second Spanish Republic.

14 Carlists believed that the Spanish crown belonged to the pretender Infante Alfonso Carlos, descended from the Bourbon Infante Carlos, Count of Molina (1788–1855).

15 The Popular Front included the Spanish Socialist Workers' Party, Communist Party of Spain, the Workers' Party of Marxist Unification, independent communists, Azaña's Republican Left, and the Republican Union Party led by Diego Martínez Barrio. It was also supported by Galician and Catalan nationalists, the Workers General Union, and the anarchist trade union Confederación Nacional del Trabajo. Many anarchists opposed the Popular Front. Burnett Bolloten, Stanley Payne, and George Esenwein, *The Spanish Civil War: Revolution and Counterrevolution* (Chapel Hill: The University of North Carolina Press, 1991), 81–367.

16 Alpert, *A New International History,* 16.

17 Buchanan, *Britain and the Spanish Civil War,* 10.

18 Enrique Moradeillos, "The Gentle General: The Official British Perception of General Franco during the Spanish Civil War," in *Republic Besieged: Civil War in Spain 1936–1939* (Edinburgh: Edinburgh University Press, 1996), 1–20.

19 Edwards, *The British Government and the Spanish Civil War,* 38.

20 Blum and the French government took the lead in proposing nonintervention in Spain. R. J. Q. Adams, *British Politics and Foreign Policy in the Age of Appeasement, 1935–39* (Stanford: Stanford University Press, 1993), 50.

21 Adams, *British Politics and Foreign Policy in the Age of Appeasement,* 51.

22 Ibid., 50–3.

23 Julián Casanova, *The Spanish Republic and Civil War* (Cambridge: Cambridge University Press, 2010), 2. See also: Robert Reid-Pharr, *Archives of Flesh: African America, Spain, and Post-Humanist Critique* (New York: New York University Press, 2016); Ariel Mae Lambe, *No Barrier Can Contain It: Cuban Antifascism and the Spanish Civil War* (Chapel Hill: The University of North Carolina Press, 2019).

24 Rajendra Prasad Dube, *Jawaharlal Nehru: A Study in Ideology and Social Change* (Delhi: Mittal Publications, 1988), 223.

25 Nationalists and Marxists increasingly pursued antithetical campaigns for independence; each, moreover, feared their own marginalization. Far from united,

Congress ideology was chaotic—an ever-evolving tug-of-war between competing discourses. Benjamin Zachariah, *Nehru* (London: Routledge, 2004), 79.

26 Sourendra Ganguly, *Leftism in India: M. N. Roy and Indian Politics 1920–1948* (Calcutta: Minerva Publishers, 1984). See also: Satyabrata Rai Chowdhuri, *Leftism in India, 1917–947* (New York: Palgrave Macmillan UK, 2007).

27 Zachariah, *Nehru*, 79.

28 Subhas Bose to Jawaharlal Nehru, March 4, 1936, in *Netaji: Collected Works: Volume 8: Letters, Articles, Speeches and Statements 1933–1937*, ed. Sisir Kumar Bose, Sugata Bose, and S. A. Ayer (Calcutta: Netaji Research Bureau, 1980), 144–5.

29 B. R. Nanda, *Jawaharlal Nehru: Rebel and Statesman* (New Delhi: Oxford University Press, 1995), 23.

30 Socialist critiques of the Mahatma discounted his critical role in politicizing the Indian proletariat. As in Europe, the rift in the Congress reflected a growing distrust between Right and Left: "[When] the party needed a united front, the Congress Socialists were embarrassing the leadership, talking of class war, frightening off potential supporters, and making new enemies." Nanda, *Jawaharlal Nehru*, 36.

31 B. R. Nanda, "Nehru and the British," *Modern Asian Studies* 30, no. 2 (1996): 474.

32 Zachariah, *Nehru*, 83.

33 To a certain extent, Nehru's presidencies in 1936 and 1937 prevented the fractionalization that began in 1938 and culminated in Bose's creation of the Forward Bloc.

34 George Joseph to Jawaharlal Nehru, July 18, 1936, Jawaharlal Nehru Papers (hereafter JNP), Nehru Memorial Museum and Library (hereafter NMML), Volume 37, pp. 57–8. First seen in Zachariah, *Nehru*, 87.

35 Critics later accused Nehru of encouraging this notion during his seventeen years as prime minister (1947–64).

36 Chanakya (Jawaharlal Nehru), "Rashtrapati" *The Modern Review of Calcutta*, November 1937, reprinted in *Selected Works of Jawaharlal Nehru*, series 1, volume 8, 520–2.

37 Ibid.

38 Nehru, *Toward Freedom*, 600. Nehru's autobiography is often revisionist and self-justificatory, making it difficult to determine whether he seriously contemplated retiring as Congress president. He was, as Sarvepalli Gopal has argued, "The only Indian politician who had an international audience, and it was he who secured for the party recognition on the world stage. Had Jawaharlal, therefore, insisted in the summer of 1936 on resigning the presidency, it is difficult to believe that Gandhi and his followers would have been shortsighted enough to let him to do." Sarvepalli Gopal, *Jawaharlal Nehru: A Biography. Vol. 1, 1889–1947* (London: Cape, 1975), 214.

39 Nehru, *Toward Freedom*, 600.

40 Ibid.

41 There existed many different strains of Indian internationalism. This chapter
    focuses primarily on Nehruvian internationalism—what Kuracina has described
    as: "The twin pillars . . . anti-imperialism and anti-fascism." Kuracina, 518–19.
    It is important to note that many scholars of South Asia have located Nehruvian
    internationalism in an imperialist understanding of world politics. Mithi
    Mukherjee, for example, has contended that Nehru's "approach to foreign relations
    . . . was not grounded in the principle of Gandhian nonviolence. It was a legacy of
    empire." Mithi Mukherjee, "'A World of Illusion': The Legacy of Empire in India's
    Foreign Relations, 1947–62," *The International History Review* 32, no. 2 (2010):
    253. For scholarship examining non-Nehruvian anti-imperialisms, see Manu
    Bhagavan, *Sovereign Spheres: Princes, Education and Empire in Colonial India*
    (Delhi: Oxford University Press, 2003); Mushirul Hasan, and Margrit Pernau,
    Regionalizing Pan-Islamism: Documents on the Khilafat Movement (New Delhi:
    Manohar, 2005); Sunil Amrith, "Asian Internationalism: Bandung's Echo in a
    Colonial Metropolis," *Inter-Asia Cultural Studies* 6, no. 4 (2006): 557–69; Dipesh
    Chakrabarty, *Provincializing Europe: Postcolonial Thought and Historical Difference*
    (Princeton: Princeton University Press, 2008); P. B. Mehta, "Still Under Nehru's
    Shadow? The Absence of Foreign Policy Frameworks in India," *India Review* 8, no.
    3 (2009): 209–33; Srinath Raghavan, *War and Peace in Modern India* (Basingstoke:
    Palgrave Macmillan, 2010); Sunil Amrith, *Migration and Diaspora in Modern
    Asia* (Cambridge: New York, 2011); Manu Goswami, "Imaginary Futures and
    Colonial Internationalisms," *The American Historical Review* 117, no. 5 (2012):
    1461–85; Manu Bhagavan, *India and the Quest for One World: The Peacemakers*
    (Basingstoke: Palgrave Macmillan, 2013); Manu Goswami, *Producing India:
    From Colonial Economy to National Space* (Chicago: University of Chicago Press,
    2013); Ali Raza, Franziska Roy, and Benjamin Zachariah, ed., *The Internationalist
    Moment: South Asia, Worlds, and World Views, 1917–39* (New Delhi: Sage, 2015);
    Venkat Dhulipala, *Creating a New Medina: State Power, Islam, and the Quest for
    Pakistan in Late Colonial North India* (New Delhi: Cambridge University Press,
    2016); Kishwar Sultana, *Politics of the All-India Muslim League, 1924–1940*
    (Karachi: Oxford University Press, 2016).

42 "Higher Status of India: Help to Spain and China, Jawaharlal's Moving Appeal,"
    The National Herald (Lucknow), November 23, 1938. Nehru founded *The National
    Herald* in Lucknow in 1938.

43 Jawaharlal Nehru, July 15–16, 1938, "A Conference on Peace and Empire Held in
    Collaboration with the London Federation of Peace and Held at Friends House,
    Euston Road," Pandit Jawaharlal Nehru: Reports on Activities 1936–1938, BL,
    India Office Records and Private Papers, L/P&J/12/293.

44 Stanley Wolpert, *Nehru: A Tryst with Destiny* (Oxford: Oxford University Press, 1996), 206.

45 Ibid.

46 Pranab Kumar Chatterjee, "The Hunger-Strike Movement of the Andaman Prisoners in 1937 and National Response," *Proceedings of the Indian History Congress* 40 (1979): 662.

47 Rudrangshu Mukherjee, *Nehru and Bose: Parallel Lives* (London: Penguin, 2014), 147.

48 Ibid.

49 "Note of Conversation between Lord Linlithgow and Mr. Jawaharlal Nehru," July 19, 1938, British Library (hereafter BL), Congress: Note of Conversation Between Linlithgow and Nehru; Correspondence Relating to India Office Records and Private Papers, IOR/L/PO/6/96. Nehru recorded his impression of the viceroy in a letter to J. B. Kripalani: "Would you believe it . . . that in the course of two hours of very frank and friendly conversation, there was no mention of Hindu-Muslim affairs or even of federation, so far as I remember. Our conversation covered a wide range of subjects. . . . We talked of independence and the Constituent Assembly and economic questions and the present international situation. . . . This will indicate to you what the basis of my talk has been." B. R. Nanda, *Road to Pakistan: The Life and Times of Mohammed Ali Jinnah* (London: Routledge, 2013), 246.

50 Mukherjee, *Nehru and Bose*, 147.

51 Preston, *The Spanish Civil War*, 141.

52 Buchanan, *Britain and the Spanish Civil War*, 8.

53 Jawaharlal Nehru, "India Looks at the World," *Asia*, January 1939.

54 Jawaharlal Nehru, "Presidential Address to the Indian National Congress at Faizpur," *Labour Monthly* 19, no. 2 (February 1937): 99.

55 Jawaharlal Nehru, *Fascism and Empire* (London: Spain-India Committee, 1937), 1–2.

56 Because General Franco deployed colonial North African troops and relied on German and Italian intervention, Republicans often portrayed the Nationalists as foreign invaders. See José Alvarez, *The Spanish Foreign Legion in the Spanish Civil War* (Colombia: University of Missouri Press, 2018).

57 Nehru's arguments echoed the Dimitrov line within the Comintern, developed during the Seventh World Congress of the Comintern (1935). Silvio Pons, *The Global Revolution: A History of International Communism 1917–1991* (Oxford: Oxford University Press, 2014).

58 Jawaharlal Nehru, July 17, 1938, "Speech at a Demonstration Held at Trafalgar Square to Mark the Second Anniversary of Hostilities in Spain," Pandit Jawaharlal Nehru: Reports on Activities 1936–1938, BL, India Office Records and Private Papers, L/PJ/12/293, File 295/26.

59　Ibid.

60　For Nehru, the urge to globalize Indian anti-imperialism was not new. In 1927, the Congress sent him to the founding of the League Against Imperialism (LAI), in Brussels, Belgium. For young revolutionaries, the LAI was a thrilling opportunity to discuss imperialism with anti-colonialists from around the world. Michele Louro, "India and the League Against Imperialism: A Special 'Blend' of Nationalism and Internationalism," in *The Internationalist Moment: South Asia, Worlds, and World Views* (London: Sage, 2015), 52.

61　The Indian medical mission (Drs. Atal, Ayub Ahmed Khan, and Manuel Rocha Pinto) served within the British Red Cross Unit.

62　Rabindranath Tagore, "The Spanish Civil War: To the Conscience of Humanity," in *The English Writings of Rabindranath Tagore: Volume Three; A Miscellany,* ed. Sisir Kumar Das (New Delhi: Sahitya Akademi, 1994), 819.

63　Roger Manvell and Heinrich Fraenkel, *Doctor Goebbels: His Life and Death* (London: Heinemann, 1960), 11.

64　Ibid.

65　"London Day by Day: Indian Music—Saraswati Puja—Abortive Communist March," *The Times of India,* January 30, 1939, 8.

66　Sehri Saklatvala was the daughter of Shapurji Saklatvala, an Indian communist and Member of Parliament. Dr. Protool C. Bhandari was the first Indian mayor of an English borough and the secretary of the Indian Committee for Food for Spain. Indira Nehru attended several of these events, and even auctioned her meenakari bracelet for 50 pounds as a donation to the Aid Spain campaign. Pranay Gupte, *Mother India: A Political Biography of Indira Gandhi* (New York: Penguin Books, 2011), 185.

67　Speech by Krishna Menon, July 17, 1938, Nehru's Activities from 1936–1938, BL, India Office Records and Private Papers, IOR: L/P&J/12/293.

68　Krishna Menon, "Indian Help for Republican Spain: A Fund in England," *The Manchester Guardian*, December 20, 1938.

69　Buchanan, *Britain and the Spanish Civil War*, 109–20.

70　Most of the children evacuated to Western Europe returned to their families after the war. Those in the Soviet Union, however, were forbidden to return by both Franco and Stalin. Many were raised in Soviet orphanages and were regularly moved during the Second World War. In 1956, three years after Stalin's death, they finally returned to Spain. Lisa A. Kirschenbaum, *International Communism and the Spanish Civil War: Solidarity and Suspicion* (Cambridge: Cambridge University Press, 2015), 198. See also Karl Qualls, *Stalin's Niños: Educating Spanish Civil War Refugee Children in the Soviet Union, 1937–1951* (Toronto: University of Toronto Press, 2020).

71　Indira Nehru to Jawaharlal Nehru, February 13, 1937, in *Two Alone Two Together: Letters Between Indira Gandhi and Jawaharlal Nehru*, ed. Sonia Gandhi (London: Hodder & Stoughton, 1992), 162.

72 Mussolini contributed 60,000 troops to the Nationalist army, while Hitler sent more than 16,000. António Salazar's *Estada Novo* regime supplied General Franco with 10,000 volunteers, in addition to logistical support for war material passing from Portugal into Nationalist territory (Nationalists often referred to Lisbon as 'El Puerto de Castile'). The Republic's only source of foreign aid was the Soviet Union. Unlike Mussolini and Hitler, however, Stalin was forced to navigate thousands of miles of ocean waters. Soviet vessels had to be outfitted with false decks, and would often have to change flags. Stalin, moreover, only gave short notice (if any) of intervention shipments, causing delays, confusion, and even theft. Although the Soviet Union provided the Republic with several modern tanks and aircraft, many of the armaments they sent to Spain were antiques—in most cases, weapons seized from past conflicts. Stanley Payne, *The Spanish Civil War* (Cambridge: Cambridge University Press, 2012), 131–48.

73 Jawaharlal Nehru, "Bombing and Kidnapping on the Frontier," in *Eighteen Months in India, 1936–1937: Being Further Essays and Writings by Jawaharlal Nehru* (Allahabad: Kitabistan, 1938), 203.

74 Alan Warren, *Waziristan, the Faqir of Ipi, and the Indian Army: The North West Frontier Revolt of 1936–37* (Oxford: Oxford University Press, 2000), 127–207.

75 In a public letter, the leader of Waziristan thanked Nehru for his support: "To the leader of the liberty-loving people and distinguished head of the Indian Nation . . . . You sir, would clearly understand that the war between us and the tyrannical Government is entirely due to their unwarranted attack on our liberties and not because of our proselytizing mania. God has plainly instructed us in the matter of religion and taught us in the Holy Book that there is no compulsion in religion. . . . You should take it from us, revered Sir, that the present situation in Waziristan is the result of excesses and the policy of aggressive conquest adopted by the Government of India and is due to no other reason. Hence so long as there is a breath of life left in us it is impossible for us to submit to slavery. With God's help may India emancipate herself from their control and may we free our land at the point of our sword." Leader of Waziristan to President Jawaharlal Nehru, February 3, 1938, A.I.C.C. Foreign Newsletter, b/18/894-T/1938, Foreign Department: Newsletter No. 31, NMML, p. 3.

76 Jawaharlal Nehru, "Interview with Fenner Brockway," Pandit Jawaharlal Nehru: Reports on Activities 1936–1938, BL, India Office Records and Private Papers, L/PJ/12/293, File 295/26.

77 Ibid.

78 During an India League Reception at Kingsway Hall on June 27, 1938, a government agent recorded Nehru as having said: "That he had been in Barcelona during several air raids: it was merely hypocritical of the British Government to hold up hands in horror over bombing in Spain and China, so long as they indulged in this identical practice

on the North West Frontier: they were, because of this, the subject of ribald comment from the whole world." India League Reception to Nehru at Kingsway Hall, June 27, 1938, Pandit Jawaharlal Nehru: Reports on Activities 1936–1938, BL, India Office Records and Private Papers, L/PJ/12/293.

79 Preston, *The Spanish Civil War*, 139.

80 Buchanan, *Britain and the Spanish Civil War*, 37.

81 Helen Graham, *The Spanish Republic at War 1936–1939* (Cambridge: Cambridge University Press, 2002), 316–17.

82 Alpert, *A New International History*, 16.

83 Graham, *The Spanish Republic at War 1936–1939*, 121.

84 Javier Rodrigo, "A Fascist Warfare? Italian Fascism and War Experience in the Spanish Civil War (1936–39)," *War in History* 26, no. 1 (January 2019): 86–104.

85 Nehru, *Toward Freedom*, 415.

86 Tom Buchanan, *The Impact of the Spanish Civil War on Britain: War, Loss and Memory* (Sussex: Sussex Academic Press, 2007), 23–42.

87 Scott Ramsay, "Ensuring Benevolent Neutrality: The British Government's Appeasement of General Franco during the Spanish Civil War, 1936–1939," *The International History Review* 41, no. 3 (2019): 604–23. See also Martin Ceadel, *Semi-Detached Idealists: The British Peace Movement and International Relations, 1854–1945* (Oxford: Oxford University Press, 2000); Talbot Imlay, *Facing the Second World War: Strategy, Politics, and Economics in Britain and France, 1938–1940* (Oxford: Oxford University Press, 2003); David Edgerton, *Warfare State: Britain, 1920–1970* (Cambridge: Cambridge University Press, 2006); Joseph Maiolo, *Cry Havoc: How the Arms Race Drove the World to War, 1931–1941* (New York: Basic Books, 2010); Helen McCarthy, *The British People and the League of Nations: Democracy, Citizenship, and Internationalism, 1918–1945* (Manchester: Manchester University Press, 2013).

88 Frank McDonough, *Neville Chamberlain, Appeasement and the British Road to War* (Manchester: Manchester University Press, 1998), 28. See also Daniel Hucker, *Public Opinion and the End of Appeasement in Britain and France* (London: Routledge, 2011), 81–7.

89 David Jorge, *War in Spain: Appeasement, Collective Insecurity, and the Failure of European Democracies Against Fascism* (London: Routledge, 2020).

90 Edwards, *The British Government and the Spanish Civil War*, 1.

91 Framke, "Political Humanitarianism in the 1930s," 69.

92 Louro, "India and the League Against Imperialism," 236.

93 Jawaharlal Nehru, *Spain! Why?* (London: The Indian Committee for Food for Spain, [1938]), 4.

94 The Indian delegation flew to Genoa and then Marseilles. Despite a letter of invitation from the Republican government, Nehru was initially blocked from

crossing the border. Eventually, after obtaining an acceptable visa, the delegation flew into Barcelona. A. A. Joyce to R. Wilberforce, "Private and Confidential Letter," The Activities of Miss Bhicoo Batlivala, BL, India Office Records and Private papers, L/I/1/1295.

95 Jawaharlal Nehru, "Homage to Spain," in *China Spain and the War: Essays and Writings by Jawaharlal Nehru* (Allahabad: Kitabistan, 1940), 62.

96 Ibid., 62–3.

97 Ibid., 63.

98 Ibid.

99 Ibid., 64.

100 "Raids Watched by Indian Congress Leader," *The Western Morning News*, June 29, 1938.

101 Jawaharlal Nehru, "Presidential Address to the Indian National Congress at Lucknow," *Labour Monthly* 18, no. 5 (May 1937): 282.

102 Framke, "Political Humanitarianism in the 1930s," 70.

103 This is one of the reasons the International Brigades played a pivotal role during the defense of Madrid. Michael Alpert, *The Republican Army in the Spanish Civil War, 1936-1939* (Cambridge: Cambridge University Press, 2013), 1–58.

104 Nehru hoped to meet Spanish prime minister Juan Negrín, but he was in Madrid.

105 Exiled from Francoist-Spain, del Vayo visited Prime Minister Nehru in New Delhi in 1957. "The Spanish Civil War," Nehru told him, "opened a cycle that will have to be closed one day with the victory of what you represent." See Julio, Álvarez del Vayo, *Give Me Combat: The Memoirs of Julio Alvarez del Vayo* (Boston: Little Brown, 1973), 123.

106 As a symbol of Indian solidarity, Nehru presented del Vayo with the flag of the Indian National Congress.

107 Nehru, "Homage to Spain," 80.

108 In September 1938, Nehru met del Vayo in Geneva. "The food problem," he later wrote, "was growing acute, and [del Vayo] begged me to help in sending food supplies from India." Nehru, "Homage to Spain," 82–3.

109 Nehru, "Homage to Spain," 81.

110 Ibid., 69.

111 Ibid., 77.

112 Ibid., 78.

113 Nehru hoped to meet with Republican generals Enrique Lister and Juan Modesto. They had been civilians prior to the war—a stonemason and tailor, respectively. The Indian delegation missed Modesto, but met with General Lister. After their meeting, Nehru was convinced "if the Republic failed in the end it was not this army that failed. It was hunger that killed it and the treachery of England and France." Nehru, "Homage to Spain," 74.

114 "La Passionaria: Spain's Modern Joan of Arc," *The Times of India*, September 24, 1936, 14.

115 La Passionaria popularized "¡No Pasarán!" (They shall not pass!) during the 1936 Siege of Madrid. In 1939, after he conquered Madrid, Franco famously declared "hemos pasado" (we have passed).

116 "La Passionaria: Spain's Modern Joan of Arc," 14.

117 Nehru, "Homage to Spain," 83–4.

118 Ibid., 85.

119 Before leaving Spain, Nehru and Republican army officers shared a toast to Indian freedom.

120 Jawaharlal Nehru, June 20, 1938, "At a Reception by the Paris Branch of Rassemblent Universel Pour la Paix, at the Cercle des Nations and Attended by M. Cachin, Leader of the French Communist Party," Pandit Jawaharlal Nehru: Reports on Activities 1936–1938, BL, India Office Records and Private Papers, L/PJ/12/293, File 295/26.

121 Nehru, *Fascism and Empire*, 2.

122 Nehru, "A Conference on Peace and Empire."

123 Framke, "Political Humanitarianism in the 1930s," 67. To distinguish himself from other John Smiths in the battalion, Huddar went by the name John Smith Irakian, despite never having been to Iraq.

124 Huddar was captured by Nationalist forces during the Battle of Gandesa (1938) and was imprisoned at San Pedro de Cardeña. One of his cellmates was Carl Geiser, author and member of the Abraham Lincoln Brigade. After a few months, Huddar was released as part of a prisoner exchange orchestrated by the British government. Tosu, Hwein-Ru and Len Tsou, *Los Brigadistas Chinos en la Guerra Civil: la Llamada de España (1936–1939)* (Madrid: Catarata, 2013).

125 Len Tsou and Nancy Tsou, "Gopal Mukund Huddar: An Indian Volunteer in the IBs," *The Volunteer: Founded by the Veterans of the Abraham Lincoln Brigade.* Last modified August 25, 2016.

126 Editorial, "Britain and Spain: What a Franco Victory Would Mean," *The Times of India*, January 4, 1939, 9.

127 Mulk Raj Anand, "Homage to Spain III: The Invincible Will to Live," *The Congress Socialist* 2, no. 21 (May 1937): 9.

128 Ibid.

129 Mulk Raj Anand, "Homage to Spain," *The Congress Socialist* 2, no. 17 (May 1937): 9. The image Anand describes is the famous El Generalisimo poster depicting Italian and German intervention in the Spanish Civil War. See Pedrero, *El Generalísimo* (Madrid: Junta Delegada de Defensa de Madrid, Delegación de Propaganda y Prensa, 1936).

130 Mulk Raj Anand, *Apology for Heroism: A Brief Autobiography of Ideas* (Bombay: Kutub-Popular, 1957), 121.

131 Alpert, *A New International History*, 177. See also Evans, Danny. *Revolution and the State: Anarchism in the Spanish Civil War: 1936–1939* (London: Routledge, 2018).

132 Graham, *The Spanish Republic at War 1936–1939*, 297.

133 Mulk Raj Anand to Saros Cowasjee, January 10, 1970, in *Author to Critic: The Letters of Mulk Raj Anand* (Calcutta: A Writers Workshop Publication, 1973), 82.

134 Anand, *Apology for Heroism*, 121.

135 *Authors Take Sides on the Spanish Civil War* (London: Left Review, 1937), 1.

136 Ibid.

137 Ibid., 4.

138 Mulk Ran Anand, in *Authors Take Sides*, 3.

139 "Food for Spain," *The Times of India*, November 28, 1938, 16.

140 Demos, "Letter to the Editor," *The Times of India*, December 12, 1938, 16.

141 An Indian in Spain, "Letter to the Editor," *Times of India*, January 11, 1937, 16.

142 Subhas Bose, "Presidential Address at the 51st Sessions of the Indian National Congress Held at Haripura in February 1938," in *Netaji: Collected Works: Volume 8: Letters, Articles, Speeches and Statements 1933–1937*, ed. Sisir Kumar Bose, Sugata Bose, and S. A. Ayer (Calcutta: Netaji Research Bureau, 1980), 30.

143 Subhas Bose to Jawaharlal Nehru, March 28, 1939, in *Congress President: Netaji Subhas Bose, Collected Works*, vol. 9, ed. Sisir Kumar Bose and Sugata Bose (New Delhi: Oxford University Press, 1995), 193.

144 March 14, 1936, "Secret, Miscellaneous 824 File on Nehru," Pandit Jawaharlal Nehru: Reports on Activities 1936–1938, BL, India Office Records and Private Papers, L/P&J/12/293.

145 Hira Lal Seth and Subhas Chandra Bose, *Personality and Political Ideals of Subhas Chandra Bose: Is He Fascist?* (Lahore: Hero Publications, 1943); Marshall J. Getz, *Subhas Chandra Bose: A Biography* (Jefferson: NC, 2002); Sugata Bose, *His Majesty's Opponent: Subhas Chandra Bose and India's Struggle against Empire* (New Delhi: Penguin Books, 2013).

146 David Darrah, "Leader of India Seeks Duce and Hitler as Allies," *The Chicago Tribune*, November 29, 1937.

147 V. S. Patil, *Subhas Chandra Bose: His Contribution to Indian Nationalism* (New Delhi: Sterling Publishers, 1988), 242.

148 For scholarship that examines the political and intellectual divide between Nehru and Bose, see Michael Brecher, *Nehru's Mantle: The Politics of Succession in India* (Westport: Greenwood Press, 1976); R. C. Pillai, *Jawaharlal Nehru and His Critics: 1923–1947: A Study With Reference to the Ideas of Nehru, Gandhi, Subhas Chandra Bose, M.N. Roy and the Communists* (New Delhi: Gitanjali Publishers, 1986); Reba

Som, *Gandhi, Bose, Nehru, and the Making of the Modern Indian Mind* (New Delhi: Penguin Viking, 2004); P. B. Mehta, "Still Under Nehru's Shadow? The Absence of Foreign Policy Frameworks in India," *India Review* 8, no. 3 (2009): 209–33; Mithi Mukherjee, "Transcending Identity: Gandhi, Nonviolence, and the Pursuit of a 'Different' Freedom in Modern India," *The American Historical Review* 115, no. 2 (2010): 453–73; Mukherjee, "A World of Illusion," 253–71; Rudrangshu Mukherjee, *Nehru and Bose* (Gurgaon: Penguin Books India, 2015).

149 Subhas Bose to Jawaharlal Nehru, March 4, 1936. Netaji Collected Works, Vol. 8, 144–5.

150 Bose, *His Majesty's Opponent*, 108. See also: Zachariah, *Nehru*, 78.

151 Jawaharlal Nehru to Krishna Menon, April 4, 1939, *Selected Works of Jawaharlal Nehru*, Vol. 9, 550.

152 Subhas Bose, "Europe Today and Tomorrow," *Modern Review*, September 1937, 318.

153 Ibid.

154 Ibid.

155 Ibid., 321.

156 Ibid., 320.

157 Ibid., 321.

158 Ibid., 320.

159 Nehru, *Spain! Why?*, 3.

160 Subhas Bose, "The Haripura Address: Presidential Address at the 51st Session of the Indian National Congress, February 1938," in *Congress President: Netaji Subhas Bose, Collected Works*, Vol. 9, 28.

161 To be sure, Nehru's shifting position reflected the ever-evolving complexities of the international situation. At the same time, it also reflected the often contradictory impulses of an anti-fascist and anti-imperialist worldview. After the outbreak of war, Nehru justified his position by contending that the war between Britain and Germany represented an imperialist conflict, rather than a war to defend freedom: "If the war is to defend the *"Status quo,"* imperialist possessions, colonies, vested interests and privilege, then India can have nothing to do with it. If, however, the issue is democracy and a world order based on democracy, then India is intensely interested in it." Jawaharlal Nehru, *What India Wants* (London: India League, 1942), 9.

162 Louro, "India and the League Against Imperialism," 235.

163 Ibid.

164 Orwell, "Homage to Catalonia," 40.

165 Carrie B. Douglas, *Bulls, Bullfighting, and Spanish Identities* (Tucson: The University of Arizona Press, 1997), 1–8.

166 Little, *Malevolent Neutrality*, 33.

167 Buchanan, *Britain and the Spanish Civil War,* 8.

168 Louro, "India and the League Against Imperialism," 237.

169 Ibid.

170 Partha Chatterjee famously argued that to colonial elites such as Nehru, "peasants were 'ignorant' and subject to 'passions' . . . . They needed to be led properly, controlled, not by force or fear, but by 'gaining their trust,' by teaching them their true interests." Partha Chatterjee, *Nationalist Thought and the Colonial World: A Derivative Discourse* (Minneapolis: University of Minnesota Press, 1993), 148. Since its inception more than four decades ago, subaltern scholarship has put forth a wide range of critical scholarship. For an introduction, see Vinayak Chaturved, *Mapping Subaltern Studies and the Postcolonial* (London: Verso, 2000); Ranajit Guha, *History at the Limit of World-History* (New York: Colombia University Press, 2003); Crispin Bates, *Subalterns and Raj: South Asian Since 1600* (New York: Routledge, 2007); Aakash Singh and Silika Mohapatra, *Indian Political Thought: A Reader* (London: Routledge, 2010); Sandipto Dasgupta, "Gandhi's Failure: Anticolonial Movements and Postcolonial Failures," *Perspectives on Politics* 15, no. 3 (2017): 647–62; Louro, *Comrades Against Imperialism*; Tariq Jazeel and Stephen Legg, eds., *Subaltern Geographies* (Athens: The University of Georgia Press, 2019); Rita Banerjee, ed., *Cultural Histories of India* (London: Taylor & Francis, 2020).

171 J. B. Kripalani, "Report of the General Secretary: Indian National Congress," January 1937, 222/63/894-C/1937, All India Congress Committee Papers: Foreign Department, NMML, 44–5.

172 Owen goes so far as to contend that public opinion in India supported fascist aggression toward Britain: "At the end of the year [1938], having assured the British left of the intensity of Congress anti-fascism, Nehru returned home. But in India, he could hardly find any allies . . . . There was little support for the Spanish republicans and a 'great deal of passive opposition' to taking in Jewish refugees." Owen, 249.

173 Louro, "India and the League Against Imperialism," 237.

3

"A Tower of Skulls"

India and the Second Sino-Japanese War

They will punctuate each thousand of the maimed and killed
with the trumpeting of their triumph,
arouse demon's mirth at the sight
of the limbs torn bleeding from women and children;
and they pray that they may befog minds with untruths
and poison God's sweet air of breath,
and therefore they march to the temple of Buddha, the compassionate,
to claim his blessings,
while loud beats the drum rat-a-tat
and earth trembles

—Rabindranath Tagore[1]

In 1915, Rabindranath Tagore wrote a letter to C. F. Andrews: "I am almost sure that Japan has her eyes on India. She is hungry . . . Japan is the youngest disciple of Europe—she has no soul—she is all science—and she has no sentiment to spare for other people than her own."[2] The following year, Tagore visited Japan. He was at once awed by its natural beauty and dismayed by its cult of modernization.[3] Tagore had long condemned the blind jingoism of Indian revolutionaries, and in Japan witnessed the apotheosis of militant nationalism.[4] At his official reception in Tokyo, he praised the Japanese nation while criticizing its state. Standing before Prime Minister Ōkuma Shigenobu, he proclaimed that "the new Japan is only an imitation of the West. This will ruin Japan."[5] A few weeks later, after a similar address denouncing Japanese militarism, the *Tokyo Asahi* reprinted Tagore's remarks under the headline: "Tagore Curses Civilization."[6]

One of the members of Tagore's welcoming committee was internationally renowned poet Yonejirō (Yone) Noguchi. A professor of English at Keio University in Tokyo, Noguchi had long admired Tagore's oeuvre. Over time, the two artists developed a warm friendship. It was through Noguchi that

Tagore came to know "the spirit of Japan, which I learned to admire in your writings and came to love through my personal contacts with you."[7] In 1938, twenty-two years after Tagore's first visit to Japan, Noguchi published a letter in *Amrita Bazar Patrika* urging Tagore to support the Japanese invasion of China. Like many Japanese propagandists, Noguchi contended that Nationalist leader Chiang Kai-shek had betrayed the Republic and created a "mistaken idea of China."[8] Japan, Noguchi argued, would liberate China's "simple and ignorant masses to a better life and wisdom."[9] From the ashes of the Republic, a revivified China would join the Japanese-led Greater East Asia Co-Prosperity Sphere.[10]

Noguchi's appeal confounded Tagore, who bemoaned the "passion of collective militarism that had overwhelmed even the creative artist."[11] In his now-famous response, Tagore denounced Japanese imperialism and its "crudely western" ethos:

> I speak with utter sorrow for your people; your letter has hurt me to the depths of my being. I know that one day the disillusionment of your people will be complete, and through laborious centuries they will have to clear the debris of their civilisation wrought to ruin by their own warlords run amok. They will realise that the aggressive war on China is insignificant as compared to the destruction of their inner spirit of chivalry of Japan which is proceeding with a ferocious severity. . . . Caught unprepared by a gigantic machinery of war, hurled upon her peoples, China is holding her own; no temporary defeats can ever crush her fully aroused spirit. Faced by the borrowed science of Japanese militarism which is crudely western in character, China's stand reveals an inherently superior moral stature."[12]

The quarrel between Tagore and Noguchi reflected wider debates over the Empire of Japan. Was it a non-Western, anti-colonial paragon? Or a synthetic facsimile of Western fascism?[13] After the Russo-Japanese War (1904–5), anti-colonialists around the world looked to Japan as an anti-imperial lodestar. Its triumph over the Russian Empire menaced Western hegemony and reawakened hopes for greater pan-Asian collaboration.[14] Three decades later, the Second Sino-Japanese War extinguished these hopes.[15] Although it threatened British hegemony, Japanese imperialism reproduced Britain's sanctimonious civilising mission. Advancing armies trumpeted an emancipatory "New East Asian Order"[16] that, in practice, brutalized innocent civilians in Shanghai, Nanjing, and elsewhere. "You are building your conception of Asia," Tagore warned Noguchi, "on a tower of skulls."[17]

The Second Sino-Japanese War culminated decades of Japanese expansion, inaugurated the Second World War, devastated China, and set the stage for the Chinese Communist Revolution.[18] It remains a source of both pride and resentment.[19] In Europe, inside-out narratives have traditionally examined British nonintervention in the conflict. Preoccupied with "financial emergency at home and acutely aware of [its] vulnerability in East Asia,"[20] the National Government believed that it would lose a two-front, intercontinental war against both Germany and Japan.[21] With little recourse, British prime minister Neville Chamberlain prioritized Europe while practicing "benevolent neutrality"[22] toward China. There was, as J. K. J. Perry has contended, "no Far Eastern Munich"[23]; China was "cast the role of heroic underdog, Japan the brutal tyrant."[24]

Seen from India, British policy in East Asia was neither benevolent nor neutral.[25] In this chapter, I contend that, seen from the outside-in, the National Government's benevolent neutrality toward China elided the British Empire's influence upon Japan. As in Ethiopia and Spain, British imperial sovereignty transcended the noninterventionism of the National Government. During Britain's imperial century, the imagined hegemony of the Pax Britannica inspired emulation from nations around the world. After the Boshin War and subsequent Meiji Restoration, the Japanese government embraced Western-style modernization. Industrialists purchased British machinery; British technical experts aided in the construction of factories; and the Imperial Japanese Navy was reorganized to resemble the Royal Navy. As in Europe, hyper-industrialization created an insatiable demand for raw materials. Expansionist government officials, pugnacious military officers, and numerous *Zaibatsu* (large business conglomerates) demanded evermore resources, impelling Japan—much like Britain, France, and Germany—to colonize non-industrialized nations.

Emulation, however, "was a prelude to competition and ultimately to confrontation."[26] European nation-states, Britain in particular, had colonized much of East and Southeast Asia. With limited avenues for expansion, Japan annexed, invaded, or asserted suzerainty over "unclaimed" and vulnerable territory, including Formosa, Korea, and Sakhalin Island. In due course, imperial cupidity demanded evermore horizons; yet this expansion could only take place at the expense of China or the Western imperial powers. Unwilling to risk war with the latter, Japan invaded the former. British imperialism thus influenced the Second Sino-Japanese War. Ideologically, the Pax Britannica represented an enchiridion for Japanese imperialists; geographically, Western imperial conquest delimited Japanese expansion to Republican China; and politically, British colonialists had debilitated the Qing and Republican governments.

For more than a century, the British Empire circled "the earth with one continuous and unbroken strain of the martial airs of England."[27] Imitation inevitably followed, particularly from those nations—like Japan—convulsed by imperialist aggression. By the turn of the twentieth century, it became popular "to link the Empire of the Rising Sun with that 'on which the sun never sets.'"[28] Amid Japanese expansion into Korea, Russia, and China, Indian anti-fascists identified significant parallels between Japanese fascism and British imperialism. Japanese pan-Asianism invoked Britain's civilising mission, and epitomized, as Tagore contended, "all the virtues of lesser Europe."[29]

The British of the East

In January 1841, during the First Opium War, several hundred Indian soldiers disembarked from the *Enterprise*, *Madagascar*, and *Nemesis*, near the mouth of the Canton River.[30] Commanded by British Major Thomas Pratt, they advanced nearly two miles before locating the upper Chuenpi Fort. As British heavy artillery occupied Chinese canons, the Anglo-Indian invasion force scaled the fort's earthen walls and overwhelmed the Qing defense. Believing rumors that the "British killed all prisoners,"[31] many Chinese soldiers refused to surrender. "A frightening scene of slaughter ensued," one participant later recalled, "despite the efforts of the [British] officers to restrain their men."[32] In the subsequent Convention of Chuenpi, the Qing Government ceded Hong Kong to the British Crown.[33]

Sino-Indian relations were complicated by the presence of colonial-Indian troops in China. Far from a periphery, India acted as a "nodal point from which peoples, ideas, goods, and institutions—everything that enables an empire to exist—radiated outward."[34] Parsi businessmen from Bombay facilitated the Opium trade, while Sikh police enforced mandates in treaty ports such as Shanghai.[35] During Chiang Kai-shek's Northern Expedition (1926–8), the promise of national unification and an end to warlordism threatened many imperialists' "privileged enclaves."[36] Colonial officials scrambled Indian troops to defend these interests, allegedly telling them "that the Chinese had vandalized Indian religious places and molested Indian women."[37]

Many Chinese anti-imperialists considered India a pitiable nation whose "internal weakness, exploited by foreign invaders, had forced it into a state of subjugation that was morally and psychologically shameful, as well as politically and economically catastrophic."[38] After the First World War, the development of global anti-imperialisms precipitated increased cooperation between India and China. The Xinhai Revolution, postwar Wilsonian Moment, and Gandhi's Champaran and Kheda satyagrahas each roused renewed calls for pan-Asianism—the "united defense of Asia against the encroachments of Western imperialism."[39] During his 1922 Presidential Address to the Congress, C. R. Das contended that "Even more important . . . is the participation of India in the great Asiatic Federation which I see in the course of formation . . . such a bond of friendship and love of sympathy and co-operation between India and the rest of Asia . . . is destined to bring about World Peace."[40]

In 1927, while attending the Congress Against Colonial Oppression and Imperialism in Belgium, Jawaharlal Nehru met with the Chinese delegation. Afterward, he lamented India's historic role in the subjugation of China: "[Indians] are bondsmen in our own household . . . far from helping China, we have to witness with shame and humiliation that our resources and manpower are being utilized by our imperialist masters to coerce China and tarnish the good name of India and make her hated by all who strive for freedom."[41] The following year, the Congress invited Soong Ching-ling—Sun Yat-sen's widow and the future vice chairman of the People's Republic of China—to attend its annual meeting in Calcutta. Colonial officials denied her a visa.[42]

Amid the rise of fascism, as Indian anti-imperialists condemned the Italian invasion of Ethiopia and the Nationalist coup in Spain, their relationships with Chinese anti-colonialists flourished. Acclaimed journalist and Guomindang leader Dai Jitao (Dai Xuantang) visited Tagore, Gandhi, and Nehru in India. Although it conflicted with their revolutionary ideology, the Chinese communist press covered Gandhi's civil disobedience campaigns in great detail.[43] Together with Tan Yun-Shan, Rabindranath Tagore founded a Sino-Indian Cultural Society in Calcutta. In April 1936, at a rally protesting Japanese truculency, Tagore urged all Indians to "fight shoulder to shoulder with our Chinese brethren to defeat the aggressors."[44] Shortly thereafter, he founded a Sino-Indian research department, the Cheena Bhavana, at his university in Santiniketan, Bengal. In a letter thanking Tagore, Chiang Kai-shek expressed his "extreme joy on the occasion of the inauguration of the Chinese Hall. We are eager to cooperate with you for the promotion of oriental culture and civilization in order to bring about peace and happiness to humanity and lead to a greater harmony of the world."[45]

Many Indians nevertheless felt ambivalent toward the Second Sino-Japanese War. For the generation of anti-colonialists that came to power before the Second World War, Japan epitomized non-Western anti-imperialism.[46] Its victory in the Russo-Japanese War (1905) captured anti-colonial imaginations. The same day he arrived in London to begin schooling at Harrow, Nehru learned of the Battle of Tsushima. "I remember well," he later reflected, "how excited I used to get when news came of the Japanese victories."[47] Japan's victory over Russia challenged Western imperialist hegemony, invalidating "several key legitimacy discourses in the Eurocentric world order."[48] Years later, as he launched his *Azad Hind* campaign to liberate India, Subhas Bose invoked the anti-imperialist legacy of the Russo-Japanese War. "This is not the first time," he argued, "that the world has turned to the East for light and guidance . . . in the creation of a new, free and prosperous East."[49]

The war itself was paradoxical. Japan defeated Russia due in part to the Anglo-Japanese Alliance—a treaty that ultimately strengthened the "Pax Britannica in the Far East."[50] Even so, Japan's ascendancy inspired hope. In 1916, during his first visit to Japan, Tagore extolled the Russo-Japanese War as an anti-imperialist cynosure:

> The first thing is the feeling of gratitude which we all owe to you—we whose home is Asia . . . . We have been repeatedly told, with some justification, that Asia lives in the past . . . . When things stood like this . . . Japan rose from her dreams, and in giant strides left centuries of inaction behind, overtaking the present time in its foremost goal. . . . In a word, modern Japan has come out of the immemorial East like a lotus blossoming in an easy grace, all the while keeping its firm hold upon the profound depth from which it sprung.[51]

At the same time, Japanese imperialism frustrated Indian anti-fascists. In 1895, during the First Sino-Japanese War, Japan invaded the island of Formosa (Taiwan). After the Russo-Japanese War, it acquired Port Arthur and the southern half of Sakhalin Island, and declared Southern Manchuria within its sphere of influence. In 1910, Japan formally annexed Korea. During the First World War, it captured Qingdao (Tsingtao), the Marshall Islands, and other German colonies, and was awarded the South Pacific Mandate by the Treaty of Versailles.[52] Finally, in 1931, Japan invaded Manchuria and created the puppet state of Manchukuo.[53] Each of these campaigns frustrated Indians who had previously praised Japanese anti-colonialism. Japan, it seemed, had forfeited its anti-imperialist legacy to become a simulacrum of the European nation-state—the "British of the East."[54]

~

In India, the outbreak of the Second Sino-Japanese War coincided with the final months of Nehru's Faizpur presidency.[55] Despite internal pressure, Nehru opted not to pursue another term. Political dissidence, bureaucratic obligations, and an ambitious travel schedule had exhausted him.[56] Nehru's withdrawal exacerbated a political schism between Marxists and Gandhian nationalists. As president, Nehru largely transcended this divide. His socialist verisimilitude and stubborn devotion to Gandhi appealed to both leftists and traditionalists, ensuring the Congress's public—if not private—unity.[57] In 1938, without Nehru, the Congress reached a turning point. It could nominate a conservative president, and further marginalize leftists, or it could recommend a socialist, and risk alienating traditionalists. Ultimately, Gandhi and the Congress chose Subhas Bose.

Bose's second presidential term—in which he challenged Gandhi and was expelled from the Congress—too often eclipses the accomplishments of his first.[58] His political program galvanized the non-Nehruvian left and anticipated many of independent India's social, political, and economic issues: "His warning about partition came true within nine years. His hope that the Congress should remain in the seat of power even after independence, has been fulfilled. . . . His plans for foreign policy, socialism and family planning were realized later."[59] Bose envisaged an industrialized India emancipated from poverty, oppression, and illiteracy. He contended that imperial connivance had divided India along religious, caste, and gender lines, and "chose to side with the underdogs, having identified the subordinated castes, the laboring masses, and women as the three oppressed collectivities who had to be empowered."[60]

Internationally, Bose's popularity soared. He toured India, appeared in newspapers across Europe, and was featured on the cover of *Time* magazine.[61] As Congress president, he promoted cultural diplomacy abroad, encouraging "cultural troupes, such as the dancers Uday Shankar and Amala Shankar, to visit Europe and disseminate Indian arts."[62] Following the death of Turkish president Kemal Ataturk, the Congress observed "Kemal Day," during which Bose offered his "friendly greeting to the emancipated people of [Ataturk's] beloved Turkey."[63] In his presidential address at Haripura, Bose promulgated the universality of Congress advocacy: "Ours is a struggle not only against British Imperialism but against world imperialism as well, of which the former is the keystone. We are, therefore, fighting not for the cause of India alone but of humanity as well."[64] Like Nehru, Bose sought to appoint Congress representatives to nations around the world—Latin America, in particular. "It is a pity," he argued, "that we have so far neglected Central and South America, where there is profound interest in India."[65] After independence, Bose envisioned these representatives serving as India's foreign diplomats.

Bose's ascension fragmented an already polarized Congress. An uncompromising anti-colonialist, he dissented from Gandhism both epistemologically and ontologically. Gandhi espoused radical nonviolence and envisioned independent India as a federation of self-sufficient agrarian communities, or *Ramrajya*.[66] Bose, by contrast, demanded a violent revolution that would topple the Raj and usher in an industrialized, modern nation-state. "We want to go not the way of China," he contended, "but the way of Turkey."[67] Together, Gandhi and Bose represented antipodean anti-colonialisms. Nevertheless, as Congress president, Bose attempted to bridge political divisions. He collaborated with Gandhi and the Working Committee and endeavored to occupy a middle ground between traditionalists and leftists. In September, however, nationalists within the All India Congress Committee (AICC) drafted a resolution criticizing socialists for "fomenting a class war in the name of defending civil liberties."[68] Leftists demanded an amendment to the resolution and even staged a dramatic walkout. Although Bose remained, Gandhi was "mightily annoyed, and said that those who had walked out should permanently leave the Congress if they could not abide by basic principles accepted by the majority."[69] Though not necessarily decisive, this episode—together with others like it—deepened political divides within the Congress.

Bosian pragmatism also contrasted with Nehruvian romanticism. Bose criticized Indian anti-fascism as intellectually myopic, and frequently proposed a "synthesis between Communism and Fascism."[70] He was, in this regard, the product of a unique "internationalist milieu"[71] in which the "intersections between socialism, communism, nationalism, pacifism, and civil liberties worldwide . . . were highly unstable."[72] Unlike Nehru, Bose subsumed ideological and philosophical exigencies within an all-encompassing anti-imperialist framework. In 1941, during the Second World War, he eluded house arrest, decamped to Berlin, and created the Indian Legion as a military unit within the German *Wehrmacht*.[73] Soldiers swore allegiance to "the leader of the German race and state, Adolf Hitler, as the commander of the German armed forces in the fight for India, whose leader is Subhas Chandra Bose."[74] Two years later, Bose allied with the Empire of Japan and revivified the Indian National Army (INA) founded by Bengali revolutionary Rash Behari Bose. In 1944, the INA attacked British India but was ultimately defeated at the battles of Imphal and Kohima.[75] Bose died the following year in a plane crash over Japanese-controlled Formosa (Taiwan). "The roads to Delhi are many," he argued just before his death, "and Delhi still remains our goal."[76]

Bose's wartime alliances have sparked fecund debates over whether he was a fascist. His Azad Hind radio addresses exhibited a problematic attraction to fascist autocracy. At the same time, he was an obdurate anti-imperialist unperturbed by ideological contradictions. He admired the rectitude of the Bhagavad Gita and Swami Vivekananda, yet often practiced realpolitik; he extolled the totalitarianism of Nazi Germany yet abhorred its racial politics; he propounded militant nationalism, yet embraced feminism and secularism; and finally, he devoted his life to Indian independence, yet entered into a military alliance with the Empire of Japan. Bosian politics existed in the interstices between these contradictions. His politics, personality, and legacy remain, among other things, a paradox.[77]

A Miserable Puppet of the West

In 1936, Mao Zedong and the Chinese Communist Party (CCP) had just completed a punishing Long March from Jiangxi to the Shaanxi province, in northwest China.[78] Exhausted, they were nevertheless "ready to tell their story to the outside world."[79] American journalist Edgar Snow traveled to the Shaanxi province in June 1936. Afforded unprecedented access to Mao, Zhou Enlai, Peng Dehuai, and Lin Biao, Snow chronicled his experiences with the CCP in *Red Star Over China*. The publication of *Red Star* coincided with the outbreak of the Second Sino-Japanese War, and provided Western audiences with a sympathetic—albeit quixotic—account of a group of peregrine "red warriors."[80] In London, it enthralled Victor Gollancz's Left Book Club, challenging prevailing depictions of Chinese inferiority—most notably, Sax Rohmer's *Fu Manchu*, "the Yellow Peril incarnate."[81] While the Spanish Civil War still figured prominently in popular British imagination, it was "no longer the only heroic struggle."[82]

More than a decade after the Second World War and the Chinese Civil War, in a preface to the second edition of *Red Star Over China*, Snow decried the quiescence of Britain and the Western allies: "The Western powers, in self-interest, were hoping for a miracle in China. They dreamed of a new birth of nationalism that would keep Japan so bogged down that she would never be able to turn upon the Western colonies."[83] Snow's criticism underscored Whitehall's equivocal, often contradictory, approach to the Second Sino-Japanese War. For nearly half a century, British foreign policy reflected "admiration for the Japanese and exasperation over their increasingly belligerent and confrontational behavior."[84] In 1902, Britain renounced its "splendid isolation"[85] to sign the First Anglo-Japanese Alliance.[86] At the Washington Naval Conference (1921–2), representatives from Britain, Japan, France, and the United States agreed to a Four-Power Treaty preserving the territorial status quo. After the Japanese invasion of Manchuria

(1931), the Foreign Office reversed course and attempted to bolster the Chinese Nationalist Government as a bulwark against Japanese expansionism. This shift in policy reflected, among other things, financial interests: "The Hongkong and Shanghai Bank and the conglomerates which were investing heavily in China in the 1930s exerted strong pressure on the Foreign Office.... [T]heir representations strengthened the government's determination to defend Britain's stake in China."[87]

Despite these efforts, Whitehall could do little to manacle Japanese expansionism. Many conservatives, moreover, discounted the immediacy of China. Prime Minister Neville Chamberlain feared that war with Japan would embolden Nazi expansionism in Europe. "We cannot ignore," he argued, "the terrible risks of putting such temptations in Hitler's way."[88] For Chamberlain, Viscount Halifax, and other leading members of the National Government, the proximity of Nazi Germany eclipsed the menace of Japan. Even chronic apostates such as Churchill contended that Britain's destiny lay "not in the Far East, not in the quarrels of the yellow peoples, but in the heart of Christendom and Europe."[89] Thus, while many in Whitehall sympathized with the Republic of China, they avoided confrontation with the Empire of Japan. As the British foreign secretary, Anthony Eden, made clear: "Unless and until the United States will join with us we could not . . . in the present state of Europe attempt any action in the Far East."[90]

The National Government nevertheless presided over a vast and often intractable empire. Whitehall did not control the ways in which the legacy, breadth, and exploitation of empire influenced individuals and nations around the world. At the same time the British government pursued nonintervention (or benevolent neutrality) in China, the British Empire emboldened Japanese expansion across East and Southeast Asia. As Congress president, Bose argued that British imperial sovereignty shaped the Japanese invasion of China. However, whereas Nehru, Tagore, and Indian anti-fascists condemned fascist imperialism, Bose equivocated, contending that fascism represented a potential ally in the war for independence. Bose, in this way, was an uncompromising anti-imperialist. Ignoring any similarities between fascism and imperialism, he maintained an almost monomaniacal devotion to Indian independence. "All possible means," he argued during the Second World War, "should be employed and the Indian people should not be hampered by any philosophical notions like Gandhian non-violence, or any sentimentalism like Nehru's anti-Axis foreign policy."[91]

As with the Spanish Civil War, Bose analyzed the Second Sino-Japanese War through a predominantly Marxist lens. "The islands which form the homeland of the Japanese race," he argued in *Japan's Role in the Far East* (1937), "are overpopulated."[92] Like many European nations, Japan had reached an economic and demographic Rubicon. Hyper-industrialization had depleted its limited natural resources. Amid the Great Depression, as austerity presaged upheaval and perhaps even revolution, the military embarked upon a program of imperial expansion. Japan, Bose contended, required "more territory for her children to settle in—more raw materials for her growing industries and more markets for her finished goods. No one will make her a present of these three things—hence the resort to force."[93]

Beginning with its invasion of Manchuria, Japan extended its military and political influence over mainland China. Bose attributed Japanese expansionism to the apocryphal Tanaka Memorial (1927)—anti-Japanese propaganda that allegedly exposed Prime Minister Tanaka Giichi's colonial ambitions:

In order to take over the world, you need to take over Asia;
In order to take over Asia, you need to take over China;
In order to take over China, you need to take over Manchuria and Mongolia.
If we succeed in conquering China, the rest of the Asiatic countries and the South
    Sea countries will fear us and surrender to us.
Then the world will realize that Eastern Asia is ours.[94]

In 1932, the military orchestrated the Shanghai Incident (January 28th Incident); the following year, it seized the Jehol (Rehe) and Chahar provinces.[95] In both instances, spurious border incidents preceded hostilities. Bose contended that Japan, much like imperialist Britain and fascist Italy, concocted these political crises: "The tactics are the same, whether one observes the north-western frontier of India or Walwal in Abyssinia or the Manchurian frontier in the Far East."[96] In 1935, after the Washington Naval Treaty expired, Japan rejected the 5:5:3 warship ratio and demanded parity with Britain and the United States. One year later, after the abortive February 26th uprising, the military-controlled government entered into the anti-Comintern Pact with Nazi Germany.[97] Bose contended that Japan's escalating bellicosity bewildered the Western Powers, whose protracted rearmament only emboldened Japanese aggression in China. "All of them [Wester Powers] are preparing feverishly and are piling up armaments and two or three years later, the outlook for Japan may be gloomy. It was, therefore, a case of 'now or never' for Japan, and she struck."[98]

Reluctant to criticize Japan, Bose instead directed his animadversions at Chiang Kai-shek and the "Western exploiting powers."[99] Perhaps this was Bose's way of propagating Japanese obloquy; Noguchi and other propagandists characterized Chiang as a "miserable puppet of the West."[100] Or perhaps the devoutly Marxist Bose loathed the virulently anti-communist Chiang. "At his heart," Bose argued, "[Chiang] is violently anti-Communist and since the split in the Kuomintang . . . has encountered consistent opposition from two quarters . . . the Western Provinces of China, known as the Chinese Soviet, and the Western Powers with their vast interests in China."[101] Bose alleged that without this opposition Chiang would likely have forsaken the Republic and negotiated nominal governance within the Greater East Asia Co-Prosperity Sphere: "Can China submit to [Japanese suzerainty] even if it brings her peace? My own view is that left to himself, Marshal Chiang Kai-shek, the Dictator of the Nanking Central Government, would have done so."[102] Ironically, Bose contended that, given the opportunity, Chiang would abandon his nation and ally with the Empire of Japan.

In *The Discovery of India*, Nehru claimed that Bose "did not approve of any step being taken by the Congress which was anti-Japanese or anti-German or anti-Italian."[103] At the same time, Bose's correspondence and speeches exhibited "no dearth of sincerity and feeling in his endeavor to dispatch the medical mission to China."[104] Bose had long panegyrized the Xinhai Revolution, contending that Sun Yat-sen was the architect not only of Republican China "but for us Indians he has a greater importance. He was one of the greatest men of Asia, nay of the whole world."[105] During Bose's presidency, the Congress organized several "All-India China" days, during which it collected foodstuffs and medical supplies for the Chinese war effort.[106] Bose urged all Indians to "make an intensive drive on these days for collecting funds."[107] The Congress even instituted a boycott of Japanese goods. In Kuala Lumpur, Chinese workers protested the Second Sino-Japanese War by drowning their tools. Management attempted to hire Indian laborers until the Congress appealed to "the Indian workers . . . to withhold their labour."[108] Almost immediately, Krishna Menon reported, "they came out of the mines . . . ."[109]

A Congress-sponsored medical mission disembarked from Ballard Pier, Bombay (Mumbai,) on September 1, 1938, with fifty-four boxes of medical supplies and one ambulance. To celebrate the occasion, the Congress organized a rally featuring Sarojini Naidu, the Chinese vice-consul, and S. A. Brelvi of the *Bombay Chronicle*. Local Chinese immigrants gave flowers to the five Indian doctors—M. Atal, M. Cholkar, D. S. Kotnis, D. Mukerji, and B. K. Basu—while an Indian boys choir sang the national anthem of China. Speaking before the assembled crowd, Bose reaffirmed his support of China: "Behind this small gift is the soul of the Indian people. . . . It is not a small thing that India is appearing on the international stage to-day as a bulwark against forces of imperialism, autocracy, and spiritual wickedness."[110]

While he sympathized with China, Bose also praised Japan. From his perspective, admiring both nations was not paradoxical, nor even irreconcilable. Describing these discordant impulses (among others), Sugata Bose has invoked a "not uncommon paradox"[111] in South Asian history: "'Men of spiritual yearnings with the strain of mysticism' were often associated with 'the cult of the sword.'"[112] Like many interwar internationalists, Bose brazenly traversed political and intellectual taxonomies. During the Second World War, in a conversation with Japanese pan-Asianist Ōkawa Shūmei, he "talked about the possibility of receiving Soviet support against the British Empire if Germany was defeated on the European front."[113] Ōkawa could not believe that Bose would support the Soviet Union. In response, Bose made clear that he was prepared "to shake hands with even Satan himself to drive out the British from India."[114] *Japan's Role in the Far East* personified this paradox; Bose simultaneously celebrated Japanese militarism while extolling Republican anti-imperialism:

> Japan has done great things for herself and for Asia. Her reawakening at the dawn of the present century sent a thrill throughout our continent. Japan has shattered the white man's prestige in the Far East and has put all the Western imperialist powers on the defensive—not only in the military but also in the economic spheres. She is extremely sensitive—and rightly so—about her self-respect as an Asiatic race. She is determined to drive out the Western Powers from the Far East. But could not all this have been achieved without Imperialism, without humiliating another proud, cultured and ancient race? No, with all our admiration for Japan, where such admiration is due, our whole heart goes to China in her hour of trial. China must still live for her own sake and for humanity. Out of the ashes of the conflict she will once again rise Phoenix-like as she has so often done in the past.[115]

Bose sympathized with China, yet eschewed denouncing Japan. His position, in this regard, paralleled that of the British government—another of the paradoxes that animated Bosian politics.

Bose nevertheless emphasized Britain's furtive role in the Second Sino-Japanese War, contending that the ubiquity of empire transmogrified China into the only viable outlet for Japanese expansion. Beginning with the Meiji Restoration, Japan embraced Western industrialization. Over time, urbanization and mechanization created an insatiable demand for raw materials. Bose contended that government and military officials instinctively looked to nations like China for economic salvation, only to discover that Western imperialists had already apportioned China's vast natural wealth:

> By that time Japan had modernised her state-machinery with the help of modern methods and had modern weapons of warfare. She found that all the big European Powers had begun to exploit China and to enrich themselves at her expense. Why, then, should not Japan, an Asiatic Power living next-door, do the same and keep out the Western Powers from draining the wealth of the East? This was the imperialist logic which started Japan on her race for expansion.[116]

During the interwar era, Japanese imperialists confronted the "ABCD Encirclement"[117]—America, Britain, China, and the Dutch East Indies. "Japanese expansion," Bose explained, "can take place only in the face of Chinese, Russian, British, or American opposition. If she expands on the Asiatic mainland, she is bound to incur the wrath of China or Russia. If she expands southward— towards the Philippine islands or Australia—she is bound to come into conflict with the United States of America or Great Britain."[118] Reluctant to wage war against the Western imperial powers, Japan invaded China.

Bose contended that British imperial hegemony shaped the trajectory of Japanese expansionism. Inveterate European empires—Britain in particular— had subjugated much of Asia. "The only alternative," Bose argued, "left to Japan for satisfying her imperialist ambitions is to expand at the expense of China."[119] The Pax Britannica had galvanized Japanese industrialization but now circumscribed Japanese expansion, forcing the burgeoning Japanese empire to invade the only remaining semi-independent, semi-industrialized nation-state. Western imperial hegemony, Bose contended, transformed China into the only means by which Japan could assert its industrial and imperial puissance: "Japan's imperialist needs and demands in the Far East can only be fulfilled if she can establish her political hegemony over China to the exclusion of the white races."[120] In China, as in Ethiopia, the ubiquity of Western imperialisms guided fascist expansionism.

While Bose denounced British imperialism, he precluded any comparison with Japanese imperialism. This obviation disassociated him from the mainstream of Indian anti-fascism, which identified profound similarities between fascism and liberal-imperialism. Interestingly, in *Japan's Role in the Far East*, Bose vaguely approximated this position, contending that Japan's imperial expansion precipitated its fascistization. "Besides the purely economic motive the Japanese are inspired by the desire to found an Empire. . . . Incidentally, then, the foundation of empires abroad enabled fascist and imperialist elements within Japanese society to come to power."[121] Bose, however, ultimately elided any comparison between fascism and imperialism—presumably because the former represented a potential ally in his war against the latter. Such inexorability often elicited fantastic allegations. Postwar critics decried Bose as the abortive "Führer of India." To be sure, Bose admired the ways in which fascist ascendancy challenged British hegemony. His wartime actions, moreover, have sparked necessary debates over his fascist proclivities. At least in 1937, however, as president-elect of the Congress, Bose repudiated Japanese fascism as a beacon for Indian independence: "Let India resolve to aspire after national self-fulfilment in every direction—but not at the expense of other nations and not through the bloody path of self-aggrandisement and imperialism."[122]

Bose remains a complicated prism from which to analyze British nonintervention in the Second Sino-Japanese War. Like Gandhi, he eludes categorization. Over the course of his life, Bose selectively adopted tenets from anti-imperialism, Hinduism, fascism, Marxism, Leninism, nationalism, and Gandhism, to name just a few. His political career encapsulated "all of the dramatic contradictions of world history in the first half of the twentieth century."[123] Perhaps the only constant in Bose's life was his pertinacious devotion to Indian independence. This idée fixe, as many scholars have contended, explicates—or at the very least, begins to explicate—his seemingly paradoxical relationship with Japan. In 1937, before British involvement in the Second Sino-Japanese War, Bose sympathized with China. Once Britain entered the conflict (1941), however, Japanese imperialism transformed into a means of toppling the Raj. It was an opportunity Bose could not resist.

Island Empires

After the Marco Polo Bridge Incident (1937), General Zhu De of the Communist Eighth Route Army wrote a letter to the Indian National Congress.[124,125] Invoking pan-Asian sentiments, Zhu urged all Indians to support the Chinese war effort: "We know that we are fighting not only the battle of the Chinese nation and the Chinese people, but we are fighting the battle of the people of all Asia. . . . It is with this consciousness that we feel justified in asking you . . . to help us in our struggle by any and all means."[126] Nehru and Foreign Affairs Department head Ram Manohar Lohia printed the letter in a pamphlet entitled *India on China* in which they contended that the Second Sino-Japanese War—much like the Second Italo-Ethiopian War and the Spanish Civil War—exhibited the similarities between fascism and imperialism:

> Why has the present order successively collapsed in Ethiopia, Spain and China? Is it because of stray incidents during manoeuvres as in China or of assassination of individuals—as in Spain? No, the causes go much deeper. . . . Fascist Italy proclaims that it must fulfil its national destiny through war and has the right and duty to build a Roman Empire in Ethiopia. Fascist Spain desires to purify and unite the Spanish nation in blood and proclaims its right and duty to protect property and religion. Militarist Japan cannot permit Chinese advancement unless under its own protection and must suppress China. to establish cooperation and stability in the East. In all these utterances, there is one common idea. Imperialism, which is the guiding principle of the present world order, must fulfil its national destiny at home and build fresh empires abroad and, perforce, resort to wars.[127]

Unlike Bose, Indian anti-fascists deliberately associated British imperialism with Japanese militarism. Lohia, in particular, contended that Japanese imperialism emulated British colonial expansion while also capitalizing upon British debilitation of Qing and Republican China. Seen from India, British imperialism and Japanese fascism were congruous ideologies inimical to freedom and self-determination. "Britain," Lohia argued, "is as much a part of the imperialist system as Japan or Italy and, far from ranging their armaments against each other, we must regard them as one solid bloc against progress and peace."[128]

After the Second Opium War (1856–60), British colonialists razed the Summer Palace (Yuanming Yuan), annexed several (additional) treaty ports, and encumbered Qing officials with the predatory Convention of Peking.[129] Half a century later, during the Boxer Rebellion (1899–1901), Britain and members of the Eight-Nation Alliance executed innocent civilians and ransacked the Forbidden City.[130] Every day for more than a year, British soldiers, civilians, and missionaries organized "loot auctions" in front of the main gate of the British Legation.[131] Even during the anti-imperialist Republican era (1912–49), "no one ideological camp prevailed; unsettling foreign influences were rampant and no single Chinese or foreign political entity could bring all Chinese territory under its control."[132] Amid a "century of humiliation,"[133] British imperialists deprecated China. Seen from India, this debilitation of the Qing and Republican states emboldened Japanese ambitions in China. As Tagore argued in *Crisis of Civilization*:

> Another great and ancient civilization for whose recent tragic history the British cannot disclaim responsibility is China. To serve their own national profit the

British first doped her people with opium and then appropriated a portion of her territory. As the world was about to forget the memory of this outrage, we were painfully surprised by another event. While Japan was quietly devouring North China, her act of wanton aggression was ignored as a minor incident by the veterans of British diplomacy.

Indian anti-fascists contended that Whitehall's nonintervention in the Second Sino-Japanese War belied the British Empire's chronic exploitation of China. British exploitation of China created an archetype for socioeconomic modernization. "Treaty privilege in China," W. G. Beasley has argued, "became a Japanese definition of success."[134] As one young Japanese nationalist explained: "America and Britain had been colonizing China for many years. China was a backward nation . . . we felt Japan should go there and use Japanese technology and leadership to make China a better country."[135]

Initially, the Japanese state adopted Western archetypes in order to defend itself "against the predation of increasingly intrusive Western powers."[136] Inevitably, however, these archetypes demanded colonial expansion. Indeed, imperialist ambition "was a logical response to [the] awareness of living in an imperialist world."[137] Imperialism demanded evermore horizons. It was—and remains—an insatiable ethos. By 1937, Japan's militarist-imperialist government—what some scholars have characterized as "fascism from above" or "Emperor fascism"—was frequently compared to fascist regimes in Europe.[138] Seen, however, from the outside-in, Japanese fascism also resembled British imperialism. "The enforced satiation of British imperialism," Lohia contended, "and the fascist conquests of Japanese imperialism differ only in the extent of their unmasked brutality."[139] In Japan, as in Italy and Germany, fascism radicalized the British imperial ethos.

Lohia contended that Japan invaded China not in defiance of British imperialism, but rather in concert with it. Confronting Japanese expansion would imperil Britain's vast Asian empire—India included. "Imperialist Powers," Lohia contended, "have to choose between attacks on their position by a colleague who has run amuck and a general destruction of the imperialist system itself."[140] Although the National Government sympathized with China, it would not jeopardize Greater Britain. As Alexander Cadogan, the Permanent Under-Secretary of State for Foreign Affairs concluded in his diary: "After tortured reflection, I'm convinced we should not help China—risk is too great."[141] With little recourse, Whitehall invoked the New Imperialist covenant— the collaborative yet adversarial entente that precluded continental war. As in Ethiopia, Lohia argued, the British government acquiesced to fascist temerity:

"The drive of Japan against China is a continuation of that of Italy and Ethiopia. The urges are the same and the interests involved are the same. . . . In 1935, Italy projects her tentacles into Ethiopia; in 1937, Japan into China."[142] Japanese expansionism challenged British imperial hegemony; yet rather than risk its empire in a continental war, Whitehall acceded—grudgingly, to be sure—to the Second Sino-Japanese War. As with the Opium Wars, the Boxer Rebellion, and the Warlord Era, China remained a nation to be partitioned by great-power imperialists.

Lohia, Nehru, and anti-fascists within the Congress opposed British foreign policy, yet were bound by it. After the Marco Polo Bridge Incident, the Raj dispatched Indian soldiers to defend British imperial interests in China. "Into this graveyard," Lohia contended, "of British, Japanese, American and French bayonets, Indian troops have been sent by the British Government."[143] In an attempt to contravene British foreign policy, Nehru visited China in August 1939, only days before the German invasion of Poland. China's pan-Asian and anti-imperialist potential had long captivated Nehru. After the 1927 Congress Against Colonial Oppression and Anti-Imperialism, he argued that the Xinhai Revolution was "not an event of local interest and importance. It is a world phenomenon of the greatest historic importance."[144] Upon Nehru's arrival at Kunming, the Guomindang organized a welcome reception with more than two hundred attendees. Across China, newspapers celebrated his anti-imperialist accomplishments. The *Yunnan Daily* hailed him as India's greatest leader. The *New China Daily* described him as a "close friend of the Chinese nation,"[145] whose visit demonstrated that "the entire Indian nation is sympathizing with us in our war of Resistance."[146] While traveling to Chongqing and Chengdu, Nehru witnessed several air raids, sitting "mostly in a darkened dug-out but peeping out sometimes to see the battle in the skies."[147] As in Spain, Nehru marveled at locals' pertinacity. Factories, schools, youth camps, and universities each found "new life and vitality"[148] under bamboo shelters.

While in China, Nehru met with Chiang Kai-shek.[149] In stark contrast with Bose, Nehru celebrated Chiang as "the supreme leader and Commander of China . . . [someone] who embodies in himself the unity of China and her determination to free herself."[150] In addition to Chiang, Nehru also met with several prominent Guomindang and CCP officials. As part of the (largely superficial) Second United Front, CCP representatives—including Ye Jianying and Bo Gu (Qin Bangxian)—collaborated with Chiang and the Guomindang.[151] Nehru also hoped to visit the CCP in Yan'an. Three months earlier, Mao had written a letter thanking Nehru, Bose, and the Congress for dispatching a medical mission: "We take this opportunity to thank your great Indian people and the Indian National Congress for the medical and material aid that you have given and hope that in the future the Indian National Congress and the Indian people will continue to help and aid us and thus together drive out the Japanese imperialists."[152] Before Nehru could travel to Yan'an, however, the outbreak of the Second World War compelled him to return to India. While limited, his experiences in Kunming, Chongqing, and Chengdu substantiated his faith in China's ultimate victory: "I found not only a race wise and profound, deep in the lore of its own great past, but also a vital people, full of life and energy, adapting themselves to modern conditions. . . . I was no judge of the military position, but I could not imagine that a people with this vitality and determination, and the strength of ages behind them, could ever be crushed."[153]

~

After the outbreak of the Second Sino-Japanese War, British public opinion sympathized with China. A poll published in the *News Chronicle* reported that 59 percent of Britons approved of strong action to defend China, while only 15 percent favored nonintervention.[154] Yet even as Chinese suffering dominated headlines, many in Britain knew little of *The Painted Veil*.[155] In August 1937, Japanese aircraft fired upon the automobile of Hughe Knatchbull-Hugessen, the British ambassador to China. A bullet pierced his ribs and grazed his spine, leaving him temporarily paralyzed.[156] After recuperating, Knatchbull-Hugessen attended a dinner party where Lady Wolverton inquired whether the Japanese pilots recognized him. "No," he answered, "I think they thought it was Chiang Kai-shek."[157] Confused, Lady Wolverton replied: "What is that?"[158]

The National Government was similarly perplexed by the Second Sino-Japanese War. Particularly after the Japanese invasion of Manchuria, Whitehall put forth a panoply of policies that reflected both their admiration and exasperation toward Japan.[159] In 1936, for example, Duff Cooper, a Churchillian anti-fascist and the British Secretary of State for War, circulated a memorandum to the cabinet entitled: "The Importance of Anglo-Japanese Friendship."[160] Preoccupied with the menace of war in Europe, Cooper warned his colleagues that British imperial interests in East Asia were "at the mercy of the Japanese."[161] To secure these interests, Cooper urged government officials to placate Japan: "It would seem a reasonable precaution, therefore, to try, by even means and even at some cost, to safeguard by amicable agreement with Japan, interests which we are unable to protect by military means."[162] As war in Europe loomed, the National Government obviated confrontation with Japan.

Committing military resources to China, Chamberlain reasoned, would only embolden Hitler in Europe and Faqir Ipi in Waziristan. Wholly committed to Europe and its empire, the British government adopted nonintervention in the Second Sino-Japanese War.

Seen from the outside-in, another interpretation of British nonintervention in the Second Sino-Japanese War emerges. At the same time the National Government adopted benevolent neutrality toward China, the British Empire shaped Japanese expansion across East Asia. British imperial sovereignty inspired Japanese imperialism, British colonial ubiquity delimited Japanese expansion to China, and British colonialists debilitated the Qing and Republican governments. To be sure, Japan's pan-Asian and anti-colonial legacy muddled Indian responses to the conflict. Subhas Bose, in particular, denounced British imperialism while eschewing any criticism of Japanese colonialism. Anti-fascists, by contrast, contended that Japanese fascism and British imperialism were interrelated. "How does it fundamentally matter," Lohia questioned, "if the fascist brutality of Japanese imperialism were exchanged for the steady suckling of British imperialism?"[163] The dissonance between Bosian pragmatism and Nehruvian anti-fascism—to say nothing of Gandhian traditionalism—led in part to Bose's resignation as Congress president (1939). Yet despite this and many other differences, Bose and Indian anti-fascists agreed that the British Empire played a significant role in the Second Sino-Japanese War. In China, as in India, imperial consequence transcended government policy.

There are limitations to this perspective. First, Indian anti-fascists overstated British influence upon Japanese modernization. Rather than simply reproducing the British Industrial Revolution, Japanese industrialization incorporated Western paradigms into its own unique cultures and traditions. Too often, anti-fascists characterized Japan as a simulacrum of the West, when in practice it often influenced and shaped the Western world. Second, perhaps because of proximity or pan-Asian idealism, Indian anti-fascists largely ignored the trans-imperial context of British nonintervention. In an empire as capacious as Britain's, events seldom occurred in isolation. At the same time British nonintervention revealed certain similarities between fascism and liberal-imperialism, it also reflected financial limitations. The only means of confronting Japanese expansion was "for Britain to step up her naval presence in the Far East, but the cost was daunting, if not prohibitive."[164] Sympathy, however genuine, could not be transformed into assistance. As early as 1932, Robert Vansittart, Permanent Under-Secretary of State for Foreign Affairs, conceded: "We are incapable of checking Japan in any way if she really means business."[165]

Despite these and other limitations, my approach underscores the similarities between the "Island Empires"[166]—imperial Britain and fascist Japan. Seen from India, the British Empire served as an archetype for Japanese fascism. As Lohia argued in *India on China*: "Japan launched upon a career of imperialism in the manner of Britain."[167]

The Delhi-Yan'an Axis

In September 1943, Robert Payne, a British journalist and former reporter for the *News Chronicle* during the Spanish Civil War, awoke to a luminous sunrise along the Yangtze River, just outside Chongqing. The mountain landscape, "so victorious, so clean and so still,"[168] reminded Payne of the "tanks of the anarquistas [Spanish anarchists] advancing towards Tarragona,"[169] in Northeast Spain. Payne frequently invoked the Spanish Civil War when describing the Second Sino-Japanese War—an approach Tom Buchanan has described as "bifocalism."[170] Payne believed that Spain and China—"twin republics assailed by fascism"[171]—formed an anti-fascist Shanghai-Madrid Axis. At times, his bifocalism even conflated the two conflicts:

> Once in Spain, travelling from Barcelona to the Ebro front, I have known the same excitement of sunrise, when the earth appears to be bathed in molten metal. There was the same shining in the air, the same air of continual and effortless expectancy, the same delight in pure being, the same feeling that the people were living their lives in an atmosphere of pure freedom. . . . But what was so curious was that even the landscape seemed the same; the same reddish-yellow earth, the same aeroplanes hidden in the fields, the same small clumps of deep green trees . . . . Even the river, though twenty times broader than the Ebro, looked familiar, and I began to search for the stumps of the stone bridge which Italian airmen and Asturian dynamiters had destroyed between them one day in May [1938].[172]

The Spanish Civil War and Second Sino-Japanese War were "more interconnected than has previously been acknowledged."[173] In May 1937, just before the Marco Polo Bridge Incident, Mao publicly declared that the CCP was "emulating you [Republican Spain] . . . by struggling against Japanese Fascism. . . . Each day our press here in the Soviet regions published reports and articles about your struggle."[174] During the Battle of Wuhan, soldiers referenced the defense of Madrid in their slogans and marches.[175] Hankow, the provisional wartime capital, was often referred to as the "Madrid or Barcelona of China."[176] In Britain, a cartoon in the *Daily Worker* depicted Spanish and Chinese laborers at opposite ends of the Shanghai-Madrid Axis, providing "more substantial resistance to the 'Rome–Berlin–Tokyo Axis' than the cowardly British government."[177]

The bifocalism conflating the Spanish Civil War and the Second Sino-Japanese War extended to India. Nehru, Lohia, and other anti-fascists identified profound similarities between China's war against Japan, the Spanish-Republican defense, and their own struggle against the British Raj. Whether fascist or imperialist, empires subjugated and exploited weaker nations. "Imperialism," Nehru contended, "shows its claws wherever it may be, in the West or in the East."[178] This perspective challenges inside-out narratives characterizing British nonintervention as the product of an overextended military, the policy of appeasement, Orientalist insouciance, or a preoccupation with Nazi Germany. Seen from the outside-in, the National Government adopted benevolent neutrality toward China at the same time the British Empire shaped Japanese expansion across East Asia. In East Asia, as in Spain, the preponderancy of the Pax Britannica transcended the impassivity of Whitehall. British imperialism acted as a paradigm for Japanese imperialists, delimited Japanese expansion to China, and debilitated the Qing and Republican governments.

Sino-Indian bifocalism also underscores the extent to which anti-colonialists from both nations considered themselves part of a transnational pan-Asian, anti-imperialist, and anti-fascist alliance. One notable traveler along the Shanghai-Madrid Axis was Indian doctor Madan Mohan Lal Atal.[179] Dispatched by the Congress to support Republican Spain, Atal was "driven by humanitarian considerations as much as by his leftist anti-fascist stance."[180] After returning to India, Atal was entrusted with leading the medical mission to China. In Wuhan, at a reception organized by the CCP and Eighth Route Army, he lauded Sino-Indian solidarity: "Today I salute my Chinese brethren for their heroic resistance to Japan. Don't see that we are just five . . . we have been sent by the Indian National Congress in the War of Resistance."[181] The following year, one of Atal's colleagues—Dr. B. K. Basu—founded the *Anti-Fascist League of Oriental Nations*.[182] General Zhu De was its chairman.[183]

In December 1942, one of the Indian doctors—Dwarkanath Kotnis—died after a series of epileptic seizures. Both the Guomindang and the CCP commemorated his contributions to the war effort. "The army," Mao publicly declared, "has lost a helping hand, let us always bear in mind his internationalist spirit."[184] In a message to India, Soong Ching-ling (Madame Sun Yat-sen) eulogized Dr. Kotnis as a symbol of Sino-Indian unanimity: "Doctor Kotnis' memory belongs not only to our two great nations but also to the noble ranks of the indomitable fighters for freedom and progress of all mankind. The future will honour him even more than the present just because it was for the future he fought and died."[185] At the Chinese funeral for Dr. Kotnis, attendees recited an elegy commemorating his magnanimity:

> You came from the shores of the warm Indian Ocean
> To brave the cold of North China,
> You fought five autumns in China, for the world of tomorrow,
> Alas! At the end of a long night, the fountain of your life ran dry,
> Oh, comrade Kotnis, our beloved, Your image will always be with us,
> And your memory will live forever in our hearts.[186]

A statue of Dr. Kotnis was erected in Shijiazhuang, Hebei. It remains an enduring symbol of an ephemeral anti-fascist, anti-imperialist, and pan-Asian alliance—the Delhi-Yan'an Axis.[187]

Notes

1 Rabindranath Tagore, "108," in *The English Writings of Rabindranath Tagore: Volume One: Poems,* ed. Sisir Kumar Das (New Delhi: Sahitya Akademi, 1994), 382. Tagore's poetry is in the public domain.

2 Tagore, *Selected Letters,* 496.

3 Tapati Dasgupta, *Social Thought of Rabindranath Tagore: A Historical Analysis* (New Delhi: Abhinav Publications, 1993), 70–107.

4 A. K. Basu Majumdar, *Rabindranath Tagore: The Poet of India* (New Delhi: Indus Publications, 1993), 100–23.

5 Quoted in Wei Liming, "Historical Significance of Tagore's 1924 China Visit," in *Tagore and China,* ed. Tan Chung et al. (Thousand Oaks, CA: Sage Publications, 2011), 32.

6 Dasgupta, *Social Thought of Rabindranath Tagore,* 82.

7 Tagore, "Letter to Yone Noguchi," 497.

8 Yone Noguchi and Rabindranath Tagore, *Poet to Poet: Full Text of Correspondence Between Yoné Noguchi and Rabindranath Tagore on the Sino-Japanese Conflict* (Calcutta: Sino-Indian Cultural Society, 1938), 1.

9 Ibid.

10 The Greater East Asia Co-Prosperity Sphere was a nebulous, imperialist network that promoted the cultural, economic, and political unity of Asian nations. As Jeremy Yellen has contended, it "must be understood as more than a simple

economic bloc, a slogan for Japanese imperialism and regional control, or the ultimate expression of a virulent pan-Asian ideology. It was also a reaction to the challenges of diplomacy and empire in the post-World War I era, and a sincere attempt to envision a new type of a political and economic order." Jeremy Yellen, *The Greater East Asia Co-Prosperity Sphere: When Total Empire Met Total War* (Ithaca: Cornell University Press, 2019), 5.

11 Tagore, "Letter to Yone Noguchi," 497.

12 Ibid., 497–9.

13 Ethan Mark, "Fascisms Seen and Unseen: The Netherlands, Japan, Indonesia, and the Relationalities of Imperial Crisis," in *Visualizing Fascism: The Twentieth Century Rise of the Global Right* (Durham: Duke University Press, 2020), 197–8.

14 Pan-Asianism was a constellation of protean ideologies selectively adapted by individuals, organizations, and governments. During the Second Sino-Japanese War, it simultaneously justified Japanese imperialism and Chinese anti-imperialism. In his analysis of pan-Asian malleability, Eri Hotta has identified three principal categories: "The first type of Pan-Asianism was of the kind that emphasized Asian commonalities in the vast philosophical dimension of Asian civilization, which included both China and India. The second type of Pan-Asianism could be defined as the kind that sought to create an alliance . . . among Asian nations, frequently, but certainly not exclusively, within the narrower geographical and cultural confines of East Asian . . . nations. Finally, the third type signifies the kind of Pan-Asianism that would become ever more enmeshed with Japan's expansionist and ultranationalist thinking, declaring Japan to be the 'Asian alliance leader' (*Ajia no meishu*) in a crusade to save the rest of Asia . . . from Western imperialism." Eri Hotta, *Pan-Asianism and Japan's War 1931–1945* (New York: Palgrave Macmillan, 2013), 7–8.

15 The Second Sino-Japanese War culminated decades of Japanese aggression. In 1937, Japanese infantry stormed the Marco Polo Bridge southwest of Beijing. Though military insignificant, the skirmish precipitated a large-scale invasion. The Guomindang, helmed by Chiang Kai-shek, had suspended its civil war against the CCP and formed the Second United Front. Each side, however, continued to vie for control in disputed Chinese territory. In the early months of the war, Japanese forces won several early victories and by 1938 had captured Shanghai and the Chinese capital of Nanking. After the fall of Wuhan, the Chinese government retreated to Chongqing. In 1939, after Chinese victories at Changsha and Guangxi, the war reached a stalemate. The Second United Front, meanwhile, continued to fracture. Open conflict between nationalists and communist forces increased, while CCP leader Mao Zedong outlined his plans for a coup against Chiang Kai-shek. By 1941, Japanese forces occupied much of northern and coastal China, but faced significant resistance in the Chinese hinterland. With little recourse, Japanese

military officials turned their attention to the United States. On December 7, 1941, Japan bombed the American naval base at Pearl Harbor, merging the Second Sino-Japanese War with the Second World War.

16 Hotta, *Pan-Asianism and Japan's War 1931–1945*, 141.

17 Tagore, "Letter to Yone Noguchi," 497.

18 Rana Mitter, *China's War with Japan, 1937–1945: The Struggle for Survival* (London: Allen Lane, 2013), 1–14.

19 Ibid.

20 Bradford Lee, *Britain and the Sino-Japanese War, 1937–1939: A Study in the Dilemmas of British Decline* (Stanford: Stanford Univ. Press, 1973), 5–6.

21 See William Roger Louis, *British Strategy in the Far East, 1919–1939* (Oxford: Clarendon Press, 1971); Ann Trotter, *Britain and East Asia, 1933–1937* (London: Cambridge University Press, 1975); Nicholas R. Clifford, *Retreat from China: British Policy in the Far East 1937–1941* (New York: Da Capo Press, 1976); Peter Lowe, *Great Britain and the Origins of the Pacific War: A Study of British Policy in East Asia 1937–1941* (Oxford: Clarendon Press, 1977); Yōichi Kibata, Anthony P. Adamthwaite, and Ian Hill Nish, *Anglo-Japanese Relations in the 1930s and 1940s* (London: Suntory-Toyota International Centre for Economics and Related Disciplines, 1986); Tim Rooth, *British Protectionism and the International Economy: Overseas Commercial Policy in the 1930s* (Cambridge: Cambridge University Press, 1993); Gaines Post, *Dilemmas of Appeasement: British Deterrence and Defense, 1934–1937* (Ithaca: Cornell University Press, 1993); Nicholas Tarling, *The Fall of Imperial Britain in South-East Asia* (Singapore: Oxford University Press, 1993); David Scott, *China and the International System, 1840–1949: Power, Presence, and Perceptions in a Century of Humiliation* (Albany: State University of New York Press, 2009); Antony Beevor, *The Second World War* (New York: Little Brown, 2013); Antony Best, *Britain, Japan, and Pearl Harbor: Avoiding War in East Asia, 1936–41* (London: Routledge, 2014).

22 J. K. J. Perry, "Powerless and Frustrated: Britain's Relationship with China During the Opening Years of the Second Sino–Japanese War, 1937–1939," *Diplomacy & Statecraft* 22, no. 3 (2011): 424.

23 Ibid.

24 Ibid., 425.

25 There is an extensive body of literature examining Indian perceptions of the Second Sino-Japanese War. For an introduction, see Sankar Ghose, *Jawaharlal Nehru, a Biography* (New Delhi: Allied Publishers, 1993); Prakash Nanda, *Rediscovering Asia: Evolution of India's Look-East Policy* (New Delhi: Lancer Publishers & Distributors, 2003); Avinash Mohan Saklani, "Nehru, Chiang Kai-shek and the Second World War," *India and China in the Colonial World* (New Delhi: Social Science Press, 2005); Cemil Aydin, *The Politics of Anti-Westernism*

   in Asia: Visions of World Order in Pan-Islamic and Pan-Asian Thought (New York:
   Columbia University Press, 2007); Pankaj Mishra, *From the Ruins of Empire:
   The Intellectuals Who Remade Asia* (New York: Farrar, Straus and Giroux, 2012);
   Masato Kimura, and Tosh Minohara, *Tumultuous Decade: Empire, Society, and
   Diplomacy in 1930s Japan* (Toronto: University of Toronto Press, 2013).

26 Olive Checkland, *Britain's Encounter with Meiji Japan, 1868–1912* (London:
   Palgrave Macmillan, 1989), 212.

27 Daniel Webster, "As a Master of English Style," in *The Great Speeches and
   Orations of Daniel Webster*, ed. Edwin Percy Whipple (Boston: Little Brown,
   1886), xxix.

28 Checkland, *Britain's Encounter with Meiji Japan*, 211.

29 Tagore, "Letter to Yone Noguchi," 497.

30 William Travis Hanes and Frank Sanello, *The Opium Wars: The Addiction of One
   Empire and the Corruption of Another* (Chicago: Sourcebooks, 2002), 118–19.

31 Ibid.

32 Ibid.

33 Although both governments abrogated the treaty, British colonial forces took
   possession of Hong Kong.

34 Thomas Metcalf, *Imperial Connections: India in the Indian Ocean Area 1860–1920*
   (Delhi: Permanent Black, 2007), 1.

35 Ibid.

36 Madhavi Thampi, "The Indian Community in China and Sino-Indian Relations,"
   in *India and China in the Colonial World*, ed. Madhavi Thampi et al. (New Delhi:
   Social Science Press, 2005), 77.

37 Ibid. As these troops arrived in China, they "were met by local Indians . . . and
   were told that they had been the victims of false propaganda. The reaction to this
   information on the part of the newly arrived troops was so great that they had to
   be hastily shifted out to Hong Kong." Thampi, "The Indian Community in China
   and Sino-Indian Relations," 77.

38 Mishra, *From the Ruins of Empire*, 219.

39 Sven Saller and Christopher W. A. Szpilman, "Introduction: The Emergence of
   Pan-Asianism as an Ideal of Asian Identity and Solidarity, 1850–2008," in *Pan-
   Asianism: A Documentary History*, ed. Sven Saller and Christopher W. A. Szpilman
   (Plymouth: Rowman & Littlefield, 2011), 2. See also Carolien Stolte, "Bringing
   Asia to the World: Indian Trade Unionism and the Long Road Towards the Asiatic
   Labour Congress, 1919–37," *Journal of Global History* 7, no. 2 (2012): 257–78.
   For scholarship that examines the Xinhai Revolution, Wilsonian Moment, and
   Gandhi's Champaran and Kheda satyagrahas, see Lee Lai Tho, and Lee Hock
   Guan, *Sun Yat-Sen, Nanyang and the 1911 Revolution* (Singapore: Chinese Heritage
   Centre, 2011); Erez Manela, *The Wilsonian Moment: Self-Determination and the*

International Origins of Anticolonial Nationalism (Oxford: Oxford University Press, 2009). Top of Form.

40 C. R. Das, *Freedom Through Disobedience* (Madras: Arka Publishing House, 1922), 37. First seen in Carolien Stolte and Harald Fischer-Tiné, "Imagining Asia in India: Nationalism and internationalism (ca. 1905–1940)," *Comparative Studies in Society and History* 54, no. 1 (2012): 73–4.

41 Jawaharlal Nehru, "The Situation in China and India's Duty," April 1927, in *The Selected Works of Jawaharlal* Nehru, ed. S. Gopal, vol. 2 (New Delhi: Orient Longman, 1972), 327.

42 Chung Tan, *Rise of the Asian Giant: The Dragon-Elephant Tango* (London: Anthem Press, 2008), 250.

43 Many within the CCP nevertheless denounced Gandhi and the INC as a bourgeois institution. See Sourendra Ganguly, *Leftism in India: M. N. Roy and Indian Politics 1920–1948* (Calcutta: Minerva Publishers, 1984); Satyabrata Rai Chowdhuri, *Leftism in India, 1917–947* (New York: Palgrave Macmillan UK, 2007).

44 Quoted in Huang I-Shu, "Sino-Indian Fraternity Between Tagore and Tan Yun-shan," in *Tagore and China*, 153.

45 Ibid.

46 Ethan Mark has contended that "although it may seem ironic in the retrospective light of a thoroughly discredited Japanese empire, the period of World War II in Asia represented a peak of transnational optimism regarding a resolution to this perennial dilemma, heralding the imminent arrival of a non-Western, alternative modernity that would reap modernity's benefits while avoiding the perils and constraints associated with a Western derivation. Envisioned in national and transnational formats, this 'Asian' alternative would harness up-to-date 'Western'-style scientific rationality, meritocracy, industrialization, and socioeconomic planning to the imagined, time-honored 'Eastern' strengths of community, morality, and spirituality. The combination would enable a controlled gallop toward national prosperity, social equity, and harmony that would steer clear of the evils, inequities, and social fragmentation of capitalism; break free of the fetters of an oppressive, static and colonially tainted 'feudal tradition'; and avoid the cataclysmic social and cultural upheaval associated with communist revolution." Ethan Mark, "'Asia's' Transwar Lineage: Nationalism, Marxism, and 'Greater Asia' in an Indonesian Inflection," *The Journal of Asian Studies* 65, no. 3 (2006): 462.

47 Jawaharlal Nehru to Indira Nehru, November 22, 1932, in *Glimpses of World History* (New Delhi: The Jawaharlal Nehru Memorial Fund, 2003), 402.

48 Cemil Aydin, *The Politics of Anti-Westernism in Asia: Visions of World Order in Pan-Islamic and Pan-Asian Thought* (New York: Columbia University Press, 2013), 72.

49 Quoted in Mitter, *Forgotten Ally*, 305.

50 Aydin, *The Politics of Anti-Westernism in Asia*, 71.

51 Rabindranath Tagore, *The Message of India to Japan: A Lecture by Sir Rabindranath Tagore Delivered at the Imperial University of Tokyo* (New York: The Macmillan Company, 1916), 7–11.

52 S. C. M. Paine, *The Japanese Empire: Grand Strategy from the Meiji Restoration to the Pacific War* (Cambridge: Cambridge University Press, 2017), 15–108.

53 Kelly Hammond, *China's Muslims & Japan's Empire* (Chapel Hill: University of North Carolina Press, 2020); Qingjun Liu, "Redefining North China during the Sino-Japanese War: The Jin–Xi Incident, 1939–1940," *Asian Studies Review* 44, no. 3 (2020): 441–58.

54 Sugata Bose, *His Majesty's Opponent: Subhas Chandra Bose and India's Struggle Against Empire* (Cambridge, MA: Belknap Press of Harvard University Press, 2011), 122. Henry Dyer used the subtitle "The Britain of the East" in his 1904 book *Dai Nippon*. Henry Dyer, *Dai Nippon: The Britain of the East: A Study in National Evolution* (London: Blackie & Son, 1904).

55 Before the Second World War, Nehru was president of the Congress in 1929–1930 (Lahore), 1936 (Lucknow), and 1937 (Faizpur).

56 Sankar Ghose, *Jawaharlal Nehru, a Biography* (New Delhi: Allied Publishers, 1993).

57 Ibid.

58 In 1939, Bose pursued a second term as Congress president against Gandhi's preferred candidate, Bhogaraju Pattabhi Sitaramayya. Although Bose won, Gandhi ultimately forced him to resign. In response, Bose created the Forward Bloc as "a forum for the more radical elements in the party. He considered this bloc to be an integral part of the Congress, and his political aim was to convert the majority within the Congress to a radical point of view." Bose, *His Majesty's Opponent*, 166.

59 V. S. Patil, *Subhas Chandra Bose: His Contribution to Indian Nationalism* (New Delhi: Sterling Publishers, 1988), 75.

60 Bose, *His Majesty's Opponent*, 10.

61 "India: Chariot of Freedom," *Time* magazine, March 7, 1938.

62 Bose, *His Majesty's Opponent*, 152.

63 Subhas Bose, "On Kemal Ataturk: Tribute to the Leader of Turkey on his death, November, 1938," in *Congress President: Speeches, Articles, and Letters January 1938–May 1939*, ed. Sisir Kumar Bose and Sugata Bose (New Delhi: Oxford University Press, 1995), 61.

64 Subhas Bose, "Presidential Address at the 51st Session of the Indian National Congress Held at Haripura in February, 1938," in *Netaji: Collected Works Volume 9: Congress President: Speeches, Articles and Letters January 1938–May 1939*, ed. Sisir Kumar Bose and Sugata Bose (Delhi: Oxford University Press, 1995), 30.

65 Ibid., 28.

66 Dennis Dalton, *Gandhi: Nonviolent Power in Action* (Colombia: Colombia University Press, 1993), 31–2.

67 Subhas Bose, "Science and Politics: Answers to Questions Posed by Meghnad Saha," in *Congress President: Speeches, Articles and Letters January 1938-May 1939*, ed. Sisir Kumar Bose and Sugata Bose (Calcutta: Netaji Research Bureau, 1995), 47.

68 Bose, *His Majesty's Opponent*, 148.

69 Ibid.

70 Ibid., 98.

71 Michele Louro, *Comrades Against Imperialism: Nehru, India, and Interwar Internationalism* (Cambridge: Cambridge University Press, 2018), 7.

72 Ibid. See also Stolte and Fischer-Tiné; Manu Goswami, "Imaginary Futures and Colonial Internationalisms," *The American Historical Review* 117, no. 5 (2012): 1461–85; Michele Louro et al., eds. *The League Against Imperialism: Lives and Afterlives* (Leiden: Leiden University Press, 2020).

73 Romain Hayes, *Bose in Nazi Germany* (New Delhi: Random House India, 2011).

74 Mike Thomson, "Hitler's Secret Indian Army," *BBC News*, September 23, 2004.

75 Christopher Bayly and Tim Harper, *Forgotten Armies: The Fall of British Asia, 1941-1945* (Cambridge, MA: The Belknap Press of Harvard University Press, 2005), 371–82.

76 Quoted in Bose, *His Majesty's Opponent*, 5.

77 Goswami, "Imaginary Futures and Colonial Internationalisms," 1475. See also Benjamin Zachariah, "Internationalisms in the Interwar Years: The Traveling of Ideas," in *The Internationalism of the Moment—South Asia and the Contours of the Interwar World*, ed. Ali Raza, Franziska Roy, and Benjamin Zachariah (New Delhi: Sage, 2015), 1–22; Joseph McQuade, "The *New Asia* of Rash Behari Bose: India, Japan, and the Limits of the International, 1912-1945," *Journal of World History* 27, no. 4 (2016): 655.

78 John Fairbank, introduction to *Red Star Over China: The Classic Account of the Birth of Communism* (Harmondsworth: Penguin Books, 1972), 1.

79 Ibid.

80 Edgar Snow, *Red Star Over China*, 95.

81 Perry, "Powerless and Frustrated," 410.

82 Ibid., 415.

83 Snow, *Red Star Over China*, 6.

84 Peter Neville, *Hitler and Appeasement: The British Attempt to Prevent the Second World War* (London: Hambledon Continuum, 2006), 62.

85 John Charmley, *Splendid Isolation? Britain, the Balance of Power and the Origins of the First World War* (London: Faber & Faber, 2013).

86 Neville, *Hitler and Appeasement*, 62.

87 Peter Cain and Tony Hopkins, *British Imperialism: 1688-2000* (New York: Longman, 2001), 612. "In the final analysis," Cain and Hopkins continue, "Britain's

interests in China were larger than those in Japan, and the Foreign Office also believed (albeit mistakenly) that, in the event of war between the two countries, China would win." Cain and Hopkins, *British Imperialism*, 612.

88 Quoted in Perry, "Powerless and Frustrated," 423.

89 Quoted in Christopher Bell, "Winston Churchill, Pacific Security, and the Limits of British Power, 1921–41," in *Churchill and the Strategic Dilemmas Before the World Wars: Essays in Honor of Michael I. Handel*, ed. John H. Maurer (London: Routledge, 2003), 67.

90 Quoted in Perry, "Powerless and Frustrated," 413.

91 Subhas Bose, *The Indian Struggle, 1935–1942* (Calcutta: Chuckervertty, Chatterjee, & Co., 1952), 26.

92 Subhas Bose, "Japan's Role in the Far East" or "The Tragedy of Japan," *Modern Review*, October 1937, Jawaharlal Nehru Papers (hereafter JNP), Nehru Memorial Museum and Library (hereafter NMML), 59.

93 Ibid.

94 Quoted in Iris Chang, *The Rape of Nanking: The Forgotten Holocaust of World War II* (New York: Basic Books, 1997), 265.

95 Mitter, *Forgotten Ally*, 27–55.

96 Subhas Bose, "Japan's Role in the Far East," 63.

97 Jeremy A. Yellen, "Into the Tiger's Den: Japan and the Tripartite Pact, 1940," *Journal of Contemporary History* 51, no. 3 (2016): 555–76; Ken Ishida, *Japan, Italy, and the Road to the Tripartite Alliance* (London: Palgrave Macmillan, 2018).

98 Ibid., 69.

99 Ibid., 61.

100 Noguchi and Tagore, *Poet to Poet*, 1.

101 Subhas Bose, "Japan's Role in the Far East," 64.

102 Ibid.

103 Thampi, "The Indian Community in China and Sino-Indian Relations," 184.

104 Ibid., 187.

105 Ibid., 184.

106 Collections during the first All-India China Day fell short of expectations. Bose believed this was due to short notice, and organized three more celebrations—July 7, 8, and 9—to mark the anniversary of the outbreak of war.

107 Subhas Bose, "Congress Medical Mission to China," in *Netaji: Collected Works Volume 9: Congress President*, 36.

108 Krishna Menon, *Why Must India Fight* (London: The India League, 1940), 9.

109 Ibid.

110 Bose, "Congress Medical Mission to China."

111 Ibid., 13.

112 Ibid.

113 Quoted in Aydin, *The Politics of Anti-Westernism in Asia*, 185.

114 Ibid.

115 Subhas Bose, "Japan's Role in the Far East," 76.

116 Ibid., 61.

117 Akira Iriye, *The Origins of the Second World War and the Pacific* (London: Routledge, 1987), 158.

118 Subhas Bose, "Japan's Role in the Far East," 60.

119 Ibid.

120 Ibid., 63.

121 Ibid.

122 Bose, "Japan's Role in the Far East," 76.

123 Bose, *His Majesty's Opponent*, 11.

124 Historians often cite the Marco Polo Bridge Incident as the start date for the beginning of the Second Sino-Japanese War. See Rana Mitter, *China's War with Japan: 1937–1945: The Struggle for Survival* (London: Penguin, 2014).

125 During the Second Sino-Japanese War, the Eighth Route Army was the fighting force of the CCP. It was led by party leader Mao Zedong and General Zhu De. Soldiers wore Chinese Nationalist uniforms and flew the flag of the Republic of China. After the Second World War (and the resumption of the Chinese Civil War), it was renamed the People's Liberation Army. Mitter, *Forgotten Ally*, 91.

126 General Chu The (Zhu De) to Jawaharlal Nehru, November 26, 1937, in *India on China* (Allahabad: All India Congress Committee, 1938), 11.

127 Ram Manohar Lohia, *India on China*, 17. Nehru and Lohia also included a cable signed by John Dewey, Albert Einstein, Bertrand Russell, and Romain Rolland condemning Japanese imperialism: "In view of wanton destruction of Oriental Civilization and for humanity peace democracy we propose peoples of all countries organize voluntary boycott against Japanese goods [*sic*] refuse to sell and load war materials to Japan cease cooperation with Japan in ways that help her aggressive policy while giving China every possible help for relief and selfdefense until Japan has evacuated all her forces from China and abandoned her policy of conquest wish Congress endorse this statement give publicity call All India join action." *India on China*, 12.

128 Lohia, *India on China*, 20.

129 Steffen Rimner, *Opium's Long Shadow: From Asian Revolt to Global Drug Control* (Harvard: Harvard University Press, 2018), 55.

130 David J. Silbey, *The Boxer Rebellion and the Great Game in China* (New York: Farrar, Straus and Giroux, 2012), 7–20.

131 Ibid., 46.

132 Anne-Marie Brady and Douglas Brown, "Introduction: Foreign Bodies," in *Foreigners and Foreign Institutions in Republican China*, ed. Anne-Marie Brady and Douglas Brown (London: Routledge, 2013), 1.

133 Stephen R. Platt, *Imperial Twilight: The Opium War and the End of China's Last Golden Age* (Toronto: Alfred A. Knopf, 2018), 8.

134 W. G. Beasley, *Japanese Imperialism: 1894–1945* (Oxford: Oxford University Press, 1987), 14.

135 Quoted in Bayly and Harper, *Forgotten Armies*, 2.

136 Paine, *The Japanese Empire*, 1.

137 Beasley, *Japanese Imperialism*, 107.

138 There is an extensive literature debating whether the interwar Japanese government was fascist. For an introduction, see Yoshiaki Yoshimi, and Ethan Mark, *Grassroots Fascism: The War Experience of the Japanese People* (New York: Columbia University Press, 1987); Stanley Payne, *A History of Fascism, 1914–1945* (Madison: University of Wisconsin Press, 1995); Louise Young, *Japan's Total Empire: Manchuria and the Culture of Wartime Imperialism* (Berkely: University of California Press, 1998); E. Bruce Reynolds, *Japan in the Fascist Era* (New York: Palgrave Macmillan, 2004); Daniel Hedinger, "Universal Fascism and its Global Legacy: Italy's and Japan's Entangled History in the Early 1930s," *Fascism* 2, no. 2 (2013): 141–60; Alan Tansman, et al., *The Culture of Japanese Fascism* (Durham: Duke University Press, 2009); Reto Hofmann, *The Fascist Effect: Japan and Italy, 1915–1952* (Ithaca: Cornell University Press, 2015); Madeleine Herren, "Fascist Internationalism," in *Internationalism: A Twentieth Century History*, ed. Glenda Sluga and Patricia Clavin (Cambridge: Cambridge University Press, 2017).

139 Lohia, *India on China*, 20.

140 Ibid., 28.

141 Quoted in Perry, "Powerless and Frustrated," 417.

142 Lohia, *India on China*, 25.

143 Ibid., 28.

144 Jawaharlal Nehru, "The Situation in China and India's Duty," April 1927, in *The Selected Works of Jawaharlal* Nehru, ed. S. Gopal, vol. 2 (New Delhi: Orient Longman, 1972), 327.

145 B. R. Deepak, *India-China Relations in the First Half of the 20th Century* (New Delhi: A.P.H. Publishing Company), 127.

146 Ibid.

147 Jawaharlal Nehru, "Diary of a Journey," in *India, Spain and the War* (Allahabad: Kitabistan, 1940), 23.

148 Ibid.

149 In 1942, the Japanese army reached Singapore, threatening colonial Burma and the Raj. The Congress refused to support British war aims unless promised independence. To support Nehru, Chiang visited India, hoping that his presence would pressure Britain into leaving India, which would then enter into the war against Japan. In a series of speeches and interview, Chiang

emphasized the importance of Sino-Indian cooperation. In his "Message to the Indian People," he articulated a vision of the two nations shared future: "I venture to suggest to my brethren, the Indian people, that in this most critical moment in the history of civilization, our two peoples should exert themselves to the utmost in the cause of freedom for all mankind, for only in a free world could the Chinese and Indian peoples obtain their freedom. Furthermore, should freedom be denied either to China or to India there could be no real peace in the world." Chiang Kai-Shek, "Message to the Indian People," *Inter-Allied Review*, March 15, 1942, 1. Chiang's visit ultimately failed. Months later, Gandhi and the Congress launched the Quit India Movement, eliminating any hope of Indian participation in the war.

150 Nehru, "Diary of a Journey," 23.

151 Mitter, *Forgotten Ally*, 73–4.

152 Mao Zedong to Jawaharlal Nehru, in *A Bunch of Old Letters: Being Mostly Written to Jawaharlal Nehru and Some Written by Him*, ed. Sunil Khilnani (New Delhi: Viking, 2005), 386.

153 Nehru, "Diary of a Journey," 24.

154 Perry, "Powerless and Frustrated," 423.

155 W. Somerset Maugham, *The Painted Veil* (London: Heinemann, 1925). The title is taken from a Percy Shelley sonnet: "Lift not the painted veil which those who live / Call Life."

156 Perry, "Powerless and Frustrated," 411–12.

157 Ibid., 411.

158 Ibid.

159 Neville, *Hitler and Appeasement*, 62.

160 Quoted in Antony Best, *Britain, Japan, and Pearl Harbor: Avoiding War in East Asia, 1936–41* (London: Routledge, 2014), 7.

161 Ibid.

162 Ibid.

163 Lohia, *India on China*, 21.

164 Cain and Hopkins, *British Imperialism*, 611.

165 Neville, *Hitler and Appeasement*, 63.

166 Ayako Hotta-Lister, *The Japan-British Exhibition of 1910: Gateway to the Island Empire of the East* (London: Routledge, 1999), 2.

167 Lohia, *India on China*, 34.

168 Robert Payne, *Chungking Diary* (London: Heinemann, 1945), 427. First seen in Tom Buchanan, "Shanghai-Madrid Axis? Comparing British Reponses to the Conflicts in Spain and China, 1936–1939," *Contemporary European History* 21, no. 4 (2012): 548–9.

169 Payne, *Chungking Diary*, 427.

170 Buchanan, "Shanghai-Madrid Axis?" 547.

171 Ibid.

172 Payne, *Chungking Diary*, 427.

173 Buchanan, "Shanghai-Madrid Axis?" 551.

174 Quoted in: Buchanan, "Shanghai-Madrid Axis?" 542.

175 Buchanan, "Shanghai-Madrid Axis?" 542.

176 Ibid.

177 Ibid.

178 Jawaharlal Nehru, *Toward Freedom: The Autobiography of Jawaharlal Nehru* (New York: The John Day Company, 1941), 411.

179 Atal was a cousin of Nehru's wife Kamala and accompanied her to Europe for medical treatment. Judith Brown, *Nehru: A Political Life* (New Haven: Yale University Press, 2003), 111.

180 Maria Framke, "Political Humanitarianism in the 1930s: Indian Aid for Republican Spain," *European Review of History* 23, nos. 1–2 (2016), 67.

181 Quoted in Deepak, *India-China Relations in the First Half*, 121.

182 In his account of the mission, Basu described several confrontations with Atal. In one such incident, on October 8, 1938, he recounted: "Before lunch, I had some altercation with Dr. Atal. I suggested that as our people had collected funds, with difficulty, for sending us here, would it not be correct for us to stay more humbly, than living extravagantly in a posh hotel. He flared up and said he could arrange my accommodation in humbler digs. As for himself, 'I have a certain standard of living.' I wonder how he would manage to keep up that standard in the north." B. K. Basu, *Call of Yanan: The Story of the Indian Medical Mission to China 1938–1943: Yin Du Yuan Hua Yi Liao Dui De Gu Shi* (Beijing: Foreign Language Press, 2003), 50.

183 Khwaja Ahmad Abbas, *And One Did Not Come Back! The Story of the Congress Medical Mission to China* (Bombay: Sound Magazine, 1944), 118.

184 Quoted in Deepak, *India-China Relations in the First Half*, 125.

185 Abbas, *And One Did Not Come Back!*, 129.

186 Quoted in Deepak, *India-China Relations in the First Half*, 125.

187 The statue of Dr. Kotnis is located in the south end of a park honoring Chinese and communist martyrs. The north and south grounds are dedicated to veterans of the Korean War and Second Sino-Japanese War. The west end honors Dr. Norman Bethune—who served as a frontline surgeon for both the Spanish Second Republic and Chinese Eight Route Army. The area devoted to Dr. Kotnis contains a small museum. Inside, his journal, medical instruments, and photos are on display. In 2013, Chinese prime minister Li Keqiang visited Mumbai and symbolically thanked the family of Dr. Kotnis—a ritual performed by every Chinese head of state. In November 2013, on the seventy-fifth anniversary of the

Indian Medical Mission, a photo exhibition dedicated to Dr. Kotnis was organized by the Chinese Consulate and Xinhua News Agency. It was held in his hometown of Vengurla, in Maharashtra. In 1946, V. Shantaram directed and starred in an adaptation of Kotnis's life, *Dr. Kotnis Ki Amar Kahani* (The Eternal Tale of Dr. Kotnis).

4

"A Triumph of Violence"[1]
India and the Munich Agreement

Through the troubled history of man
Comes sweeping a blind fury of destruction
And the towers of civilization topple down to dust.
In the chaos of moral nihilism
Are trampled underfoot by marauders

The best treasures of Man heroically won by the martyrs for ages.

Come, young nations,
Proclaim the right for freedom,
Raise up the banner of invincible faith.
Build bridges with your life across the gaping earth
Blasted by hatred
And march forward.

Do not submit yourself to carry the burden of insult upon your head,

Kicked by terror,
And dig not a trench with falsehood and cunning
To build a shelter for your dishonoured manhood;
Offer not the weak as sacrifices to the strong
To save yourself.

Rabindranath Tagore
Ahbhan (A Call) in *Poems on Munich*
Published by the Indo-Czechoslovak Cultural Society, New Delhi[2]

In December 1940, Mohandas K. Gandhi, the spiritual leader of the Indian campaign for independence, wrote a letter to Adolf Hitler. "Dear Friend," he began, "that I address you as a friend is no formality. I own no foes."[3] For more than a year, fascist bellicosity had overwhelmed Europe. Hitler had conquered Poland, Lithuania, France, the Low Countries, and Scandinavia; the Luftwaffe blitzed London in an unprecedented terror-bombing campaign; and the Royal Italian Army besieged French and British colonies in the Horn of Africa.[4] The scope of devastation bewildered Gandhi. Devoted to swaraj ("self-rule"[5]) and satyagraha ("truth force"[6]), he implored Hitler to renounce the "science of destruction"[7] and embrace ahimsa, or nonviolence:

> We have found in non-violence a force which, if organized, can without doubt match itself against a combination of all the most violent forces in the world. . . . It is a marvel to me that you do not see that [violence] is nobody's monopoly. If not the British, some other power will certainly improve upon your method and beat you with your own weapon. You are leaving no legacy to your people of which they would feel proud. They cannot take pride in a recital of cruel deed, however skillfully planned. I, therefore, appeal to you in the name of humanity to stop the war. . . . If you attain success in the war, it will not prove that you were in the right. It will only prove that your power of destruction was greater.[8]

Hitler never received the letter; Government of India censors intercepted it.[9] Gandhi's appeal nevertheless exhibited the extent to which he coalesced Western political ideologies.[10] Violence, he argued, animated Western modernity. Whether conservative, liberal, Marxist, or fascist, Europe's great powers worshipped the power of destruction.[11] "To arm India on a large scale," Gandhi explained in *Hind Swaraj*, "is to Europeanize it."[12]

In the years after the Nazi seizure of power, Hitler increasingly menaced Europe with war. He rearmed the Wehrmacht, remilitarized the Rhineland, intervened in the Spanish Civil War, and orchestrated the Austro-German Anschluss.[13] Finally, in 1938, he demanded the annexation of ethnic Germans living in the Sudetenland (a borderland stretching across Western Czechoslovakia).[14] As Europe braced for war, British prime minister Neville Chamberlain organized a four-power conference and—together with Hitler, Mussolini, and Édouard Daladier—negotiated the fate of the Sudetenland.

The Munich Agreement has since sparked impassioned—if often sententious—debate.[15] In May of 1940, as the British retreated from Dunkirk, three frustrated politicians denounced British foreign policy. Writing under the pseudonym Cato, Michael Foot, Peter Howard, and Frank Owen vituperated Chamberlain and the policy of appeasement: "[They] took over a great empire, supreme in arms and secure in liberty, and they conducted it to the edge of annihilation."[16] After the Second World War, Winston Churchill similarly argued that appeasement constituted a feckless betrayal of British civilization.[17] An appeaser, he magniloquently quipped, "hopes that if he feeds the crocodile enough, the crocodile will eat him last."[18] In 1962, revisionist A. J. P. Taylor courted controversy by contending that Chamberlain—restricted, as he was, by an overextended empire, an anemic economy, and obstreperous anti-war public opinion—acted pragmatically.[19] In recent years, scholars have arrived at something of a middle ground, contending that Chamberlain confronted political, economic, and military crises, yet also misapprehended Nazi temerity.[20]

Taken together, orthodox, revisionist, and middle ground (or counter-revisionist) scholarship has characterized the Munich Agreement as an extraordinary, momentous event. Even revisionists such as Taylor—who depicted appeasement as a recurrent British policy—have affirmed (and reaffirmed) its historical gravity: "[Munich] was a triumph for all that was best and most enlightened in British life; a triumph for those who had preached equal justice between peoples; a triumph for those who had courageously denounced the harshness and short-sightedness of Versailles."[21] Seen, however, from India, Munich was neither momentous nor extraordinary. In this chapter, I contend that, seen from the outside-in, the Munich Agreement was not an ineluctable—perhaps injudicious—compromise between disparate political systems, but rather another instance of Europe's imperial great powers negotiating the sovereignty of smaller nations. It was, as Jawaharlal Nehru argued, imperialism practiced in Europe.[22]

Absent representation from Prague, Chamberlain forsook the self-determination of a "far away country . . . of whom we know nothing."[23] Czechoslovakia suffered from imperial intrigue in much the same way as India, yet because it was in Europe—and populated by white Europeans—it was (eventually) deemed an unprecedented tragedy. For Indian anti-fascists, British connivance exhibited the similitude between fascism and liberal-imperialism. Both the British and Nazi empires exalted racial superiority, economic exploitation, and industrialized violence while, at the same time, repudiating the self-determination demanded by the Congress.[24] Seen from India, the Munich Agreement resembled the Scramble for Africa, Treaty of Versailles, Great Game, and Open Door Policy. "We resist British imperialism," Gandhi explained in his letter to Hitler, "no less than Nazism. If there is a difference, it is in degree."[25]

A Mild Hindu and the Vigorous Prussian

In January 1933, German president Paul von Hindenburg appointed Adolf Hitler chancellor of Germany. One month later, on February 27, Dutch communist Marinus van der Lubbe set the Reichstag (German Parliament) on fire.[26]

Hitler and the Nazis accused van der Lubbe of participating in a Comintern conspiracy and convinced President Hindenburg to enact the Reichstag Fire Decree. The state nullified civil liberties, censored publications, and imprisoned political opponents—most notably, the KDP (German Communist Party). In March, with the opposition mostly jailed or expelled, the Nazis—together with the Centre Party, German National People's Party, and other members of the assembly—passed the Enabling Act. Hitler was invested with plenary powers, the constitution was essentially (though not officially) abrogated, and the Weimar Republic was transmogrified into a "barbarous utopia."[27]

Around the world, anti-imperialists lamented the Nazi seizure of power. "Hitler and his Nazis have triumphed in Germany," Nehru wrote after the Enabling Act, "and their victory [is] a victory of counter-revolution."[28] In 1933, the Gestapo arrested Bengali communist Saumyendranath Tagore for allegedly "planning the assassination of Hitler."[29] Upon his release from prison, Tagore fled to Paris, where he publicly vilified the Reichstag Fire Decree, Nazi anti-Semitism, and the insouciance of the imperialist great powers, Britain and France:

> Comrades, let me warn you all not to have any illusion about the imperialist governments. If you think that these governments would really do anything to put an end to the brutal Nazi regime in Germany, you are wholly mistaken. They will do nothing. . . . The time for long speeches is over. The time for action has come, the time for the revolutionary action.[30]

With each Nazi triumph—currency stabilization, Strength Through Joy, and the Night of Long Knives—the state increasingly persecuted enemies of the Reich.[31] Indian anti-fascists sympathized with the victims of this tyranny. Jews, in particular, were not a recondite people unknown to the Congress. Prominent anti-colonialists—including M. N. Roy, B. Shiva Rao, and R. K. Nehru—married Jewish refugees from Europe.[32] Additionally, many Western-educated Indians had learned the wretched history of European anti-Semitism.[33] In a pamphlet entitled *An Appeal to Students*, S. C. Dutta—convener of an All-India Anti-Fascist Students' Conference—decried the Nazi racial state:

> In Germany an offensive against Jews was set into motion. They were sacked, deprived of their jobs and turned out of Germany. Thousands of Jews were murdered in cold blood. Free thinking has been totally stopped. Papers against the government have been confiscated, Anti-Nazis have been exiled, murdered or sent to concentration camps, children were snatched from their parents, husbands beaten into pulp before their wives and young girls freely molested.

Fascism is brute force. . . . It drags back humanity to dark ages of barbarism and slavery.[34]

Even Subhas Bose, who would eventually abscond to Nazi Germany and command the Indian Legion as a military unit within the Wehrmacht, denounced Nazi anti-Semitism. "Having lived in Germany," he wrote after *Kristallnacht*, "I know that the teaching of racial science on a nation-wide scale has prepared the Nazi psychologically for such a pogrom. When the Nazis are taught to regard Jews as vermin, it is small wonder that their conscience does not revolt against organised brutality against innocent and unarmed people."[35]

Before the Second World War, the Congress Working Committee (CWC) encouraged persecuted Jews to seek employment in India.[36] It even considered granting asylum to Jewish refugees. Devoid, however, of financial and institutional resources, and internally admonished—problematically, to be sure—for seeking to transform India into an "asylum of Jews,"[37] the CWC withdrew the proposal. The Congress nevertheless forwarded dozens of applications to prospective employers. "I am Hungarian," one candidate wrote to the Congress, "descending from Jewish ancestors. . . . The political tide having turned against Non-Aryans in Central Europe I have decided to emigrate and my Indian friends whom I consulted persuaded me to offer my services to the INC."[38] Nehru and the CWC coordinated with the German Jewish Aid Committee and several other organizations.[39] A dozen or so Jewish émigrés ultimately settled in India.

The British government, meanwhile, appeased Nazi truculence.[40] In May 1937, upon his ascension to prime minister, Neville Chamberlain confronted numerous challenges, including a ponderous rearmament scheme,[41] desiccating empire,[42] vociferous anti-war sentiments,[43] the French government "behaving like a pricked balloon,"[44] and a looming Anglo-German War that would, in all likelihood, lead to millions of deaths and a potential Bolshevik revolution in Germany.[45] Chamberlain, in this regard, was a devout anti-communist.[46] His "profound antipathy towards the Soviet Union was one of the most consistent features of his personal diplomacy."[47] Indeed, radical opinion "took little convincing that Chamberlain would sooner see Hitler overrun Europe than find himself fighting Fascism as an ally of the Soviet Union."[48] In Spain, Chamberlain preferred the Nationalists to a Soviet satellite; and in Central Europe, he preferred Hitler to Stalin (at least before the Nazi invasion of Bohemia and Moravia).[49] Privately, Chamberlain rhapsodized over "the far reaching plans which I have in mind for the appeasement of Europe and Asia and for the ultimate check to the mad armament race, which if allowed to continue must involve us all in ruin."[50]

Territorially and demographically, the British Empire remained a powerful—albeit recalcitrant—institution. As prime minister, Chamberlain needed only to maintain the status quo. "We have got all that we want—perhaps more," a 1926 Foreign Office memorandum acknowledged, "Our sole object is to keep what we have and to live in peace."[51]

Anti-imperialists had long associated fascism in Europe with colonialisms across Africa and Asia. Pan-African Marxist George Padmore contended that Nazism emulated the racialized violence of the Amritsar Massacre, the Boxer Rebellion, and the South African War. "British imperialists," he argued, "treat the Negro masses like Nazis treat the Jews."[52] In India, anti-fascists similarly maintained that British appeasement exhibited the similarities between fascism and liberal-imperialism. "Fascist aggression," the Congress Socialist Party argued at the Haripura (1938) session:

> Has increased and an unabashed defiance of international obligations has become the avowed policy of fascist powers. British foreign policy, in spite of its evasions and indecisions, has consistently supported the fascist powers in Germany, Spain and the Far East and must, therefore, largely shoulder the responsibility for the progressive deterioration of the world situation.[53]

The fulcrum connecting India and Germany was Britain. Seen from Whitehall, India was an imperative possession and Germany a paramount concern. Each nation, moreover, represented an extraordinary challenge. Nazi Germany radicalized British colonial violence, while Gandhian satyagraha exposed its untenability. From the British perspective, these challenges were remarkably similar. In 1936, after Hitler remilitarized the Rhineland, Thomas Stopford "put the question"[54] to the home secretary, John Simon: "Is there not a certain similarity between Hitler and Gandhi?"[55] Viscount Halifax, a former viceroy of India and one of the architects of appeasement, enthusiastically agreed. Both men had the same "strong inferiority complex, the same idealism, the belief in the divine mission to lead his people and the same difficulty with unruly lieutenants."[56] Two years later, during the Czechoslovakian crisis, Halifax admitted to relying on his experiences with Gandhi when negotiating with Hitler.[57] "The main difference," he later explained, "is that a mild Hindu is probably less alarming than the vigorous Prussian."[58] Halifax characterized Gandhi as an obdurate, reactionary ideologue hellbent on undermining British paramountcy. He understood Hitler in much the same way.

The rise of Hitler coincided with the physical decline of Gandhi. By 1938, years of overexertion had exhausted the Mahatma.[59] Aged sixty-nine, he "personally confronted many of the dilemmas of advancing age—deteriorating health, declining energy, the challenge of a new generation of political activists with backgrounds, experiences, priorities, and ideals very different from those with whom he had worked in 1920 or even in 1928-1931."[60] Many of Gandhi's earliest satyagrahis had perished or retired. At the same time, a younger generation of anti-colonialists increasingly gravitated toward Marxism—not Gandhian swaraj—as their liberating creed. Some privately scorned the Congress's de rigueur pledge of nonviolence; others publicly demanded a violent proletarian revolution. Although widely adored, Gandhi presided over a contentious Congress: "It was difficult to control, often divided, and full of people who had little time for his spiritual vision and its implications and denied the primacy of nonviolence in all relationships."[61] Amid crises in Ethiopia, Spain, and China, "we find Gandhi, an aging man, struggling to come to terms with failing strength, a changing environment, and the apparent limitations, errors, and blindness of those close to him."[62]

Gandhi nevertheless remained devoted to nonviolence. It was, he argued, "made of stern stuff. It is firmer than the firmest metal known to the scientists. . . I will not have the power of non-violence to be underestimated in order to cover my limitations or weaknesses."[63] In the years before the Second World War, this conviction propelled Gandhi onto the global stage. With each international crisis, Nazism ostensibly required a violent response. Around the world, pacifists, peace advocates, and anti-imperialists looked to Gandhi for a nonviolent panacea to fascist pugnacity. Could Gandhism rehabilitate Nazi rancor? According to the Mahatma, there could be no other way, for only "non-violence has greater power than Hitler's or Mussolini's force."[64]

Peace without Honor

In 1937, Herman Göring—Supreme Commander of the Luftwaffe and one of the most powerful figures in Nazi Germany—organized a hunting exhibition in Berlin. Göring formally invited Viscount Halifax, an avid hunter mordantly dubbed "Holy Fox"[65] by Churchill. While in Germany, Halifax visited the Berghof, a sprawling mountain chalet in the Obersalzberg, near Berchtesgaden. Upon his arrival, a narrow path leading up the entryway had been cleared of snow. "As I looked out of the car window," Halifax later recalled, "I saw in the middle of this swept path a pair of black-trousered legs, finishing up in silk socks and pumps."[66] Assuming this was the footman, Halifax moved to hand him his coat until the German foreign minister, Konstantin von Neurath, hissed from inside the car: "*Der Führer! Der Führer!*"[67] Looking up, Halifax realized that "higher up, the trousers passed into a khaki tunic with swastika armlet."[68] The footman was Adolf Hitler.

During the nearly day-long meeting with Halifax, Hitler was splenetic. Ivonne Kirkpatrick, first secretary at the embassy in Berlin, described him as a "spoilt, sulky child."[69] After lunch, Hitler perked up while discussing *The Lives of a Bengal Lancer*—an Orientalist 1935 film in which British soldiers defend the Northwest Frontier against Muslim *frondeurs*.[70] According to Kirkpatrick, Hitler "liked this film because it depicted a handful of Britons holding a continent in thrall. That was how a superior race must behave and the film was compulsory viewing for the S.S."[71] Afterward, Halifax recounted his experiences as viceroy of India—particularly the Gandhi-Irwin Pact (1931). In a portentous response, Hitler criticized the British government for propitiating Indian anti-imperialists. "Shoot Gandhi," he told a nonplussed Halifax, "and if that does not suffice to reduce them to submission, shoot a dozen leading members of Congress; and if that does not suffice, shoot 200 and so on until order is established. You will see how quickly they will collapse as soon as you make it clear that you mean business."[72]

Hitler's recommendation underscored the extent to which fascism radicalized colonial ideologies. After the Nazi seizure of power, Germany was a "never-ending struggle for preeminence within a coalition—micro-tug-of-wars between party and state, fascists and conservatives, and leader and party."[73] The state, moreover, required the illusion of driving momentum (racial in character) or else risked fading into authoritarianism.[74] In the pursuit of a "permanent revolution,"[75] radicalization was inescapable. Year after year, Hitler menaced Europe with war. He rearmed the German Wehrmacht, remilitarized the Rhineland, intervened in the Spanish Civil War, and demanded an Anschluss with Austria.

Nazi violence bewildered Gandhi. Hitler abhorred nonviolence, racial tolerance, self-determination, and the universal protection of human rights. "The philosophy," Gandhi contended, "for which the two dictators [Hitler and Mussolini] stand calls it cowardice to shrink from carnage. They exhaust the resources of poetic art in order to glorify organized murder. There is no humbug about their word or deed. They are ever ready for war. There is nobody in Germany or Italy to cross their path. Their word is law."[76] Gandhi maintained that fascism—much like imperialism, liberalism, and other Western ideologies— required evermore "destructive knowledge."[77] In India, the quintessence of Western civilization had enslaved millions. Gandhi thus repudiated Western conceptions of independence and developed his own discourse of freedom "anchored not in the Western notion of freedom, but rather in the Indic—Hindu, Buddhist, and Jain—discourses of renunciative freedom (moksha and nirvana in Sanskrit)."[78] Swaraj emancipated body, mind, and soul; it was antithetical to violence. "We will not die killing," Gandhi argued, "though we might be killed. It is a novel experiment, I know."[79]

Like many anti-fascists, Gandhi identified a profound interrelation between fascism and liberal-imperialism. Hitler and the Nazis were a "revised edition of [Europe's] so-called democracies . . . an answer to [British and French] misdeeds."[80] During the First World War, both Britain and Germany committed "falsehoods, exaggerations and inhumanities."[81] The Treaty of Versailles, however, only punished Germany. Britain expanded its empire, annexing Iraq, Transjordan, Mandatory Palestine, and many former German colonies.[82] Gandhi contended that Hitler instinctively challenged this inequity. As Führer, he refortified the Wehrmacht, presided over a totalitarian wartime economy (in peacetime), exploited "lesser races," and arrogated lebensraum— or "living space." He radicalized British imperialism, Gandhi argued, in order to defeat it: "The so-called democracies have . . . misappropriated other people's lands and have resorted to ruthless repression. What wonder [that] Hitler and company have reduced to a science the unscientific violence their predecessors had developed for exploiting the so-called backward races for their own material gain?"[83]

In 1938, after orchestrating the Anschluss with Austria, Hitler affixed his imperialist gaze upon the Sudetenland—a borderland in Western Czechoslovakia containing a significant number of ethnic Germans. On September 24th, after his second abortive meeting with Chamberlain, Hitler issued the Godesberg Memorandum. Unless the government in Prague relinquished the Sudetenland, Germany would invade. "It is a *de facto* ultimatum," Czech diplomat Jan Masaryk protested, "of the sort usually presented to a vanquished nation and not a proposition to a sovereign state which has shown the greatest possible readiness to make sacrifices for the appeasement of Europe."[84] As the deadline approached, Europe braced for a second Great War. Gas masks were apportioned and trenches dug. However, at the eleventh hour, Chamberlain requested a third and final meeting with Hitler. "If at first you don't concede," members of the Foreign Office quipped, "fly fly fly again."[85]

Chamberlain, Hitler, Mussolini, and Daladier arrived in Munich on September 29th. Like the Moirai, these great-power imperialists decided the fate of the Sudetenland.[86] The Czechoslovakian delegation "was not allowed in the conference hall and had to await its destiny in the adjacent room."[87] Guileless in his rapprochement of Hitler, Chamberlain ultimately surrendered the Sudetenland to Germany and, in return, received a pledge of Anglo-German unanimity—"peace for our time." The following morning, as an exultant crowd mobbed his aircraft at Heston Aerodrome, Chamberlain proclaimed:

> The settlement of the Czechoslovakian problem which has now been achieved is, in my view, only the prelude to a larger settlement in which all Europe may find peace. This morning I had another talk with the German Chancellor, Herr Hitler, and here is the paper which bears his name upon it as well as mine. Some of you, perhaps, have already heard what it contains but I would just like to read it to you: "We regard the agreement signed last night and the Anglo-German Naval Agreement, as symbolic of the desire of our two peoples never to go to war with one another again."[88]

The Munich Agreement has since epitomized Chamberlain's fecklessness. "The umbrella," wartime pundits sardonically argued, "had been mightier than the sword."[89] At the time, however, Chamberlain was hailed as a brilliant statesman.[90] "No conqueror returning from a victory on the battlefield," *The Times* proclaimed, "has come adorned with nobler laurel."[91] After his panegyric at Heston Aerodrome, Chamberlain returned to London. "The streets," he later wrote, "were lined from one end to the other with people of every class, shouting themselves hoarse, leaping on the running board, banging on the windows & thrusting their hands in to the car to be shaken."[92] In an "exceptional honour,"[93] Chamberlain joined the king and queen on the balcony at Buckingham Palace. Afterward, King George VI celebrated Munich as "a magnificent effort."

Seen from the outside-in, the Munich Agreement—rather than a noble laurel or, in the lachrymose words of Churchill, "the end of the British Empire"[94]— was simply imperialism practiced in Europe. It was not momentous, nor even inimitable. As with the Scramble for Africa, Europe's great powers redrew their maps in order to forestall world war. Whether fascist or imperialist, they annexed and ultimately forsook the self-determination of the Sudetenland. Munich, Indian anti-fascists contended, was yet another imperial transaction— another Berlin Conference (1884), Brussels Conference (1890), or Paris Peace Conference (1919).

Gandhi contended that the Munich Agreement revealed the moral turpitude of Western politics. Europe's great powers had colonized much of Africa and Asia, yet still yearned for additional horizons. Inevitably, their cupidity led them to covet the vulnerable nations around them. Munich, Gandhi argued, reflected the extent to which European colonialisms had finally turned inward: "It does appear to me that small nationalities cannot exist in Europe with their heads erect. . . . They must become vassals. Europe has sold her soul for the sake of a seven days' earthly existence. The peace Europe gained at Munich is a triumph of violence; it is also its defeat."[95] During his triumphal return from Germany, Chamberlain invoked Benjamin Disraeli securing the New Imperialist covenant at the Berlin Conference (1884). "For the second time in our history," Chamberlain proclaimed outside Downing Street, "a British Prime Minister has returned from Germany bringing peace with honour. I believe it is peace for our time."[96] Gandhi disagreed. Together, Hitler and Chamberlain had betrayed Czechoslovakian swaraj. The Munich Agreement, much like the Berlin Conference, was an imperial negotiation—"peace," Gandhi argued, "without honour."[97]

As in Ethiopia, Spain, and China, the INC condemned fascism and imperialism. Nehru visited Prague in August, one month before the Munich Agreement. He was in Geneva—the headquarters of the League of Nations— during Chamberlain's final meeting with Hitler. Together with Gandhi and the Congress, Nehru excoriated Munich as a "triumph of brutal reaction."[98] Whitehall, he contended, invoked the New Imperialist covenant—the collaborative yet adversarial entente that precluded continental war—in order to preserve its increasingly precarious hegemony: "The Congress records its entire disapproval of the British foreign policy culminating in the Munich Pact. . . . This policy has been one of the deliberate betrayal of democracy, repeated breach of pledges, the ending of the system of collective security and cooperation with the Governments which are avowed enemies of democracy and freedom."[99] In London, Rajani Palme Dutt contended that Chamberlain had undermined collective security, forsook Czechoslovakian self-determination, and evinced the interrelation between Nazi Germany and imperialist Britain. Rather than preserve peace, Dutt argued, the Munich Agreement guaranteed war:

> The alliance of Chamberlain and his tool, Daladier, with Hitler and Mussolini has dealt a heavy blow to peace and democracy in Europe. . . . They have presented Hitler with strategic and economic domination of all Central and Southeastern Europe: they have frightened away every smaller state from the side of the Western democracies, whose "friendship" had been proved in the hour of trial more deadly than the open enmity of fascism: and now they seek to clamp down Europe under a fascist directory.[100]

In the aftermath of the Munich Agreement, more than a hundred thousand Czechoslovakians, and even several thousand ethnic Germans, fled the

Sudetenland. Indian anti-fascists decried this mass migration. In arrogating lebensraum—or "living space"—Hitler espoused the imperial ethos that had despoiled India. Indeed, seen from India, Munich represented the apotheosis of fascist-imperialist avariciousness. "I feel so humiliated and helpless when I contemplate all this," Rabindranath Tagore bemoaned, "humiliated to see all the values, which have given whatever worth modern civilisation has, betrayed one by one and helpless that we are powerless to prevent it. Our country is itself a victim of these wrongs. . . . I can only remind those who are not yet wholly demented that when men turn beasts they sooner or later tear each other."[101]

Tagore visited Prague in 1921 and again in 1926. Czechoslovakian artists, novelists, and scholars had long extolled his artistry. *Gitanjali*, in particular, "meant so much especially for the Czech soldiers during the bad days of the Great War."[102] Tagore's sojourns sparked considerable cross-cultural collaboration.[103] Composers Leos Janacek and J. B. Foerster set his poems to music, Prague Radio honored him with a message of goodwill and peace on Christmas Eve (1937), his plays were staged in Prague, and Indologists Moritz Winternitz and Vincene Lesny visited Santinektan as guest lecturers.[104] After the Munich Agreement, Tagore vilified fascist-imperialist perfidy. "I can only offer profound sorrow," he wrote in a telegram to Czechoslovakian president Edvard Beneš, "on behalf of India and myself at a conspiracy of betrayal that has suddenly flung your country into a tragic depth of isolation and I hope that this shock will kindle a new life into the heart of your nation leading her to moral victory and unobstructed opportunity of perfect self-attainment."[105] In India, more than one hundred Czechoslovakian émigrés formed the Czechoslovakian Society of Calcutta (branches later opened in Bombay, Lahore, and Hyderabad). Its aim, articulated in wartime by honorary president John F. Bartos, was "to stand steadfastly behind the Czechoslovak Government in London, to help by all their means the Czechoslovak and Allied cause to win this war, [and] to fulfill all the obligations to their country as well as towards the country on whose soil they now live—India."[106]

~

Winston Churchill remains a lionized anti-appeaser. During and after the Second World War, he cultivated a mythos as one of the few conservatives to have divined the Hitlerian menace.[107] After the Munich Agreement, he purportedly declared: "You [Chamberlain] were given the choice between war and dishonour. You chose dishonour, and you will have war." Churchillian anti-appeasement has since come to epitomize the exigency of confronting, rather than conciliating, tyrants. It has been invoked—often mendaciously—to justify British military intervention in the Korean War (1950–3), Mau Mau Insurgency (1952–6), Suez Crisis (1956), Falklands War (1982), Gulf War (1990–1), and the Iraq War (2003).[108]

In *the Gathering Storm,* Churchill depicted his "Wilderness Years"—or time without a government position (1929–39)—as the product of his stentorian anti-appeasement. He was correct; however, the anti-appeasement that kept him from power was not directed toward Germany, but rather India. For years, Churchill predicted—often in eschatological terms—that the Government of India Act (1935) would destroy the British Empire. He prophesized doom at its mere mention.[109] Yet when the act passed, "nothing happened. Rarely had a politician been proved so hopelessly wrong, after nearly wrecking his own political party in the process."[110] Afterward, when Churchill once again predicted doom—this time over the Hitlerian peril—conservatives ignored him.[111] During the Second World War, Stanley Baldwin's "biographer, G.M. Young asked the former prime minister what had kept Churchill out of the running for any cabinet office and alienated from his party, Baldwin answered in one word: 'India.'"[112] In 1929, F. E. Smith (Lord Birkenhead), Churchill's closest friend, first used "appeasement" as a pejorative when he calumniated the "appeasers of Gandhi."[113] The following year, Churchill used the term while discussing the Raj with a German diplomat. By 1933, "he was already using it to describe British policy toward Hitler."[114]

Churchill considered Nazism and Gandhism desultory ideologies unmoored from Western traditions. He was the most ardent, if not most clamorous, opponent of appeasing their demands. Seen, however, from the outside-in, Churchill reviled Nazism and Gandhism because the former radicalized British imperial violence while the latter exposed the hypocrisy of British civilization. Churchill, Indian anti-fascists contended, loathed appeasement not out of a chivalric commitment to freedom, democracy, and self-determination, but because it threatened British imperial hegemony. In the case of Hitler, his criticism was righteous; in the case of Gandhi, it was rancorous, vainglorious, and reactionary. Put simply, Churchill—the acclaimed *Last Lion,* a man who *Walked with Destiny*—was right about Hitler and wrong about Gandhi.[115] These campaigns should be mentioned in tandem.

Fascism, moreover, was not—as Churchill contended—unmoored from Western traditions, but rather the apotheosis of its imperial avidity. Colonialism had despoiled Africa, Asia, and the Americas; at long last, its radicalization imperiled Europe. Munich, Indian anti-fascists argued, was not an unprecedented nor even momentous occurrence. It was an imperial transaction similar to the Scramble for Africa and, eventually, the partition of India (1947). Gandhism, by contrast, was indeed unmoored from Western traditions. Demanding swaraj, Gandhi created a political, spiritual, and cultural movement that repudiated Western, Orientalist, and imperialist discourses. This renunciation of British paramountcy unnerved, and often incensed, Churchill. In 1931, during the Round Table Conferences that culminated in the Gandhi-Irwin Pact, Churchill maligned Gandhi as "A seditious Middle Temple lawyer, now posing as a fakir of a type well known in the east, striding half-naked up the steps of the viceregal palace . . . to parley on equal terms with the representative of the King-Emperor."[116]

Gandhism subverted British imperial hegemony while at the same time exposing the violence animating—and sustaining—the civilising mission. It also evinced the uncomfortable extent to which fascism and liberal-imperialism were interrelated. In 1943, Prime Minister Churchill exacerbated a calamitous Indian famine by denying food import requests. Between two and five million Bengalis perished in what some scholars have called the Bengali Holocaust.[117] When the secretary of state for India, Leo Amery, requested assistance, Churchill pitilessly replied: "Famine or no famine, Indians will breed like rabbits."[118] Eventually, the Delhi government sent Whitehall a detailed description of the devastation. Echoing—obliquely, to be sure—Hitler's disquieting exchange with Halifax, Churchill is alleged to have responded: "Then why hasn't Gandhi died yet?"[119] Churchill's insouciance toward the Bengal Famine underscored the similarities between liberal-imperialism and fascism. Even as they warred against one another, the governments of Hitler and Churchill privileged white Europeans, callously perpetrated the deaths of millions of "lesser" human beings and harbored voracious imperial ambitions. Nazi Germany undeniably represented a far more extreme—and unprecedented—manifestation of imperialism. Similarities nevertheless existed.

You Do Not Know Hitler

In July 1937, Nazi *Schutzstaffel* (SS) officer Captain Roland von Strunk visited Gandhi at his ashram in Shegoan. A propagandist for the Reich Ministry of Public Enlightenment and Propaganda, Strunk was interested in *Sarvodaya* (self-sufficient communalism) and, in particular, Gandhi's critiques of industrialization and Western medicine. As he entered the ashram, Strunk was shocked to see Hermann Kallenbach, a German Jew, sitting "barebodied and in a khadi dhoti."[120] After their interview, Gandhi implored Strunk to explicate "why the Jews are being persecuted in Germany."[121] It was "the Jews," Strunk responded, "who overran Germany after the War, who ousted Germans from their jobs, and who 'guided' the fight against Hitler."[122] Even so, Strunk confessed that "we [the Nazis] have just overdone it. That's the mistake revolutions always do."[123]

Strunk marched with Mussolini's soldiers during the Second Italo-Ethiopian War and served as "Hitler's Special Agent"[124] to General Franco during the Spanish Civil War.[125] He witnessed fascist savagery firsthand and had grown weary of it: "Oh, there is such a lot of hate in Europe. And it has reached its climax in Spain. It is cruel, heartless, stupid, inhuman—this Spanish War. It can't be compared with any other war."[126] During their interview, Strunk was flummoxed by Gandhi's desire to adapt European warfare. "Though I am opposed to war," the Mahatma explained, "there is no doubt that war induces reckless courage. Well, without ever having to engage in a war I want to learn from you the art of throwing away my life for a noble cause. But I do not want that excessive desire of living that Western medicine seems to encourage in man."[127] Gandhi believed that satyagrahis should immolate themselves rather than commit violence. In adapting European warfare, he sought to capture the essence of martyrdom— apotheosized, as it was, in the culture of Western militarism. Political ideologies such as fascism, liberalism, and imperialism asserted their authority by monopolizing state violence. Gandhi reclaimed this sovereignty by encouraging satyagrahis to welcome death. Willingly receiving violence denuded the state of its coercive power. Somewhat paradoxically, Gandhi embraced death in order to emancipate life.[128]

Gandhi has since been criticized for his renunciative philosophy and, in particular, his exhortations to German Jews. He never did, as George Orwell observed, "specialize in avoiding awkward questions."[129] He welcomed them, often to his detriment. Amid the rise of fascism, Gandhi contended that satyagraha would peacefully resolve crises in Ethiopia, Spain, and China. During the Second World War, he contended that Britons should prostrate themselves before Nazi soldiers:

> You want to kill Nazism? You will never kill it by its indifferent adoption. . . . I hope you do not wish to enter into such an undignified competition with the Nazis. I venture to present you with a noble and braver way, worthy of the bravest soldier. . . . You [Britain] will invite Herr Hitler and Signor Mussolini to take what they want of the countries you call your possessions. Let them take your beautiful island, with your many beautiful buildings. You will give all these

but neither your souls, nor your minds. If these gentlemen choose to occupy your homes, you will vacate them. If they do not give you free passage out, you will allow yourself man, woman and child, to be slaughtered, but you will refuse to owe allegiance to them.[130]

Gandhi believed that satyagraha would countervail Hitlerian violence—that the Wehrmacht, *Einsatzgruppen*, and other Nazi soldiers would behave in much the same way as British colonial officials. Hitler, however, radicalized imperial violence; he worshipped race.[131] In urging Britain to "let Herr Hitler and Signor Mussolini to take what they want," Gandhi conflated fascism and liberal-imperialism, rather than understanding them as consanguineous iterations of the Western imperialist ethos. To some extent, this mischaracterization reflected the palisades of British censorship, as well as Gandhi's deteriorating health. By 1938, he had stopped touring, limited his correspondence, and only read newspaper headlines.[132] Even so, conflating fascism and liberal-imperialism diminished the unprecedented—and tragic—atrocities of the Hitlerian regime. Nazism remains a singular evil.

In the wake of the Munich Agreement, Gandhi sympathized with the victims of fascist-imperialist connivance. Invoking the New Imperialist covenant, Europe's great powers partitioned Czechoslovakia in order to preclude—or at the very least, forestall—war. Gandhi nevertheless criticized the government in Prague for seeking assurances from imperial powers: "In spite of all the goodwill in the world England and France cannot save them [Czechoslovakia]. Their intervention can only mean bloodshed and destruction such as has never been seen before."[133] If, instead, the Czechoslovakian people had adopted satyagraha, they would have obviated the tragedy at Munich: "I have the hardihood to say that if [Czechoslovakia] had known the use of nonviolence as a weapon for the defence of national honour . . . they would have spared England and France the humiliation of suing for a peace which was no peace."[134] Germany would likely invade the Sudetenland, perhaps even Bohemia and Moravia. Gandhi, however, maintained that nonviolent civil disobedience would bewilder Nazi soldiers. Czechoslovakian satyagrahis would immolate themselves en masse, compelling the Nazi war machine to confront its malignity. "[It would] be a glorious victory for the Czechs," Gandhi argued, "and the beginning of the fall of Germany."[135]

Fascism had perfected the "science of destruction."[136] Resistance on these terms was futile. The government in Prague, Gandhi contended, should espouse "an alternative [satyagraha] which had proved its effectiveness under somewhat similar circumstances."[137] Nonviolence transformed the "mass mind"[138]—first unconsciously, then consciously. It was, Gandhi insisted, the only righteous form of resistance:

> What would Republican Spain gain if it had Franco's resources, or China if she had Japan's skill in war, or the Czechs if they had the skill of Herr Hitler? I suggest that if it is brave, as it is, to die to a man fighting against odds, it is braver still to refuse to fight and yet to refuse to yield to the usurper. If death is a certainty in either case, is it not nobler to die with the breast bared to the enemy without malice against him within?"[139]

Gandhi envisioned his satyagrahis as an army of nonviolent warriors. In Czechoslovakia, these soldiers would sacrifice themselves before Nazi bayonets. Eventually, Gandhi argued, their sacrifice, together with that of others, would countervail Nazi antipathy.

Gandhi could not fathom an irredeemable soul. Everyone, even the most violent Nazis, "show in their family circles . . . tenderness, affection, consideration and generosity."[140] Satyagraha appealed to this tenderness; it bridged differences with empathy and overwhelmed enmity with munificence. Hitler, Gandhi argued, only knew violence. A satyagrahi would locate his compassion and use it to counterpoise Nazi bellicosity. If uncertain, Czechoslovakians or German Jews needed only to examine South African and Indian civil disobedience campaigns. The circumstances, Gandhi contended, were identical: "It is hardly necessary for me to point out that it is easier for the Jews than for the Czechs to follow my prescription. And they have in the Indian satyagraha campaign in South Africa an exact parallel. There the Indians occupied precisely the same place that the Jews occupy in Germany."[141]

Zionists, Westerners, and even some Indians criticized Gandhi for conflating British and Nazi persecution. "Even during the days of General [Reginald] Dyer's brutal administration," Hayim Greenberg argued, "there did not reign that bestiality and 'moral anesthesia' which characterise the Germany of today."[142] Satyagraha presumed a moral and philosophical equivalence between Nazism and British imperialism. Hitler, however, radicalized British colonial violence. In India, the Raj permitted protests, demonstrations, anti-colonial propaganda, and—apart from tragedies such as the First War of Indian Independence (Indian Rebellion of 1857) or the Jallianwala Bagh Massacre—refrained from the spectacle of public persecution. These affordances were unimaginable in Nazi Germany. "If we took India," Hitler remarked during the war, "the Indians would certainly not be enthusiastic, and they'd not be slow to regret the good old days of English rule!"[143]

Greenberg alleged that Gandhi's appeals for Czechoslovakian and Jewish civil disobedience exhibited the provinciality of swaraj. Gandhism was crafted to combat the peculiarities of British imperialism; it assumed its tormentors were capable of empathy and compassion. Hitler, however, was not the British viceroy. "You do not know Hitler and Mussolini," one visitor to Sabarmati Ashram warned Gandhi: "They are incapable of any kind of moral response."[144] Renowned philosopher Martin Buber contended that even as British colonialism brutalized the subcontinent, it was bound (at least in India) by certain constraints:

> Jews are being persecuted, robbed, maltreated, tortured, murdered. And you, Mahatma Gandhi, say that their position in the country where they suffer all this is an exact parallel to the position of Indians in South Africa. . . . Do you know of the torments in the concentration camp, of its methods of slow and quick slaughter. . . . Do you think perhaps that a Jew in Germany could pronounce in public one single sentence of a speech such as yours without being knocked down?[145]

Buber maintained that satyagraha undermined British imperialism by virtue of demographics. Indians far outnumbered British colonial officials. Civil disobedience thus awed a timorous minority—one susceptible to such demonstrations ever since the Indian Rebellion of 1857. In Germany, by contrast, Jews comprised less than 1 percent of the population. Nazism, moreover, was pitiless. Storm troopers assaulted, imprisoned, and murdered protestors. "A Jewish Gandhi in Germany," Greenberg famously argued, "should one arise could 'function' for about five minutes—until the first Gestapo agent would lead him, not to a concentration camp, but directly to the gallows."[146] Gandhi believed that the fervency of individual satyagrahis persuaded even the most benumbed hearts. His philosophy, critics argued, was predicated upon the spectacle of self-sacrifice. Practitioners needed to be seen and heard—conditions unimaginable in Nazi Germany.

Gandhi believed that Greenberg, Buber, and other critics misunderstood his conception of nonviolence. He acknowledged that a Jewish Gandhi, as Greenberg alleged, would "function for five minutes before a Gestapo agent led him to the gallows." Gandhi, however, argued that satyagraha's potency lay not in its presentation, but rather its magnanimity:

> I must say that I see no reason to change the opinion I expressed in my article. . . .
> As the writer says, "a Jewish Gandhi in Germany . . . would be promptly taken to the guillotine." But that will not disprove my case or shake my belief in the efficacy of ahimsa. I can conceive the necessity of the immolation of hundreds,

if not thousands, to appease the hunger of dictators who have no belief in ahimsa.[147]

Gandhi contended that the death of a Jewish Gandhi would galvanize German Jews. Friends and family would follow in his example; and hundreds, in turn, would follow in theirs. Eventually, thousands of Jewish satyagrahis would immolate themselves, compelling individual Germans to confront the maliciousness of anti-Semitism.

Gandhi believed in the universality of nonviolence. He could not fathom a circumstance in which he would sanction violence. Even as Nazi Germany degenerated into a genocidal state, Gandhi urged German Jews to sacrifice themselves. Nazism, in this regard, represented the ultimate test of nonviolence. It created an inscrutable paradox in which its devotion to violence compelled its opponents to even greater violence. Such cruelty bewildered Gandhi. Even as he proposed nonviolence in Czechoslovakia, Germany, and elsewhere, he bemoaned its potential repercussions:

Although I have been experimenting with it [nonviolence] for fifty years, I have no cut-and-dry answers to all the questions. When I start thinking what I would have done if I had been in Spain now or in China or Austria, and if Hitler had attacked these countries and I found men and money being drained away, my head starts reeling.[148]

Nazism was impenetrable—at once devoted to imperialist violence yet seemingly immune to compassion. Such acrimony challenged Gandhian satyagraha. "The tyrants of old," Gandhi admitted before the war, "never went so mad as Hitler seems to have gone."[149]

~

In *The Communist Manifesto,* Karl Marx and Friedrich Engels contended that modern bourgeois society "with its relations of production, of exchange, and of property, a society that has conjured up such gigantic means of production and of exchange, is like the sorcerer, who is no longer able to control the powers of the nether world whom he has called up by his spells."[150] Liberals, imperialists, fascists, and communists each sought to harness these protean energies; each failed to create the utopia they envisioned. Change, revolutionaries discovered, was an imperfect and fragmentary process. Resistance, the (often imagined) counterrevolution, predominated. Too often, the revolutionary state resorted to violence in order to preserve the revolution.

Whereas Western ideologies such as communism and fascism administered this violence, Gandhism received it. It inverted traditional power structures so that individuals, rather than the state, retained hegemony. For Gandhi, death was the utopia, rather than its means. Nazism, the French Revolution, and the Russian Revolution each radicalized death. "That is the mistake," Captain Strunk argued, "revolutions always do." Swaraj also radicalized death; satyagrahis asserted their individual hegemony by relinquishing life. Gandhi prescribed nonviolence to Czechoslovakians and German Jews not out of pitilessness, but love. This was— and remains—the paradox of revolutions: to preserve the cherished life, one must sacrifice it. Imperialists, fascists, and communists each sacrificed millions to preserve their utopias. Gandhi proposed the same, not because he longed to see Czechoslovakians or German Jews annihilated—as Hitler did—but because he wanted to set them free.

Buber, Greenberg, and other critics discounted the ubiquity of violence within colonial societies. The British Raj administered, controlled, and was created by violence.[151] Antagonists "continually challenged the narrative of the Pax Britannica and breached the security of the empire's defenses."[152] Gandhism, moreover, was not simply the absence of violence, but rather a revolutionary cosmology—a "potential inherent in every kind of action, personal as well as political."[153] Like most modern political ideologies, Gandhism endeavored to remake its followers. This transformation, however, was not accomplished through violence—as with fascism—but by its abnegation. Gandhi radicalized nonviolence in order to wrest sovereignty from a colonial state which, as Max Weber, Michele Foucault, and others have argued, monopolized violence.[154] Embracing self-immolation liberated the satyagrahi from the machinery of imperial oppression. There was power in choosing death, as opposed to having it thrust upon you.

Gandhi nevertheless misunderstood the profundity of Nazi antipathy. His conviction in the universality of satyagraha blinded him to the particularities of British and Nazi colonialisms. Although compassionate, his exhortations to Czechoslovakians and German Jews were misguided. As Buber, Greenberg, and other critics argued, British colonialism and Nazism were not the same. Nazism was an execrable barbarism unprecedented in modern European history. Urging nonviolence against it was injudicious, if not temerarious. Gandhi nevertheless persisted. After the Second World War, when asked about the Holocaust, he told Louis Fischer: "Hitler killed five million Jews. It is the greatest crime of our time. But the Jews should have offered themselves to the butcher's knife. They should have thrown themselves into the sea from cliffs. . . . It would have aroused the world and the people of Germany. . . . As it is they succumbed anyway in their millions."[155]

My Nonviolence Seems Almost Impotent

Six months after the Munich Agreement, Hitler invaded what remained of Czechoslovakia. Nazi ambitions, Whitehall discovered, were prodigious. Munich has since come to epitomize the pusillanimity of appeasing dictators. "[It] remains," as Daniel Hucker has argued, "a dirty word."[156] Chamberlain, however, was constrained by myriad factors.[157] As he himself understood it: "France was hopelessly unreliable, America would do nothing useful to help anywhere, the Soviets were interested only in damaging the capitalist powers, and the Dominions would not fight over irrelevant squabbles in central Europe."[158] Additionally, the British "public's unrestrained joy and relief in the aftermath of Munich persuaded him that appeasement enjoyed widespread popular support."[159] Overwhelmed by domestic, imperial, and foreign complications, Chamberlain appeased Hitler.[160]

Seen from India, the Munich Agreement exhibited the interrelation between fascism and liberal-imperialism. One of the most irreconcilable characteristics of British liberalism was that "even as it held freedom to be the highest goal that a man or a society could aspire to, it was also the flag-bearer of British colonialism. British liberals saw no contradiction in fighting for democracy or self-government at home and for colonies abroad."[161] Indian anti-fascists, and Gandhi in particular, challenged this hypocrisy not by maligning Chamberlain's obsequiousness, nor by celebrating appeasement as a "triumph for all that was best and most enlightened,"[162] but rather by criticizing Whitehall's invocation of the New Imperialist covenant. Seen from the outside-in, the Munich Agreement—in addition to a feckless betrayal of British diplomacy, a shrewd political maneuver that facilitated rearmament, a product of limited alternatives, and a reflection of British anti-communism—was also an imperial negotiation between Europe's great powers. As in Spain and China, Chamberlain forsook the self-determination of the Sudetenland. He "betrayed Czechoslovakia," Nehru argued, "and [threw] her to the Nazi wolves."[163]

With each successive war crisis, Gandhi languished. The inexorability of death bewildered him. "I have been hesitating," he confessed in a statement to the press, "to say anything on the impending world crisis. . . . I know that many in the West believe that my word does carry weight. I wish I shared their belief."[164]

Gandhi nevertheless wrote to Hitler. For years, supporters had implored him to appeal to the Führer. Only months before the German invasion of Poland (1939), he acquiesced and wrote his first letter to Hitler:

> Friends have been urging me to write to you for the sake of humanity. But I have resisted their request, because of the feeling that any letter from me would be an impertinence. Something tells me that I must not calculate and that I must make my appeal for whatever it may be worth. It is quite clear that you are today the one person in the world who can prevent a war which may reduce humanity to the savage state. Must you pay that price for an object however worthy it may appear to you to be? Will you listen to the appeal of one who has deliberately shunned the method of war not without considerable success? Anyway I anticipate your forgiveness, if I have erred in writing to you.[165]

Upon the outbreak of war, Gandhi sympathized with Britain, France, and the victims of fascist pugnacity. His opposition to British imperialism was institutional; he defied England but loved Englishman.[166] He even wept at the thought of London's destruction: "And as I was picturing before him [Viceroy Linlithgow] the Houses of Parliament and the Westminster Abbey and their possible destruction, I broke down. I have become disconsolate. In the secret of my heart I am in perpetual quarrel with God that He should allow such things to go on. My non-violence seems almost impotent."[167]

In his declaration of war against Germany, Chamberlain contended that "It is the evil things we shall be fighting against—brute force, bad faith, injustice, oppression, and persecution."[168] Seen from India, the outbreak of the Second World War divided Europe's "blood brothers"[169]—fascism and imperialism. Initially, many in the Congress supported Britain. Nazism radicalized the British imperial ethos; it exalted racialized violence. The Raj, however, declared war on Germany without consulting the Congress. Whitehall, moreover, refused to consider independence in exchange for Congress support of the British war effort. In response, anti-fascists questioned how Chamberlain—and later Churchill—could claim to defend democracy while opposing self-determination in India. "It must be clearly understood," Nehru argued, "that we are not going to be pawns in imperialist adventures, nor are we prepared to help governments which will betray democracy whenever they have a chance to do so."[170] After the abortive Cripps Mission (1942), Gandhi inaugurated his Quit India Movement. "We shall either free India," he famously declared, "or die in the attempt."[171] The Congress could not fortify its oppressor; it would not preserve imperialist enslavement. Though at war with one another, Europe's great powers each sought to expand—

or at the very least, maintain—their colonial empires. Seen from India, Britain and Nazi Germany fought not for self-determination, but brute force, bad faith, injustice, oppression, and persecution. They were, as Gandhi argued, more alike than either cared to admit.

Notes

1 Mohandas K. Gandhi, "Logical Consequence," October 8, 1938, in *The Collected Works of Mahatma Gandhi* (CWMG), vol. 79 (New Delhi: Publications Division Government of India, 1999), 98.

2 Rabindranath Tagore, "Ahbhan (A Call)," in *Munich Betrayal and India's Stand Against Fascism* (New Delhi: Embassy of the Czechoslovak Socialist Republic in collaboration with the Indo-Czechoslovak Cultural Society, 1978), 4. Tagore's poetry is in the public domain.

3 Mohandas K. Gandhi, "Letter to Adolf Hitler," December 24, 1940, in CWMG, vol. 79, 453.

4 Germany had also conquered Romania, Latvia, Estonia, and Finland. Thomas Childers, *The Third Reich: A History of Nazi Germany* (London: Simon & Schuster, 2017), 562–8; Andrew Stewart, *Victory: The Second World War and the East Africa Campaign* (New Haven: Yale University Press, 2016), 48–94.

5 Swaraj meant "more than just independence. 'Self-rule' required what the *Bhagavad-Gita* and Upanishads demanded, knowledge of the individual self. Only this knowledge could produce a higher form of spiritual freedom, that is, freedom from the illusion of separateness and freedom to realize the universal self." Dennis Dalton, *Mahatma Gandhi: Nonviolence Power in Action* (New York City: Colombia University Press, 1993), 3.

6 Gandhi drew a "sharp distinction between satyagraha and 'passive resistance' because the latter allowed for 'internal violence,' the harboring of enmity and anger among resisters even when they commit no physical violence." Dalton, *Mahatma Gandhi*, 9.

7 Gandhi, "Logical Consequence," 98–9.

8 Gandhi, "Letter to Hitler," 455.

9 This was Gandhi's second letter to Hitler; the first was dated July 23, 1939.

10 Much of Gandhian ideology is beyond the scope of this chapter. For scholarship examining his conception of independence, see B. R. Nanda, Puran Chandra Joshi, and Raj Krishna, *Gandhi and Nehru* (Delhi: Oxford University Press, 1979); Dennis Dalton, *Indian Idea of Freedom: Political Thought of Swami Vivekananda, Aurobindo Ghose, Mahatma Gandhi, and Rabindranath Tagore* (Gurgaon, Haryana: Academic Press, 1982); Partha Chatterjee, *The Nation and Its Fragments:*

Colonial and Postcolonial Histories (Delhi: Oxford University Press, 1997); Ranajit Guha, *Dominance without Hegemony: History and Power in Colonial India* (Cambridge: Cambridge University Press, 1997); Ajay Skaria, "Gandhi's Politics: Liberalism and the Question of the Ashram," *South Atlantic Quarterly* 101, no. 4 (2002): 955–86; B. R. Nanda, *Three Statesmen: Gokhale, Gandhi, and Nehru* (Delhi: Oxford University Press, 2004); Mithi Mukherjee, "Transcending Identity: Gandhi, Nonviolence, and the Pursuit of a 'Different' Freedom in Modern India," *The American Historical Review* 115, no. 2 (2010): 453–73; Sudhir Chandra, *Gandhi: An Impossible Possibility* (New York: Taylor & Francis, 2016); Ramachandra Guha, *Gandhi: The Years That Changed the World, 1914–1948* (London: Knopf Doubleday, 2018).

11 Gandhi, "Letter to Hitler," 455.

12 Mohandas K. Gandhi, *Hind Swaraj* (Madras: Ganesan, 1921), 60.

13 Richard Evans, *The Third Reich in Power* (New York: Penguin Books, 2005), 612–712.

14 Jackson J. Spielvogel and David Redles, *Hitler and Nazi Germany: A History* (New York: Routledge, 1988), 158.

15 David Valladares, "Tragedy or Betrayal? Interwar Europe and British Appeasement," *History: Reviews of New Books* 48, no. 2 (2020): 29–32.

16 Michael Foot, Peter Howard, and Frank Owen, *Guilty Men* (London: Penguin, 1940), 17. The title *Guilty Men* referred to fifteen public figures: Neville Chamberlain, Sir John Simon, Sir Samuel Hoare, Ramsay MacDonald, Stanley Baldwin, Lord Halifax, Sir Kingsley Wood, Ernest Brown, David Margesson, Sir Horace Wilson, Sir Thomas Inskip, Leslie Burgin, Earl Stanhope, W. S. Morrison, and Sir Reginald Dorman-Smith. After publication, the term "Guilty Men" became synonymous with anyone that had supported appeasement.

17 Winston Churchill, *The Second World War, Volume 1: The Gathering Storm* (New York: Houghton Mifflin Company, 1948). For similar arguments, see Lewis Namier, *Diplomatic Prelude, 1938–1939* (London: The Macmillan Press, 1948); John Wheeler-Bennett, *Munich: Prologue to Tragedy* (New York: Duell, Sloan and Peace, 1948); Alan Bullock, *Hitler: A Study in Tyranny* (New York: Harper Perennial, 1952).

18 Martin Gilbert, *Winston Churchill and Emery Reves: Correspondence, 1937–1964* (Austin: University of Texas Press, 1997), 230.

19 A. J. P. Taylor, *The Origins of the Second World War* (New York: Touchstone, 1961). For similar arguments, see Keith Feling, *Life of Neville Chamberlain* (North Haven: Shoe String Press, 1946); Keith Robbins, *Munich: 1938* (London: Cassell & Company, 1968); Martin Gilbert, *The Roots of Appeasement* (New York: New American Library, 1966); Donald Cameron Watt, *How War Came: Immediate Origins of the Second World War, 1938–1939* (London: Mandarin, 1989).

20 Paul Kennedy, *The Rise and Fall of the Great Powers* (New York: Random House, 1989); Robert Caputi, *Neville Chamberlain and Appeasement* (Selinsgrove, PA: Susquehanna University Press, 2000); Ian Kershaw, *Making Friends with Hitler: Lord Londonderry, the Nazis, and the Road to War* (New York: The Penguin Group, 2004); Peter Neville, *Hitler and Appeasement: The British Attempt to Prevent the Second World War* (London: Hambledon & London, 2007); Tim Bouverie, *Appeasement: Chamberlain, Hitler, Churchill, and the Road to War* (London: Tim Duggan Books, 2020); Andrew David Stedman, *Alternatives to Appeasement: Neville Chamberlain and Hitler's Germany* (London: Bloomsbury Academic, 2020). There is, moreover, a recent push to move beyond elite actors, and examine social, cultural, material, and emotional aspects of the Munich Agreement. As Julie Gottlieb, Daniel Hucker, and Richard Toye have argued, "Most analyses [of the Munich Agreement] focus on the policy makers . . . . Within this framework, different stories can be woven depending on the answers provided to certain overarching questions. Were the decisions taken right or wrong? Were the policies pursued justified or unjustified? Was there a viable alternative? These questions encourage either/or responses, cultivating a binary debate that is both compelling and seductive." Julie Gottlieb, et al., "Introduction," in *The Munich Crisis, Politics and the People*, ed. Daniel Hucker, Julie Gottlieb, and Richard Toye (Manchester: Manchester University Press, 2021), 3. See also Julie Gottlieb, *'Guilty Women,' Foreign Policy, and Appeasement in Inter-War Britain* (Basingstoke: Palgrave Macmillan, 2015).

21 Taylor, *The Origins of the Second World War*, 189.

22 Jawaharlal Nehru, *Toward Freedom: The Autobiography of Jawaharlal Nehru* (New York: The John Day Company, 1941), 358.

23 Frank McDonough, *Neville Chamberlain, Appeasement, and the British Road to War* (Manchester: Manchester University Press, 1998), 126.

24 Mark Mazower, *Hitler's Empire: Nazi Rule in Occupied Europe* (New York: Penguin, 2008), 553–604.

25 Gandhi, "Letter to Hitler," 455.

26 Historians have since debated whether van der Lubbe acted alone or if he was involved in a Nazi plot to consolidate power: William L. Shirer, *The Rise and Fall of the Third Reich: A History of Nazi Germany* (New York: Simon & Schuster, 1960); Detlev Peukert, *Inside Nazi Germany: Conformity, Opposition, and Racism in Everyday Life* (New Haven: Yale University Press, 1987); Ian Kershaw, *Hitler, the Germans, and the Final Solution* (New Haven: Yale University Press, 2009); Danny Orbach, *The Plots Against Hitler* (New York: Houghton Mifflin, 2016).

27 Michael Burleigh and Wolfgang Wippermann, *The Racial State: Germany, 1933–1945* (Cambridge: Cambridge University Press, 1991), 3.

28 Jawaharlal Nehru, *Glimpses of World History: Being Further Letters to His Daughter, Written in Prison, and Containing a Rambling Account of History for Young People* (New York: The John Day Company, 1942), 912.

29 Saumyendranath Tagore, *Hitlerism: The Aryan Rule in Germany* (Calcutta: Ganashakti Publishing House, 1933), 102. After his release from prison, Tagore fled Germany and returned to India, where he founded the Communist League (later the Revolutionary Communist Party of India).

30 Ibid., 87.

31 The Law for the Prevention of Genetically Diseased Offspring instituted forced sterilization; the Law for the Protection of German Blood prohibited marriage and extramarital intercourse between Jews and Germans (or kindred blood); and the Reich Citizenship Law stripped Jews of German citizenship. Non-Aryans were barred from civil-service and government regulated industries, while those that fled were forced to surrender their assets. Shirer, *The Rise and Fall of the Third Reich*, 188–278.

32 P. R. Kumaraswamy, *India's Israel Policy* (New York: Columbia University Press, 2010), 51.

33 "It is one of the wonders of history," Nehru wrote in *Glimpses of World History*, "how the Jews, without a home or a refuge, harassed and persecuted beyond measure, and often done to death, have preserved their identity and held together for over 2000 years." Nehru, *Glimpses of World History*, 51.

34 S. C. Dutta, "Pamphlet Written by S. C. Dutta, Convener of the 'All India Anti-Fascist Students' Conference," *M.N. Roy Papers 1940–1942*, Nehru Memorial Museum and *Library* (NMML), 90/1/1940-1942, Part II Section I.

35 Quoted in Yulia Egorova, *Jews and India Perceptions and Image* (London: Routledge, 2006), 39. Bose founded the Indo-Czech Association in Prague in 1934, and met with Edvard Beneš on numerous occasions.

36 As one proponent put it: "Is it possible for India to do its part in the solution of [the Jewish] question to its own profit? Would it not be clever to use the opportunity of getting now people of highest knowledge and industrial efficiency for the evolution of Indian national economies?" "India's Industrialization. Scope of Gaining Service of Jewish Experts. An Opportunity for India," *All India Congress Committee Papers: First Installment*, NMML, 45/F.D.42/909-E-1938-1939, 46.

37 Subhas Bose criticized the CWC's efforts, contending that Nehru's plan would transform India into an "asylum for the Jews." Nehru disagreed. "I am surprised to learn," he wrote to Bose, "that you felt so strongly about this as, so far as I remember, you did not express yourself definitely at the time." Kumaraswamy, 51–2.

38 Dr. L. I. Stux to the Indian National Congress, March 28, 1939, "Application from Jews for Vacancies in the A.I.C.C.," *All India Congress Committee Papers: First Installment*, NMML, 45/F.D.42/909-E-1938-1939.

39 Gandhi supported the Congress's plan. "I boycott foreign goods," he wrote to
    Nehru, "not foreign ability. And I feel keenly for the persecuted Jews. As a concrete
    proposal I suggest your collecting the names of the most deserving ones and
    making it plain to them that they must be prepared to throw in their lot with
    us and accept our standard of living." Mohandas Gandhi, "Letter to Jawaharlal
    Nehru," August 31, 1938, in CWMG, vol. 73, 425.

40 Adrian Phillips, *Fighting Churchill Appeasing Hitler: How a British Civil Servant
    Helped Cause the Second World War* (London: Biteback Publishing, 2019).

41 Britain was not "a military-technological superpower in the interwar years for
    there was then no such thing; but it could claim to be the most powerful of
    the great powers. It had certainly lost its pre-eminent place as a naval power to
    non-European powers, but it was still the strongest." David Edgerton, *Warfare
    State: Britain, 1920–1970* (Cambridge: Cambridge University Press, 2006),
    58. Whitehall nevertheless grappled with the political, social, and cultural
    ramifications of rearmament: "Confounded by runaway German rearmament the
    liberal democracies struggled with the problem of how to arm themselves against
    the escalating threat of total war without succumbing to totalitarianism." Joseph
    Maiolo, *Cry Havoc: How the Arms Race Drove the World to War, 1931–1941* (New
    York: Basic Books, 2010), 4.

42 The First World War and the Russian Revolutions did "much to destabilize and
    challenge the old world order of the late nineteenth century, and politicians and
    activists participated in an emerging discourse on the imagined futures of a new
    world of greater equality, justice, and peace. Mobilization for national sovereignty,
    working class rights, suffrage, civil liberties, pacifism, disarmament, and anti-
    racism grew dramatically in the 1920s and 1930s as a consequence of the war's
    failure to challenge global and local inequalities." Michele Louro, *Comrades Against
    Imperialism: Nehru, India, and Interwar Internationalism* (Cambridge: Cambridge
    University Press, 2018), 7–8.

43 Public opinion, Daniel Hucker has argued, "was evidently volatile with regard
    to Nazi Germany." Daniel Hucker, *Public Opinion and the End of Appeasement
    in Britain and France* (London: Routledge, 2011), 84. By 1938, "both the peace
    movement and public opinion [in Britain] had started to polarize. One current
    of opinion was drawn to the pole of accommodation: many *pacifists* advocated
    peaceful change; many defencists supported appeasement; unprecedented
    numbers of pacificists threw in their lot with the Peace Pledge Union and other
    new associations; and a section in the far left still favoured war resistance. Another
    current of opinion was attracted by the opposite pole of containment: the leaders
    of the LNU still supported collective security even though they now understood
    that it required rearmament; many socialists *pacifists* came to advocate a 'peace
    front' of the progressive states against the fascist ones; and those defencists who

shared the concerns of Winston Churchill, since 1929 a backbencher, called for more energetic rearmament." Martin Ceadel, *Semi-Detached Idealists: The British Peace Movement and International Relations, 1854–1945* (Oxford: Oxford University Press, 2000), 326. See also Helen McCarthy, *The British People and the League of Nations: Democracy, Citizenship, and Internationalism, 1918–1945* (Manchester: Manchester University Press, 2013).

44　Quoted in David Faber, *Munich, 1938: Appeasement and World War II* (New York: Simon Schuster, 2008), 282.

45　Talbot Imlay, *Facing the Second World War: Strategy, Politics, and Economics in Britain and France, 1938–1940* (Oxford: Oxford University Press, 2003).

46　Chamberlain distrusted the Soviet Union. "Our chief trouble," he explained in a letter to his sister, "is with Russia. I confess to being deeply suspicious of her. I cannot believe that she has the same aims and objects that we have or any sympathy with democracy as such. She is afraid of Germany & Japan and would be delighted to see other people fight them. But she is probably very conscious of her own military weakness and does not want to get into a conflict if she can help it. Her efforts are therefore devoted to egging on others but herself promising only vague assistance." Neville Chamberlain to Hilda Chamberlain, in *The Neville Chamberlain Diary Letters: Volume 4, the Down Street Years, 1934–1940*, 412.

47　Robert Self, "Introduction," in *The Neville Chamberlain Diary Letters: The Downing Street Years, 1934–1940* (Aldershot: Ashgate, 2002), 18.

48　Ibid.

49　David Jorge, *War in Spain: Appeasement, Collective Insecurity, and the Failure of European Democracies Against Fascism* (London: Routledge, 2020).

50　Neville Chamberlain to unknown, October 30, 1937. *Records of the Cabinet Office*, British National Archives (NA), 140/149/34. As Daniel Hucker has noted: "The British saw the press as a barometer of public opinion. The personal papers and diaries of contemporary politicians often refer to newspaper editorials, and perceptions of opinions were garnered largely from such sources. However, whereas [French prime minister] Daladier focused on criticism, Chamberlain preferred to dwell on the positives." Hucker, *Public Opinion and the End of Appeasement in Britain and France*, 29.

51　Quoted in Paul Kennedy, "The Tradition of Appeasement in British Foreign Policy 1865–1939," *British Journal of International Studies* 2, no. 3 (1976): 205.

52　George Padmore, "British Imperialists Treat the Negro Masses Like the Nazis Treat the Jews," *Labor Action* 5, no. 42 (1941): 4.

53　Indian National Congress, "Foreign Policy and War Danger: Resolution Passed at the 51st Session of the Indian National Congress at Vithalnagar-Haripura," in *Peace and Empire: Jawaharlal Nehru Presidential Address at the Conference on Peace and Empire* (London: India League, 1938), 28.

54 Arthur Herman, *Gandhi and Churchill: The Epic Rivalry That Destroyed an Empire and Forged Our Age* (New York: Bantam Books, 2008), 418.

55 Ibid.

56 Ibid.

57 Ibid.

58 Ibid., 419. Hitler was not Prussian.

59 Judith Brown, "The Mahatma in Old Age: Gandhi's Role in Indian Political Life, 1935–1942," in *Congress and Indian Nationalism: The Pre-Independence Phase*, ed. Richard Sisson and Stanley Wolpert (Berkley: University of California Press, 1988), 272. In 1935, Gandhi's "health collapsed completely and he had to stay in bed, refraining from all writing, dictation, and correspondence. Although he agreed to rest for two months, his blood pressure was still erratic, and to compound this problem he had to have all his remaining teeth extracted . . . . [Later, in 1937,] his blood pressure rocketed . . . and in the last week of October [1937] he collapsed in Calcutta." Brown, "The Mahatma in Old Age," 272.

60 Ibid., 271.

61 Ibid., 282.

62 Ibid., 274.

63 Mohandas Gandhi, "Conundrums," September 25, 1939, in CWMG, vol. 76, 357.

64 Mohandas Gandhi, "Speech at Edward's Mission College, Peshawar," May 5, 1938, in CWMG, vol. 73 (New Delhi: Publications Division of Government of India, 1999), 147.

65 Benjamin Carter Hett, *The Nazi Menace: Hitler, Churchill, Roosevelt, Stalin and the Road to War* (New York: Henry Holt, 2020), 174.

66 Ibid., 58.

67 Ibid.

68 Ibid.

69 Ibid.

70 Ibid.

71 Ivone Kirkpatrick, *The Inner Circle: Memoirs* (London: Macmillan, 1959), 97.

72 Hett, *The Nazi Menace*, 62.

73 Robert Paxton, *The Anatomy of Fascism* (London: Allen Lane, 2004), 121.

74 Ibid.

75 Ibid., 148.

76 Mohandas K. Gandhi, "If I Were a Czech," October 6, 1938, in CWMG, vol. 74, 89.

77 Mohandas K. Gandhi, "Speech at Vidyamandir Training School, Wardha," April 21, 1938, in CWMG, vol. 73, 115.

78 Mukherjee, "Transcending Identity," 454.

79 Mohandas K. Gandhi, "Interview to Captain Strunk," July 3, 1937, in CWMG, vol. 71, 404.

80 Ibid.

81 Mohandas K. Gandhi, "What to Do?" April 15, 1939, in CWMG, vol. 75, 248.

82 P. J. Cain and A. G. Hopkins, *British Imperialism: 1688–2015* (London: Routledge: 2016), 441–526.

83 Gandhi, "What to Do?" 248.

84 Quoted in Igor Lukes, *Czechoslovakia Between Stalin and Hitler: The Diplomacy of Edvard Beneš in the 1930s* (Oxford: Oxford University Press, 1996), 239.

85 Faber, *Munich, 1938*, 391.

86 P. E. Caquet, *The Bell of Treason: The 1938 Munich Agreement in Czechoslovakia* (New York: Other Press, 2018).

87 Sidorov Andrei Yu, "International Relations in Europe in 1938: The Munich Conference; The Collapse of the Versailles System," in *History of International Relations and Russian Foreign Policy in the 20th Century*, ed. Anatoly Torkunov, William Wohlforth, and Boris Martynov (Newcastle: Cambridge Scholars Publishing, 2020), 211.

88 Neville Chamberlain, "Peace for Our Time," September 30, 1938, *Records of the Prime Minister's Office*, NA, 1-266A/132/ 35.

89 Quoted in Neville, *Hitler and Appeasement*, xi.

90 Chamberlain could "legitimately regard opposition as confined to a minority, albeit a vocal one. Conservative dissidents failed to provide a united front and the prospect of forming a cross-party opposition with the Labour and Liberal parties was fleeting and short-lived." Hucker, *Public Opinion and the End of Appeasement in Britain and France*, 82.

91 Quoted in Faber, *Munich, 1938*, 1.

92 Quoted in Robert Self, *Neville Chamberlain: A Biography* (London: Ashgate, 2006), 325.

93 Ibid., 40.

94 Quoted in Herman, *Gandhi and Churchill*, 429.

95 Mohandas K. Gandhi, "Logical Consequence," 98.

96 Chamberlain, "Peace for Our Time."

97 Mohandas K. Gandhi to C. F. Andrews, October 5, 1938, in CWMG, vol. 76, 89.

98 Jawaharlal Nehru, *China, Spain, and the War* (Allahabad: Kitabistan, 1940), 112.

99 Indian National Congress, "Resolution of Foreign Policy Adopted by Congress at Tripuri," in *Munich Betrayal and India's Stand Against Fascism*, 54.

100 Rajani P. Dutt, "After Munich: No Defeatism! Rally the Peace Forces!" *New Masses* (London), October 1938.

101 Stanislava Vavroušková, "India and Czechoslovakia Between the Two World Wars: A Study of Cultural Contacts and Exchange of Ideas," *Archív Orientální* 75, no. 3 (2007): 268.

102 Ibid., 265. Similarly, Jan Baroš contended that "the Great Indian poet Rabindranath Tagore in his very first visit to Prague won the hearts of the Czechs. This exchange

of culture, exchange of thoughts and ideas, this spiritual association with each other bore rich fruits. An Oriental Institute was established in Prague, with a number of prominent Indians and Czechoslovaks at the helm of affairs. Reputed Indian scholars and educationists lectured in the Carolinum, the oldest University north of the Alps, in Prague." Jan Baroš, *India and Czechoslovakia* (Calcutta: Baptist Mission Press, 1943), 37.

103 Indian Professor Benoy Kumar Sarkar argued that a "profound identity" existed between Indian and Czechoslovakian cultures: "Both among Indians and Czechs an important item of cultural life is to be found in the attempt to distinguish between the old and new ideals or the ancient and the modern view-points. As a modern representative of ideology we may take Masaryk . . . . A Bengali intellectual coming into contact with these Czech views would be at once reminded of one of Masaryk's senior contemporaries, Bankim Chatterji (1838–94). In Chatterji's novels and essays published in Bengali language, we come across the self-same analysis of the distinctions between ancient and modern ideals as one finds in Masaryk." Benoy Kumar Sarkar, "Czech Ideals Through Indian Eyes," in *India and Czechoslovakia*, ed. Jan Baroš, 34–5.

104 S. Radhakrishnan, *Rabindranath Tagore: A Centenary, Volumes 1861–1961* (New Delhi: Sahitya Akademi, 1961), 365. After the Munich Agreement, Tagore wrote a letter to Lesny expressing his sadness over the betrayal of Czechoslovakia: "It was sad to read in your letter all the news about the great betrayal of your magnificent people at the hands of England and France. I met Mr. Nehru a few days back. He was in Central Europe at the time of the tragic happenings and he gave me a graphic description of the woes of the mutilation of Czechoslovakia." See: Rabindranath Tagore to Vincene Lesny, February 14, 1939, in *The English Writings of Rabindranath Tagore: Volume Three, a Miscellany*, ed. Sisir Kumar Das (New Delhi: Sahitya Akademi, 1996), 54.

105 Rabindranath Tagore, "Message of Rabindranath Tagore to the President of the Czechoslovak Republic," in *Munich Betrayal and India's Stand Against Fascism*, 54.

106 Cenek Valenta, "The Calcutta Czechoslovaks," in *India and Czechoslovakia*, 115.

107 Richard Toye, "Churchill, Munich and the Origins of the Grand Alliance," in *The Munich Crisis, Politics and the People*, 128.

108 Gerald R. Hughes, *The Postwar Legacy of Appeasement* (London: Bloomsbury, 2014).

109 Herman, *Gandhi and Churchill*, 417.

110 Ibid.

111 Ibid., 418.

112 Ibid.

113 Ibid., 419.

114 Ibid.

115 William Machester, *The Last Lion: Winston Spencer Churchill Alone, 1932–1940* (New York: Bantam Books, 1988); Andrew Roberts, *Churchill: Walking with Destiny* (London: Penguin, 2018).

116 Guha, *Gandhi*, vi.

117 Madhusree Mukerjee, *Churchill's Secret War: The British Empire and the Ravaging of India during World War II* (New York: Basic Books, 2010).

118 Herman, *Gandhi and Churchill*, 513.

119 Shashi Tharoor, *Inglorious Empire: What the British Did to India* (London: Scribe, 2017), 160.

120 Gandhi, "Interview to Captain Strunk," 406. First seen in Faisal Devji, *The Impossible Indian: Gandhi and the Temptation of Violence* (Cambridge: Harvard University Press, 2012), 185.

121 Ibid.

122 Ibid.

123 Ibid.

124 Gabrielle Ashford Hodges, *Franco: A Concise Biography* (New York: Thomas Dunne, 2000), 114.

125 Strunk also reported on the Japanese invasion of Manchuria (1931).

126 Gandhi, "Interview to Captain Strunk," 406. On two separate occasions, Strunk protested to General Franco about the mass murder of Republican prisoners of war. "These atrocities," American journalist John Whitaker reported, "were always denied abroad by the propaganda bureau. They were rarely denied in Spain by the Spaniards or by the Germans and Italians. Captain Strunk told me twice of protests he made personally to Franco, who made a *pro forma* denial. Franco's answer in each instance was the same. Franco said, with a knowing smile, 'Why, this sort of thing can't be true—you have got your facts wrong, Captain Strunk.'" John Whitaker, *We Cannot Escape History* (New York: Macmillan, 1943), 111–12.

127 Gandhi, "Interview to Captain Strunk," 405.

128 Swaraj required absolute nonviolence. Anyone opposed to it—even those, like Congress leftists, only superficially committed to it—perpetuated violence.

129 George Orwell, "Reflections on Gandhi," in *A Collection of Essays* (New York: Houghton Mifflin Harcourt, 1970), 177.

130 Mohandas K. Gandhi, "To Every Briton," July 2, 1940, in CWMG, vol. 78, 387.

131 Michael Mann, *Fascists* (Cambridge: Cambridge University Press, 2004), 139–76.

132 Brown, "The Mahatma in Old Age," 272.

133 See Mohandas K. Gandhi, "If I Were a Czech," 89.

134 Gandhi, "Logical Consequence," 98–99.

135 Mohandas K. Gandhi, "Discussion with Christian Missionaries," December 12, 1938, in CWMG, vol. 74, 311.

136 Gandhi, "Logical Consequence," 98–9.

137 Mohandas K. Gandhi, "Why Not Great Powers?" November 5, 1938, in CWMG, vol. 74, 193.

138 Citation.

139 Gandhi, "Logical Consequence," 100.

140 Gandhi, "What to Do?" 248.

141 Gandhi, "The Jews," November 20, 1938, in CWMG, vol. 74, 239. Gandhi argued that South African president Paul Kruger, much like Hitler, justified state-sponsored persecution on religious and racial grounds: "President Kruger used to say that the white Christians were the chosen of God and Indians were inferior beings created to serve the whites. A fundamental clause in the Transvaal constitution was that there should be no equality between the whites and coloured races including Asiatics. There too the Indians were consigned to ghettos described as locations. The other disabilities were almost of the same type as those of the Jews in Germany. The Indians, a mere handful, resorted to satyagraha without any backing from the world outside or the Indian Government. Indeed the British officials tried to dissuade the satyagrahis from their contemplated step. World opinion and the Indian Government came to their aid after eight years of fighting. And that too was by way of diplomatic pressure not of a threat of war." Gandhi, "The Jews," 241.

142 Hayim Greenberg, "An Answer to Gandhi," in *The Inner Eye: Selected Essays, Volume 1* (New York: Jewish Frontier Association, 1953), 233. In April 1919, Brigadier-General Reginald E. Dyer ordered his Gurkha and Balochi soldiers to open fire on a peaceful demonstration at the Jallianwala Bagh public gardens in Amritsar. For almost ten minutes, Dyer's troops fired as civilians desperately evacuated. After the soldiers had nearly exhausted their ammunition supply, hundreds lay dead and thousands more wounded. Kim Wagner, *Amritsar 1919: An Empire of Fear & the Making of a Massacre* (New Haven: Yale University Press, 2019), 74–207.

143 Adolf Hitler, "India or the Control of Europe," in *Hitler's Secret Conversations, 1941–1944*, ed. Hugh Redwald Trevor-Roper and Gerhard L. Weinberg (New York: Enigma Books, 2013), 153.

144 Gandhi, "Discussion with Christian Missionaries," 311.

145 Martin Buber to Mahatma Gandhi, February 24, 1939, in *The Letters of Martin Buber: A Life of Dialogue,* ed. Nahum Norbert Glatzer (New York: Schocken Books, 1991), 476.

146 Greenberg, "An Answer to Gandhi," 233.

147 Mohandas K. Gandhi, "The Jewish Question," May 22, 1939, in CWMG, vol. 75, 415.

148	Mohandas K. Gandhi, "Speech at Gandhi Seva Sangh Meeting," March 27, 1938, in CWMG, vol. 73, 53.

149	Gandhi, "The Jews," 239–240.

150	Karl Marx and Friedrich Engels, *The Communist Manifesto* (Auckland: The Floating Press, 2009), 15.

151	Tharoor, *Inglorious Empire*, 1–36.

152	Antoinette Burton, *The Trouble with Empire: Challenges to Modern British Imperialism* (Oxford: Oxford University Press, 2015), 1.

153	Devji, *The Impossible Indian*, 5.

154	Max Weber, *Economy and Society*, edited by Guenther Roth and Claus Wittich (Berkeley: University of California Press, 1968); Michele Foucault, *Discipline & Punish: The Birth of the Prison* (New York: Vintage, 1977). See also Devji, *The Impossible Indian*, 185–192.

155	Louis Fischer, *The Life of Mahatma Gandhi* (New York: Harper, 1950), 348.

156	Hucker, *Public Opinion and the End of Appeasement in Britain and France*, 3.

157	Jessi Gilchrist, "'Clouds of Mutual Suspicion:' Neville Chamberlain and Appeasement in the Mediterranean," *The International History Review* 44, no. 2 (2021): 1–18.

158	Self, "Introduction," 20.

159	Hucker, *Public Opinion and the End of Appeasement in Britain and France*, 133.

160	Bruce Strang, "Sir Alexander Cadogan and the Steward-Hesse Affair: Assessments of British Cabinet Politics and Future British Policy, 1938," *The International History Review* 43, no. 3 (2021): 657–76.

161	Mukherjee, "Transcending Identity," 472.

162	Taylor, *The Origins of the Second World War*, 189.

163	Nehru, *China, Spain, and the War*, 98.

164	Mohandas K. Gandhi, "Statement to the Press," August 27, 1939, in CWMG, vol. 76, 273.

165	Mohandas K. Gandhi, "Letter to Adolf Hitler," July 23, 1939, in CWMG, vol. 76, 156–7.

166	Gandhi, *Hind Swaraj*, 18–19.

167	Gandhi, "Statement to the Press," September 5, 1939, in CWMG, vol. 76, 311–12.

168	Quoted in *British War Aims: A Collection of Extracts form Speeches Delivered by H.M. Ministers in the United Kingdom Between 3ʳᵈ September, 1939, and 31ˢᵗ March, 1940* (London: H.M. Stationery Office, 1940), 16.

169	Jawaharlal Nehru, *Fascism and Empire* (London: Spain-India Committee, 1937), 1–2.

170	Jawaharlal Nehru, "The Betrayal of Czechoslovakia," in *Munich Betrayal and India's Stand Against Fascism*, 64–5.

171	Mohandas K. Gandhi, "Speech at A.I.C.C. Meeting," in CWMG, vol 83, 197.

5

"A War for the Future of the World"[1]

India and the Outbreak of the Second World War

The Great One comes,
sending shivers across the dust of the Earth.
In the heavens the trumpet,
in the world of man the drums of victory are beaten.
the hour has arrived for the great Birth.
Today the gates of night's fortress crumble into the dust—
On the crest of awakening dawn assurance of new life proclaims "Fear Not."
The great sky resounds with paeans of victory to the Coming of Man.

—Rabindranath Tagore
Crisis in Civilization[2]

In 1920, Manabendra Nath Roy left Mexico and embarked upon a pilgrimage to the newly created Russian Socialist Federative Soviet Republic.[3] Mikhail Borodin had invited Roy to attend the Second World Congress of the Communist International (Comintern). At the time, Roy was an auspicious global revolutionary. He had protested the Partition of Bengal, participated in the Indo-German Conspiracy, and helped found the *Partido Socialista Obrero* (later the Mexican Communist Party).[4] In due course, he would collaborate with C. R. Das, Vladimir Lenin, Joseph Stalin, and Mao Zedong, and hold the distinction of being accused in three major conspiracy cases—Howrah (1910), Kanpur (1924), and Meerut (1929).[5]

Roy arrived in Moscow three months before the Second International and quickly established himself as an anti-colonial virtuoso. Before the congress, Lenin forwarded Roy a preliminary draft of his *Theses on the National and Colonial Question* with the note: "Com. Roy, for criticism and suggestions."[6] That same day, Roy met Lenin for the first time. "You are so young," the Bolshevik leader quipped, "I expected a grey-bearded wise man from the East."[7] During their meeting, Lenin confessed his limited understanding of non-Western anti-imperialisms, and consulted with Roy several times before the congress.[8] He even urged Roy to prepare a concomitant treatise—later adopted as *Supplementary Theses on the National and Colonial Question.*

During the fourth session of the Second International, the congress debated "National and Colonial Questions." Lenin proposed an orthodox-Marxist program of supporting the self-determination of subject nationalities and liberation movements, arguing that anti-colonial activism would disrupt the flow of colonial capital. Eventually, Europe's bankrupt imperial states would collapse, and from their ashes a proletarian revolution would inaugurate an egalitarian world order. Roy supported Lenin's dialectic, save for one issue—Gandhi. Lenin deemed him revolutionary; Roy, however, considered him a reactionary demagogue.[9] "Gandhi," Roy wrote in his memoirs, "was the crucial point of difference. Lenin believed that, as the inspirer and leader of a mass movement, he was revolutionary. I maintained that, a religious and cultural revivalist, he was bound to be a reactionary socially, however revolutionary he might appear politically."[10] Roy contended that Gandhi and an incipient capitalist—or bourgeois—class promulgated nonviolence in order to suppress revolutionary activism. Rather than vanquish imperialism, the Congress would preside over a transfer of power from British colonialists to Indian colonialists. Gandhi, Roy argued, would betray the Indian revolution.

Twenty years later, during the Second World War, Roy believed that Gandhi had fulfilled this prophecy. After the failed Cripps Mission, Gandhi launched his Quit India Movement (1942).[11] He sabotaged the Indian revolution, Roy argued, by opposing a righteous anti-fascist conflict. In Ethiopia, Spain, China, and Czechoslovakia, the Congress had vilified British nonintervention (or appeasement). British imperialism, the Congress maintained, had encouraged—or at the very least, condoned—fascist expansionism. During the Second World War, however, British prime minister Neville Chamberlain finally confronted fascist bellicosity. He did as the Congress had demanded, only to then be criticized for it. Such hypocrisy, Roy contended, evinced the retrogression of Gandhian ideology:

The attitude of the Indian nationalist movement towards this war should have been entirely different from that of the Congress. And indeed, originally, it was different. Ever since 1929, and particularly since 1936, the Indian National Congress time and again condemned Fascism as the greatest menace to human progress, and sympathized with the victims of

Fascist aggression. By making those declarations and expressing sympathy with the victims of Fascist aggression, the Congress committed itself to active participation against Fascism, unless all those pronouncements and resolutions were empty words. Even when the war was declared, the Congress was prepared to participate in it. Mahatma Gandhi himself declared in favour of unconditional support for this war. Later on, he said he meant only moral support; but if this war is bad, moral support for it is certainly even worse than material support.[12]

Roy is a Daedalean lens from which to analyze the outbreak of the Second World War. Many of his assertions were remarkably prescient; many more were not. During the conflict, Roy remained characteristically aloof—criticized by anti-colonialists for supporting British imperial anti-fascism and repudiated by British colonial officials for his relentless anti-colonialism.[13] A sibylline, and often impenetrable anti-imperialist, Roy's experience of the Second World War differed from traditional South Asian narratives: Congress imprisonment, the British-Indian Army, the China-Burma-India Theatre, the Indian National Army, and the Muslim League campaign for Pakistan, to name just a few.

Inside-out scholarship has traditionally depicted the outbreak of the Second World War as a clash between fascist villainy and liberal-imperialist rectitude (however limited).[14] At the same time, orthodox-Marxist scholarship has characterized the first years of the war as an internecine imperialist struggle, transformed only by the revolutionary anti-fascism of the Soviet Union (1941).[15] Finally, scholars of empire have examined the paradox of anti-imperialist participation in the Second World War. In India, in particular, anti-colonialists could support Britain—fortifying the depredatory system that had despoiled South Asia—or Nazi Germany, whose racialized, opprobrious, and expansionist ideology had radicalized the colonial ethos.[16] Roy's understanding of the outbreak of the Second World War challenged—yet in quintessential Royian fashion, reconstituted—each of these interpretations. Defying inside-out traditionalists, he characterized the war as a clash between rival, albeit dissimilar, malefactors. Unlike orthodox Marxists, however, Roy considered Nazism the more immediate menace and urged revolutionary forces around the world to support British imperial anti-fascism. Lastly, Roy reconciled—or at the very least, circumvented—the paradox of anti-imperialist participation by contending that subject nationalities should support Britain because the devastation of war would devitalize its empire and precipitate an era of decolonization.

Roy's understanding of the Anglo-German War was a farrago of ingenuity and inscrutability. He often mischaracterized—or calumniated—inside-out, Marxist, anti-colonial, and other non-Royian interpretations of the war. At the same time, however, he articulated a trenchant understanding of the war that was substantiated by postwar events and, perhaps more importantly, remains a useful lens from which to analyze the conflict. In this chapter, I contend that, seen from the outside-in, the outbreak of the Second World War was not a Manichean conflict between liberal probity and fascist malignity, nor a good war, but rather a calamitous civil war between Europe's imperial great powers.[17] It was nevertheless righteously anti-fascist—in that Nazism was a singular malignancy—and imaginably anti-imperialist, insomuch as the wartime enervation of the British Empire augured an era of decolonization. Although on the periphery of the Indian independence movement, Roy propounded a unique conception of anti-fascism that reconstituted the tenets of British anti-fascism—defined primarily by the annihilation of Nazi Germany—around Indian tenets of anti-imperialism and decolonization. "The fight against Fascism," he argued, "will not be won, Hitlerism will not be overthrown, unless the advent of a revolution is regarded as a necessity, not for any particular section of society, but for mankind in general."[18] Perhaps more than any other nation, India understood the Second World War across an ethical spectrum.[19] Roy epitomized this complexity. A devout anti-imperialist, he urged progressive forces around the world to support the British Empire so that it would destroy fascism and, in the process, itself.

Hamlet without the Prince of Denmark

In May 1941, Independent Member of Parliament Eleanor Rathbone published an open letter entitled "Some Indian Friends."[20] For more than eight months, England had endured the "indescribable chaos"[21] of the Nazi Blitz. Thousands of civilians had perished, while more than a million homes had been destroyed. The Congress, meanwhile, refused to support the British war effort unless guaranteed unconditional independence. Frustrated, Rathbone vilified the Congress—Jawaharlal Nehru in particular—for abetting Nazi aggression: "Was the absence of formal consultation [before the Viceroy declared war], even if a bad mistake, so inexcusable under the stress of great emergency that it should condition your whole attitude and turn you from potential allies of ours into actual allies of the aggressors, for that is what in effect you are."[22]

Rathbone's letter provoked an impassioned response from Rabindranath Tagore. Aged seventy-nine, the Poet suffered from numerous health concerns. Upon reading "Some Indian Friends," he erupted in "a final explosion of wrath."[23] Forsaking retirement, Tagore dictated a response reminiscent of his 1937 letter to Yone Noguchi:

> I have been deeply pained at Miss Rathbone's open letter to Indians. . . . What have the British who have held the purse strings of our nation for two centuries and exploited its resources done for our poor people? I see famished bodies crying for bread, village women digging up mud for drinking water, since wells are even scarcer in the villages than schools. I sympathize with the English population today itself in danger of starvation, but when I see the whole might of the British navy engaged in convoying food vessels to England and recollect that I have seen our people perish of hunger and not even a cartload of rice brought from the neighboring district I cannot help contrasting British at home with British in India. . . . I see riots raging throughout the country. When scores of Indian lives are lost, property looted, women dishonored, mighty British arms take no action, only British voice is raised from overseas to chide us for unfitness to put our house in order.[24]

For centuries, imperial ideologies had plundered Indian wealth, civilization, and culture. Now, as they foundered in a war against an imperial co-conspirator, British imperialists appealed to Indian magnanimity. Supporting Britain, they argued, was righteous. In a final paroxysm of anti-imperialist effulgence, Tagore decried British hypocrisy: "[the] British hate the Nazis for merely challenging their world mastery and Miss Rathbone expects us to kiss the hand of her people in servility for having riveted the chains on ours."[25] He died two months later.

The debate over Congress intervention reflected Indians' multifarious understandings of the Second World War. It was at once righteous yet nefarious; imperialist yet emancipatory; and finally, distant yet imperative. As Gandhi and the Congress advocated noncooperation, South Asians participated in nearly every theatre of war. The British-Indian Army served in Africa, Asia, and Europe; Subhas Bose and the Indian National Army led a Japanese-supported invasion of Imphal and Kohima; and as much of Europe suffered under fascist persecution, millions in Bengal perished from a historic famine.[26] Across India, the war "flattened out the pretensions of empire, making ceremonial and ritual excesses look archaic. It mobilized women, workers, and the urban middle class in new ways. It heightened nationalism, so that older forms of transnational solidarity became dated and obsolete."[27] No longer is the British war effort "simply an island story of heroic, plucky

England fighting against Nazi-occupied Europe."[28] India shaped the war and was, in turn, transformed by it.

In England, the rise of fascism transformed the Raj from an imperial panoply into a strategic necessity. India formed "the backbone of British defence east of the Suez."[29] It provided soldiers, natural resources, and unmatched financial leverage. With each Nazi triumph, imperialists increasingly silenced appeals for self-determination or dominion status. Military and "strategic reasoning gained weight in the armoury of arguments of the 'die-hard' imperialists and could not be easily discarded."[30] The impending war nevertheless created a colonial crisis. Congress noncooperation could potentially destabilize the Raj and cause negative propaganda repercussions in neutral nations— the United States, in particular. Any concessions, by contrast, would entail considerable "modification of the Government of India Act, with foreseeable complications."[31]

After the Nazi invasion of Poland, the Congress offered Viceroy Linlithgow its full cooperation in exchange for unconditional independence. India, Nehru proclaimed, would not defend imperial cupidity:

> If the war is to defend the "*Status quo,*" imperialist possessions, colonies, vested interests and privilege, then India can have nothing to do with it. If, however, the issue is democracy and a world order based on democracy, then India is intensely interested in it. . . . But there is an inherent an ineradicable conflict between democracy for India or elsewhere and imperialism and fascism. If Great Britain fights for the maintenance and extension of democracy, then she must necessarily end imperialism in her own possessions, establish full democracy in India, and the Indian people must have the right of self-determination. . . . A free, democratic India will gladly associate herself with other free nations for mutual defence against aggression and for economic co-operation.[32]

Nehru and the Congress implored Linlithgow to declare his "war aims," or postwar plan for India. A skilled obfuscator, Linlithgow contended that any such declarations were premature.[33] Circumstances were certain to evolve; declarations, he argued, concerning a single nation might aggravate international relations: "Such a definition can only come at a later stage in the campaign, and that when it does come, it cannot be a statement of the aims of any single ally. There may be many changes in the world position and in the situation that confronts us before the War comes to an end."[34] Nehru later described Linlithgow as "Heavy of body and slow of mind, solid as a rock and with almost a rock's lack of awareness."[35]

As early as its Madras meeting (1927), the Congress proclaimed that it would not support another imperialist conflict.[36] The Raj nevertheless repudiated Congress promulgations. Linlithgow declared war on Germany without consulting Congress leaders, and purposefully withheld his postwar vision of India.[37] He believed that the Congress would understand the war as he did—that "they would share the same fears about German expansionism, the same need to defeat fascism, and would unquestioningly support the prioritization of war."[38] "Our moral case is so strong," he argued shortly after the outbreak of war, "it ought, I feel, to make an appeal to anyone who is prepared to approach it with an open mind."[39] To be sure, the Second World War profoundly affected Indian anti-colonialists. Fascism radicalized Britain's colonial ethos; it glorified racial violence. When war erupted between imperialist Britain and Nazi Germany, many in the Congress—including Nehru and Gandhi—instinctively supported Britain. At the same time, anti-colonialists could not sustain, or perpetuate, colonial oppression. Ultimately, the Congress resolved that its position would be determined by Chamberlain and the National Government. If Linlithgow relinquished the Raj and asseverated unconditional independence (after the war), the Congress would support the British war effort. Whitehall, however, refused to surrender the Raj, leaving the Congress with a difficult decision: "Cooperation, or non-cooperation which might eventually turn into confrontation."[40]

The Congress ultimately chose noncooperation. "For the last four years," Abul Kalam Azad declared during his presidential address (1940):

> The world resounded with cries of democracy and freedom. . . . But the moment India raised this question, the reality behind these utterances was unveiled. Now we are told that . . . safeguarding the freedom of nations is the aim of this war; but that this is confined within the geographical limits of Europe. The peoples of Asia and Africa should not dare to have any such hopes.[41]

Many Indian anti-fascists believed that fascism and liberal-imperialism were interrelated. As Indo-British newspapers detailed Nazi racial discrimination, signs saying "Whites Only" were on display in railway stations and waiting rooms across India.[42] Hazratgani, the "main thoroughfare of Lucknow, where glass-fronted shops lined the streets, and diners enjoyed the city's famous biryanis, was out of bounds to Indians during certain hours of the day and they were banned from walking on certain sections of the pavements."[43] Seen, moreover, from the outside-in, British nonintervention had facilitated fascist imperialism in Ethiopia, Spain, China, and Czechoslovakia. Whether fascist or imperialist, Neville Chamberlain, Benito Mussolini, and Adolf Hitler had negotiated the sovereignty of millions.[44] Now, anti-fascists contended, Whitehall implored colonies it had long-tormented to support a war for imperialist supremacy.

In 1942, the Imperial Japanese Army occupied British Burma (formerly part of the Raj). Fearing Indian collaboration, Whitehall dispatched Sir Stafford Cripps to negotiate Congress support of the British war effort. Cripps was a compelling intermediary. A Marxist and Labour MP, he maintained convivial relationships with Gandhi, Nehru, and several other Congress leaders. Cripps, however, did not guarantee independence, merely dominion status and the right to frame a constitution by the constituent assembly. Though sincere, his "haste, vagueness, and shifting position dashed all hopes to the ground."[45] As the *Bharatadevi* of Madras put it: "The proposed transfer of all power minus defence will be like playing Hamlet without the Prince of Denmark."[46] Like many European anti-fascists, Cripps harbored an unconscious imperialism. "There are many men in Europe," Ram Manohar Lohia argued, "who, in spite of all their sincere professions of racial equality, cannot rid themselves of the white man's burden. It is part of their sub-conscious make-up . . . Sir Stafford Cripps is one of them."[47] Cripps's proposals were ultimately too radical for Whitehall and too conservative for the Congress. Dominion status, Gandhi famously quipped, was "drawing a post-dated cheque on a crashing bank."[48]

After the failure of the Cripps Mission, the Congress gathered at Wardha and drafted a resolution demanding independence. Gandhi organized a Quit India civil disobedience campaign, urging all Indians "to go the fullest length under ahimsa. Complete deadlock by strikes and other non-violent means. Satyagrahis must go out to die not to live. They must seek and face death."[49] "We shall either free India," Gandhi proclaimed, "or die in the attempt."[50] The Raj swiftly responded. Gandhi, Nehru, and the CWC were arrested. The Indian Imperial Police seized property, censored newspapers, and imprisoned protestors. Colonial officials, Nehru contended during his trial at Gorakhpur Prison, "[had adopted] every disruptive and reactionary tendency . . . . [Their] forcible realisations of money for the war from even the poor of India, and their repeated affronts to Indian nationalism, are such that we can never forget them or ignore them."[51] Colonial officials transformed the Raj into a totalitarian regime—what many anti-colonialists decried as British fascism. The Defense of India Act (1939) invested policemen and civil servants with unprecedented power, and the state systematically deployed its security apparatus for internal defense.[52] Although resistance continued throughout the war, Congress anti-colonialists were incarcerated—cut off from the world—for nearly three years.

The Armed Conflict Which Nobody Wanted

Born Narendra Nath Bhattacharya, M. N. Roy grew up fascinated by the writings of Bankim Chandra Chattopadhyay and Swami Vivekananda. After the Partition of Bengal (1905), he participated in the national protests against British imperialism. During the First World War, the architects of the Indo-Germany Conspiracy ordered Roy to obtain foreign armaments and capital for a violent anti-colonial revolution. When the scheme foundered, Roy fled to Japan, where he crossed paths with Chinese Nationalist Sun Yat-sen (in exile after an abortive Guomindang revolution). Pursued by the *Kempeitai* (Japanese secret police), Roy fled to the United States—first California, then New York.

While at the New York Public Library, Roy developed an interest in the revolutionary oeuvre of Marx and Engels. Menaced, however, by British agents, Roy decamped to Mexico, where he was welcomed by President Venustiano Carranza. In 1919, Roy helped found the *Partido Comunista Mexicano* (Mexican Communist Party). Through these efforts, he came to shelter Mikhail Borodin—a prominent Comintern agent wanted by the US Secret Service. In discussions with Borodin, Ignazio Santibanez, Evelyn Trent, and others, Roy experienced an intellectual and philosophical awakening:

> Mexico was the land of my rebirth. It is true that before coming there I had begun to feel with ideas and ideals of my earlier life. But it was during my stay in Mexico that the new vision became clear and the dissatisfaction with a sterile past was replaced by a conviction to guide me in a more promising future. It was more than a change of political ideas and revolutionary ideals, I acquired a new outlook on life; there was a revolution in my mind—a philosophical revolution which knew no finality.[53]

In 1920, Borodin invited Roy to attend the Second World Congress of the Comintern. After publishing his *Preliminary Draft of Theses on the National and Colonial Questions,* Roy served on the Comintern's presidium for eight years and was a member of the Political Secretariat, the Executive Committee, and the World Congress.

In 1927, Joseph Stalin ordered Roy and Borodin to lead an agrarian revolution in China. Ideological dissidence between the Comintern and the CCP—exacerbated by Chiang Kai-shek's Northern Expedition and the outbreak of the Chinese Civil War—ultimately frustrated Roy's efforts.[54] He returned to Moscow in 1928, amid the dissolution of the United Opposition. Denied a meeting with Stalin, as well as treatment for an infected ear, Roy fled the Soviet Union and took refuge with Willi Münzenberg—one of the organizers of the League Against Imperialism.[55] Shortly thereafter, *The Inprecor*, a monthly Marxist magazine, announced Roy's expulsion from the Comintern.

In 1930, after almost twenty years abroad, Roy returned to India. Six months later, colonial police arrested and imprisoned him without a trial. Anti-colonialists later smuggled his written defense out of prison and published it with the title: *I Accuse! From the Suppressed Statement of Manabendra Nath Roy on Trial for Treason.* Roy's philippic condemned the illegality of his incarceration: "The law under which I am charged," he argued:

> Has no force of law in the modern civilized sense of the term. . . . The British government . . . is an instrument of predatory imperialism foisted upon this country by violence. There can be no progress, prosperity and liberty for the Indian people until this foreign domination is overthrown. The charge against me is absurd. This trial is a form of violence.[56]

Sentenced to six years in prison, Roy ultimately served five. Torturous living conditions inflicted lasting damage to his heart, kidneys, and ears.

While incarcerated, Roy followed political developments in Germany, Ethiopia, Japan, China, and the Soviet Union. During the Spanish Civil War, he criticized Anglo-French nonintervention, arguing—much like Indian anti-fascists—that it exhibited the interrelation between fascism and liberal-imperialism:

> How could the Blumians [followers of French prime minister Léon Blum] be such confounded fools! Don't they see that the noose is relentlessly closing on their own accursed necks, with the aid and connivance of the "democratic" powers, for the pleasure of whom they are selling their souls, and themselves assisting the rape of democracy? The French Republic is doomed, unless, some miracle happens. What could possibly save her when the African hordes of Franco would be on the Pyrenees to close up the ring. . . . This is the tragic result of the policy of kowtowing before those who found in non-intervention the most effective manner of helping the victory of Fascism in Spain.[57]

In November 1936, British imperial police discharged M. N. Roy from Dehra Dun prison. The INC immediately admitted him as a member.[58] The following year, during his presidential address at Faizpur, Jawaharlal Nehru welcomed "comrade M.N. Roy" as "one of the bravest and ablest of India's sons of the present generation," who "has just come to us after a long and most distressing period in prison."[59] At Nehru's request, Roy recovered in Allahabad, where he published a weekly newspaper, *Independent India.*

While in Allahabad, Roy had his first meeting with Mohandas K. Gandhi. Beforehand, Vallabhbhai Patel, Rajendra Prasad, and Bhulabhai Desai offered Roy an annual stipend and a seat on the CWC in exchange for his unqualified support of the Mahatma.[60] Roy refused and, after his meeting with Gandhi, resolved to challenge Congress orthodoxy. Months later, during a presidential address to the United Provinces Youth Conference in Sitapur, Roy made his position clear: "The revolt against imperialism is being miscarried simply because it has not been consciously backed up by a far-reaching revolt, a social revolt. Be the standard bearer of a social revolt, and you will qualify yourself for leading the struggle for national liberation more effectively than those wedded to an antiquated philosophy and a reactionary social outlook."[61] That same year, Gandhi recommended that Roy "render mute service"[62] to the campaign for Indian independence.

Roy founded the League of Radical Congressmen as a revolutionary soviet within the Congress. "We stand," he proclaimed during an AICC meeting in Bombay, "for a revolution inside the Congress, a revolution in outlook, a revolution in methods, a revolution in its structure—so that it can become the leader of the revolution which must take place in our country to establish the freedom needed for the progress and prosperity of the nation."[63] Roy modeled his revolution after the Jacobins of the French Revolution. He believed that a constituent assembly should seize power from the Indo-British bourgeoise (Gandhi and the Congress) and establish a democratic dictatorship to actualize—and defend—the revolutionary state. The Raj was an "old decayed structure: it is ugly; it is breeding filth and disease, vitiating the life of the whole nation."[64] Reform, Roy contended, would only perpetuate Indian enslavement. Emancipation required revolutionary violence.[65]

While serving on the Comintern's presidium, Roy lamented the rise of fascism. After his expulsion from the Soviet Union, he wrote several articles for *Gegen Den Strom* criticizing the Third Period "social-fascist" doctrine for fracturing leftist politics and discomfiting anti-fascist militancy: "While the official [Soviet] leaders furiously denounce 'right' opportunism, the real danger to threaten the international proletarian revolutionary movement lies in the surging development of fascism."[66] Roy contended that Stalin's "'putschist' tactics"[67] betrayed Leninist orthodoxy. Auguring the Dimitrov line at the Seventh World Congress, he urged the Comintern to organize latitudinous anti-fascist coalitions.[68]

Roy considered Mussolini and Hitler the denouement of philosophical reaction, or counterrevolution. Frightened by the inexorability of revolutionary activism, the bourgeoise radicalized Hegelian idealism and pseudo-scientific disciplines such as positivism, new-realism, and empiricism.[69] They united "the disillusioned petty-bourgeois masses in a fanatical army, demagogically led in the paradoxical crusade for galvanizing the chains of their own slavery."[70] Fascism, Roy contended, was reactionary violence unencumbered by "a logical system of ideology."[71] In recent years, scholars have convincingly argued that fascism possessed an intelligible—if not distinct—ideology. Like many Marxists, Roy almost exclusively analyzed socioeconomic structures, which fascists largely preserved. He ignored political, cultural, and spiritual transformations, reducing fascism (erroneously) to a manifestation of reactionary violence.[72] Its only purpose, Roy maintained, was "keeping their hands free to wield any weapon in their bloody crusade against forces making for the liberation of society from the vulgar materialism of capitalist civilization."[73]

Upon the outbreak of the Second World War, Roy understood fascism in less conventionally Marxist terms. His expulsion from the Soviet Union had precipitated a creeping disillusion with dialectical materialism.[74] After the war, he would develop a new philosophy, Radical Humanism, which "believed that a commonwealth of morally and spiritually liberated individual is the fundamental requirement for the realization of a better and healthier society."[75] In 1940, amid this metamorphosis from Marxism to Radical Humanism, Roy propounded a sui generis interpretation of the Second World War. It was not, he argued, an ideological struggle between British magnanimity and Nazi villainy— as many in England understood it—nor simply an internecine imperialist conflict, but rather an international civil war. Roy believed that neither Hitler nor Chamberlain wanted war. Germany demanded *lebensraum* in the East, not a pyrrhic struggle against a global empire. Similarly, if drawn into an Anglo-German conflict, the British government would likely be debilitated by the social, material, and imperial sacrifices necessary to prosecute such an arduous war. Even if successful, an enervated British Empire would be susceptible to anti-imperialist agitation. Roy maintained that the outbreak of the Second World War was an accident—the product of jingoistic rabidity, rather than a fascist conspiracy. By extending a defense guarantee to Poland, Whitehall inadvertently militarized the revolutionary crusade against fascism. This miscalculation, Roy argued, represented an opportunity to extirpate the twin evangelists of counterrevolution—fascism and imperialism. By supporting the British war effort, Indian anti-colonialists could obliterate political reactionism (fascism) while, at the same time, the vicissitudes of war would likely devitalize the British Empire. The Anglo-German War, Roy argued, was righteous, insomuch as its destructiveness would shatter European imperial hegemony and precipitate Indian independence.

Like the Comintern, Roy contended that the Anglo-German War did not pit fascist iniquity against democratic probity. The oppression and disenfranchisement of the British Empire belied any claim to rectitude, or even democracy: "Apart from the fundamental consideration that an imperialist State cannot be really democratic, the fact is that even parliamentary democracy has been practically abolished in England ever since the formation of the 'National Government [1931]."'[76] Roy believed that the governments of England and France harbored fascist proclivities. Immediately upon the outbreak of war, British prime minister Neville Chamberlain curtailed civil liberties and imprisoned thousands of suspected dissidents. Democracy, Roy argued, "was but a mere formality. Why discard it so long as it camouflaged totalitarianism in operation?"[77] Similarly, after the Molotov-Ribbentrop Non-Aggression Pact (1939), French prime minister Édouard Daladier—a former paraclete of the French Popular Front (1936–8)—outlawed the *Parti communiste français* and threatened its leaders with execution.[78] Both Britain and France, Roy maintained, were autocratic, or at the very least undemocratic. The war, consequently, was not an ideological struggle between fascism and democracy. Whitehall's incipient totalitarianism undermined Churchill's claim of "a war undertaken in the name of liberty."[79]

Unlike the Comintern, Roy contended that the Second World War was not an internecine imperialist conflict. Shortly after the German invasion of Poland, Stalin—in a meeting with Georgi Dimitrov, General Secretary of the Comintern—contended that "a war is on between two groups of capitalist countries . . . for the redivision of the world, for the domination of the world! We see nothing wrong in their having a good hard fight and weakening each other."[80] Roy dismissed this interpretation as "superficial."[81] Fascist states, he maintained, were not necessarily imperialistic; economic differences—the availability of capital, in particular—differentiated them. "Owing to their expansionist tendencies," Roy argued, "the Fascist States have been called imperialist States. But territorial expansion is not the characteristic feature of modern Imperialism. The United States of America is a typical, first-class, modern imperialist country; yet, to conquer colonies politically has not been, as a rule, its policy."[82] In Britain, France, and the United States, surplus capital for export animated imperialist expansion. Fascism, by contrast, seized power during a crisis of capitalism. In Germany, for example, the Nazi *Machtergreifung* occurred only after the global depression had popularly invalidated the Weimar Republic. After securing control of the state,

Hitler and the Nazis invested all surplus capital into revivifying the Wehrmacht. These expenditures, however, left them with scarcely any capital to purchase raw materials. Economic self-sustenance, Roy insisted, motivated German bellicosity: "Autarchy is the peculiar principle of Fascist economy . . . . Modern imperialism is the outcome of prosperity. Therefore, Fascist economy provides no foundation for modern imperialist expansion."[83] Nazi expansionism, he argued, "may be analogous to Roman Imperialism, but certainly not to British Imperialism."[84]

Roy believed that capitalist plenitude animated imperialism, while capitalist hardship precipitated fascism. This conclusion, as Mark Mazower and other scholars have demonstrated, too neatly dichotomized these ideologies. They were interrelated, as well as mutually constitutive.[85] Roy nevertheless insisted that they were complimentary. Germany and Britain, he argued, were not imperial competitors: "Instead of any rivalry, there has been a systematic cooperation between England and Germany ever since the signing of the Locarno Pact in 1924."[86] Roy maintained that Europe's leading imperialist rivalry was between France and Britain. France emerged from the Great War with "tremendous imperialist potentialities."[87] In a particularly baseless claim, Roy alleged that Whitehall countenanced the rise of Nazism in order to subvert French imperial hegemony. Neville Chamberlain, he argued, appeased Hitler in order to advance British foreign policy: "The Nazis triumphed in Germany, on the one hand, as an open challenge to the French military hegemony of Europe and, on the other hand, as the bulwark against the spread of Bolshevism. In both these respects, they were welcome to British diplomacy."[88] Using this specious analytical framework, Roy contended that the Anglo-German War was not—as Stalin maintained—an internecine capitalist-imperialist conflict. Chamberlain and the British government had encouraged fascist pugnacity:

> It is well known how, ever since the invasion of Abyssinia, England refused to raise a finger to resist repeated Fascist aggressions. In every single occasion of those successive acts of aggression—Abyssinia, Spain, Austria, Czechoslovakia— England could call a halt if she wanted. Terribly alarmed by the growing military power of Germany, and also by the expansionist policy of Italy, France would have readily joined England in any action against Fascist aggression. Then, the Soviet Union was always there, ready to throw in her weight on the side of democracy and freedom. Yet, it was British diplomacy which did not allow any concerted anti-Fascist action.[89]

The rise of Germany destabilized Europe's traditional balance of power. It transformed France, Britain's leading imperialist rival, into a middling power subservient to British diplomacy. "Fascism," Roy argued, "instead of being a new rival to British Imperialism, has served as an instrument in its hand."[90]

Roy's critiques of inside-out and orthodox-Marxist interpretations were misleading, if not erroneous. However, at the same time he (spuriously) criticized others, Roy propounded a novel—and occasionally incisive—understanding of the war. In the tradition of Marx and Hegel, he contended that history proceeded in stages and, accordingly, that historical epochs determined the character of a war. Those waged in the age of bourgeois revolutions established or defended the national state; those fought in the era of New Imperialist expansion colonized "uncivilised" nations; and those undertaken in the epoch of universal capitalist prosperity expanded Western empires. Finally, Roy argued, capitalism "decays, and the world enters into the period of revolution. The wars in that period usually prepare the ground for impending revolutions; therefore, in that period, capitalist States do not deliberately prepare for an armed conflict among themselves."[91] Roy believed that wars waged in the era of revolution undermined capitalist hegemony. To preserve the existing order, liberal-imperialist and fascist governments eschewed conflict; Chamberlain thus appeased Hitler.

With some notable exceptions, the British aristocracy suppressed progressive and revolutionary forces—anti-imperialism, liberalism, socialism, and feminism, to name just a few. According to Roy, British conservatives understood that, in the course of an Anglo-German War, counterrevolutionary forces in both nations would be destroyed. They thus schemed to obviate any conflict. After the German invasion of Poland, however, Whitehall had little recourse but to declare war on fascism. Nazi truculency compelled Britain to extend a defense guarantee to Poland, which Hitler promptly violated. This blunder, Roy argued, accidentally obtruded a revolutionary war upon the counterrevolutionary British government:

> German troops marched into Poland before her protectors had sanctioned her violation. That was bad manners; the Nazis had been very useful, but they should not be allowed to become too much of a nuisance. They should be taught to behave. But the halt was called when it was too late. Meanwhile, the Poles had spoiled the delicate situation irreparably. Unexpectedly, they had taken into their head to resist German invasion. The fat was on the fire. The situation was out of hand. For the sake of prestige, England had to declare war, and France had no option but to follow suit. An accidental combination of circumstances provoked the armed conflict which nobody wanted.[92]

Anticipating the scholarship of A. J. P. Taylor, Roy contended that, rather than a Manichean struggle or archetypal imperialist conflict, the Second World War was an accident—one possible outcome after more than a decade of nationalist bluster.[93] Progressives had long combatted counterrevolutionary forces. This struggle took place within each country and around the world; it was, as Roy maintained, an international civil war. By invading Poland, Hitler inadvertently militarized this conflict. He forced Whitehall to join with revolutionary forces in annihilating the "most dangerous spearhead of international counterrevolution, namely, Fascism."[94]

Roy contended that because the Anglo-German War erupted in the age of revolution—in defiance of the machinations of counterrevolutionary forces—it would undermine capitalist-imperialist hegemony. Indeed, seen from the outside-in, the Second World War was revolutionary, even as its primary belligerents were reactionary: "When neighbouring countries are armed to the teeth . . . armed conflicts of more or less serious nature may be precipitated by . . . some unfortunate miscalculation. That sort of war, however, is not an imperialist war; it is an internecine conflict, bound to weaken both the parties involved and thus open the floodgates of revolution."[95] Capitalist-imperialist cupidity had exploited non-Western nations for more than a century. After European colonizers conquered much of Africa, Asia, and the Americas, they turned their predatory gaze inward, upon each other. The First World War, Roy argued, produced capitalist-imperialist prosperity (Britain and France) and rancorous capitalist decline (Italy and Germany). In due course, the latter embraced autarchic expansionism—or fascism—and terrorized the victorious imperialists with a calamitous civil war. At long last, Roy maintained, a primordial struggle heralded the end of European hegemony. Wielding industrialized weaponry, Europe's great powers would destroy one another: "It is the type of conflict," Roy argued, "which marks the turning points of history. It is the paroxysm of death of a doomed social order and, at the same time, the birth-pang of a new."[96]

Roy believed that after the Second World War India would enter into an age of revolution. The essential precondition, however, was the eradication of fascism. Indeed, a peremptory Nazi triumph would sanctify political reactionism; a pyrrhic British victory, by contrast, would extirpate fascism and, in all likelihood, subvert British imperial hegemony. Fervent, perhaps even monomaniacal in his pursuit of the latter, Roy urged progressive forces around the world to support the British war effort: "It is a war for the future of the world. If the British Government happens to be a party to this war, why should the fighters for human liberty be ashamed of congratulating it for this meritorious deed, perhaps inadvertently committed, and recognise it is an ally in a noble cause."[97] For more than a decade, Indian anti-fascists had grappled with the quandary of a potential Anglo-German War. Should they support Britain—fortifying the imperial Moloch that had plundered the subcontinent—or Nazi Germany, whose racialized animus radicalized British imperialism? Roy circumvented this dilemma by contending that a British victory would result in the destruction of its empire. In an era where many anti-colonialists struggled to repudiate both British imperialism and German fascism, Roy argued that to be anti-imperialist was to support the self-destructive impulse of British anti-fascism: "Are we, then, to support imperialism? The question is altogether irrelevant. Here is an occasion wherein astute fighters for freedom and democracy can push Imperialism perhaps to the extent of destroying the bloodiest weapon of its own creation, and thus rendering itself vulnerable to the coming revolutionary onslaught."[98]

After Gandhi inaugurated his Quit India campaign, British imperial police imprisoned thousands of anti-colonialists. Owing to his ardent anti-fascism, Roy was exempted.[99] Colonial officials nevertheless distrusted his support of the British war effort: "The short-sighted and die-hard reactionaries who still happen to be the rulers of this country, often tell us: 'You are anti-fascist; that is alright. But what about Russia?'"[100] Imperialists in both England and India loathed Bolshevism. These "purblind gentlemen," Roy argued, failed to see the Soviet Union as a potential anti-fascist ally: "Those who, throughout the world really wish the defeat of Fascism and save the world from a relapse into barbarism, must enter into an alliance with the Soviet Union."[101] Roy believed that until Whitehall embraced the revolutionary potency of the Soviet Union, Nazi soldiers would overwhelm Europe. "If I can support the British war effort," he reasoned, "British imperialists can support the Soviet Union."

~

In 1928, after his failed mission to China, Roy returned to Moscow amid the power struggle between Lenin, Leon Trotsky, and Grigory Zinoviev. Isolated, and increasingly fearful for his safety, Roy absconded to Germany, where he attributed his fall from grace to the misadventure in China as well as his (often vociferous) critiques of Comintern policy. He had denounced Bolshevik Eurocentrism, Stalin's agglomeration of power, and the program—reconstituted since the publication of *Supplementary Theses*—of supporting anti-colonial nationalist movements such as the Congress:

> I consider this policy to be a fatal mistake, and, therefore, have criticized it as such. This is the cause of my expulsion, from the Communist International. I have been expelled from the Communist International not only owing to

my opposition to its present Indian policy; I have taken a leading part in the opposition to the entire policy of the present leadership of C.I. [Communist International]."[102]

Across Europe, thousands of former socialists marched under fascist banners. The Comintern meanwhile quibbled over policy. It was preoccupied, Roy argued, with bureaucratic and vainglorious self-interest, and had "become the greatest internal menace to the Proletarian Revolution."[103]

More than a decade after Roy's expulsion from the Comintern, the doctors of the Congress-sponsored medical mission to China met with communist leader Mao Zedong. During their conversation, Mao asked: "What is Loy doing?"[104] Confused, the doctors replied that they did not know anyone by that name. Mao went on to describe the Shanghai Massacre and the Defense of Wuhan, before again mentioning Mr. Loy—the tall Indian representative of the Communist International. One of the doctors, B. K. Basu, remembered "that in Chinese 'R' was pronounced as 'L' . . . I enquired 'Are you referring to M.N. Roy? He has recently been released from a long imprisonment and is now working with Pandit Nehru' . . . Mao listened and made a mild understatement. 'A lot of damage was done to the great revolution.'"[105]

Roy was a brilliant, contumacious revolutionary who experienced astonishing successes and, as Mao noted, disconcerting failures.[106] He devoted himself to proletarianism, yet refused to make any of the compromises Stalin, Mao, and Nehru considered necessary. A contemporary of Gandhi, he never possessed a similar following. It "was always Gandhi and never Roy who dominated the Indian nationalist movement."[107] Upon the outbreak of war, Roy mischaracterized fascism as an exclusively reactionary phenomenon and discounted the consanguinity between fascism and liberal-imperialism. To be sure, Roy criticized the persecution, cupidity, inequality, and racism of both phenomena. He simply understood them as a divergent articulation of capitalist prosperity (imperialism) or torpidity (fascism). This misleading contention discounted the uneasiness—and at times, antipathy—between the British and German governments. They were, as inside-out scholarship has ably demonstrated, inimical.[108]

While Roy faltered in his assessment of what the war was not, he propounded a fascinating interpretation of the Second World War that reconciled the tension between Indian anti-imperialism and British anti-fascism. Seen from the outside-in, the Anglo-German War would shatter European hegemony and precipitate Indian independence; it was revolutionary, even as its primary belligerents were counterrevolutionary. Roy was wrong about many things, but about this he was right. In 1945, a grueling Allied victory rendered Europe's imperial powers economically, politically, and morally insolvent. Although anything but ineluctable, India attained independence two years later. Roy's analysis was, and remains, a stunning achievement.

A Matter of Life and Death

In 1189, the Holy Roman Emperor, Frederick I Barbarossa, inaugurated the Third Crusade against Saladin's Muslim armies in Jerusalem. Seven hundred years later, Hitler and the Wehrmacht "embarked on a fresh crusade, this time against the Soviet Union, the heartland of hated Bolshevism."[109] In place of Frederick I's ironclad knights, Hitler deployed panzers, aircraft, and armored infantry. Never "before or since had there been a war like this one."[110]

In a radio broadcast on the day of the invasion, British prime minister Winston Churchill claimed that Nazi ambitions encompassed India:

> So now this bloodthirsty guttersnipe must launch his mechanized armies upon new fields of slaughter, pillage and devastation. . . . And even the carnage and ruin which his victory, should he gain it—though he's not gained it yet—will bring upon the Russian people, will itself be only a stepping stone to the attempt to plunge four or five hundred millions who live in China and the three-hundred fifty million who live in India into that bottomless pit of human degradation over which the diabolic emblem of the swastika flaunts itself. It is not too much to say here this pleasant summer evening that the lives and happiness of a thousand million additional human beings are now menaced with brutal Nazi violence.[111]

Churchill's magniloquence was intended, in part, to secure Indian support for the British war effort.[112] Soviet Russia's capaciousness, however—to say nothing of its pertinacious defense—increasingly overwhelmed the Wehrmacht. Far from "carnage and ruin," India functioned as "an extended British sphere . . . in which some subjects could find sanctuary."[113] Colonialists, in particular, "felt indulged and fortunate compared to their relatives in Britain. Here they were protected by large whitewashed villas, long lawns, servants and drivers, and could acquire all manner of goods on the black market."[114]

After Operation Barbarossa, Congress anti-colonialists approached the war in one of two ways. First, Gandhian nationalists—and even many Marxists— protested the conflict. To be sure, many anti-colonialists sympathized with the Allied war against fascism. Nehru even asseverated its revolutionary character: "The world war is obviously part of a great revolution that is taking place throughout the world. . . . These aggressors are out to impose a tyranny far worse than any that has existed and therefore in any event they should be opposed."[115] Anti-colonialists nevertheless believed that a British victory would fortify—perhaps even enlarge—the Raj. Many in the Congress, including Gandhi, had supported Britain during the First World War. Afterward, the League of Nations' mandate system facilitated British imperial expansion in West Asia.[116] Congress anti-colonialists would not be manipulated again. "It would be ridiculous," J. B. Kripalani argued, "for a slave country to take up cudgels for the liberty of other nations."[117]

For years, Indian anti-fascists contended that British nonintervention in Ethiopia, Spain, China, and Czechoslovakia had emboldened fascist aggression. British prime ministers Stanley Baldwin and Neville Chamberlain had invoked the New Imperialist covenant—the collaborative yet adversarial entente that precluded continental war—in order to preserve the British imperial hegemony. Inevitably, however, the bellicosity intrinsic to both fascism and liberal-imperialism escalated beyond control. For imperialism, but particularly fascism, conquest begot evermore conquest. By countenancing fascist expansionism, Ram Manohar Lohia argued, Whitehall precipitated the global war that now threatened its existence: "British foreign policy must also be held responsible for encouraging the forces of evil as in the Italo-Ethiopian, Spanish and China-Japan wars and, thus, for hastening a world war. India, therefore, can have nothing to do with a war whose object may in any way be the continuance either of imperialism or fascism."[118] Compelled—by circumstances, colonial officials, and the vicissitudes of war—to support fascism or liberal-imperialism, the Congress instead demanded that the British Quit India.[119] "The time has come," Nehru argued, "to put an end to the idea of empire . . . India must be accepted and treated as a free country on terms of equality. Any other course leads to conflict and misfortune for all concerned."[120]

A second, much smaller group of Congress anti-colonialists saw the war as an opportunity to topple the Raj. Most famously, the Axis powers furnished Subhas Bose with material and military resources for an anti-imperialist invasion of India. In an Azad Hind radio broadcast from Berlin, Bose averred that all Indians should exploit the conflict in order to advance anti-imperialist interests: "The three [Axis] Powers are determined to defeat and destroy British imperialism. It is the task of the rising generation of the Indian people . . . to utilize the present international crisis to the fullest extent, so that out of the ashes of the British Empire may rise a free and liberated India."[121] Debates have since arisen over whether Bose was fascist.[122] Like Rash Behari Bose, Mohan Singh, and other opportunist anti-colonialists, Bose hoped the Anglo-German War would debilitate, or fracture, the British Empire. He sought independence at any cost.[123]

Roy criticized both approaches. Rather than support the British war effort—and the eradication of the British Empire—Congress anti-colonialists organized vainglorious protests or joined with the apotheosis of counterrevolution. "It is not permissible," Roy argued:

> For the fighters for democracy and freedom, not only in Europe, but throughout the world, including India, to be indifferent about the outcome of the conflict and its possible developments. . . . No sensible person can talk of freedom and democracy, and at the same time not admit that the fall of Hitlerism and the elimination of the Fascist menace in general will greatly contribute to the triumph of the cause of freedom and democracy."[124]

Roy quit the Congress in 1940. To a certain extent, he never belonged in it. He had long contemned Gandhian nonviolence. After his resignation, Roy reorganized the League of Radical Congressmen—previously a subsidiary within the Congress—into the independent Radical Democratic Party (RDP). Like Roy, members publicly criticized Gandhi's Quit India campaign. After renouncing the Congress, Kunwar Anand Singh, Chief Whip of the Congress Assembly in the United Provinces, denounced the "succession of blunders which has reduced the once powerful mass organisation to its present helpless state of demoralization and disintegration."[125] In a letter to Singh, Nehru pithily responded: "Clearly a person who thinks or has thought, as you do, has no place in an organisation like the Congress."[126]

In speeches and demonstrations across India, Roy contended that the Quit India Movement betrayed Indian anti-imperialism.[127] For nearly a decade, the Congress had propounded an anti-fascist and anti-imperialist foreign policy. Nehru, Gandhi, and others staged protest marches, organized medical missions, and visited war-torn nations. Upon the outbreak, however, of the Anglo-German War, the Congress espoused isolationism. It forsook anti-fascist internationalism, Roy argued, in order to advance nationalist anti-colonialism:

> For many years, along with all progressive elements throughout the world, the Indian nationalist movement was opposed to Fascism. Time and again, Congress expressed their abhorrence for this menace to human civilization, and passed resolutions condemning Fascist aggression and sympathizing with

the victims of Fascism. From press and platform, the British Government was accused for conniving with the Fascist dictators, for betraying democracy in Spain, in China, in Czechoslovakia. . . . When at last this war broke out, Fascism had already grown so strong that it appeared to be almost too late. When France surrendered, it appeared that Fascism would conquer the whole of Europe and perhaps the whole of the world. At that moment, it was imperative for all the fighters for freedom, democracy and progress throughout the world to pool all their resources for a desperate effort to defeat the Fascist monster, because a victory of Fascism, or even appeasement on the terms of the Fascist dictators, would make the whole world a victim of Fascist terror and brutalization, and would throw back humanity into the dark ages of medievalism. If we have condemned Fascist aggression in Spain, in China, Austria and Czechoslovakia and sympathized with the victims, and even supported them to the extent of sending men and money and medical aid, why should our attitude suddenly change in the present gigantic fight against the bulwark of Fascism in Europe?[128]

Roy claimed that the Anglo-German War exhibited the opportunism of Congress's anti-fascism. For years, anti-colonialists contended that fascism radicalized the racism, exploitation, and violence of British colonialism. "The British Empire is imperialist," Nehru claimed during the Sudetenland Crisis, "and that encloses fascism."[129] Yet when these political ideologies warred against one another, Congress retreated into nationalist isolation. Quit India, Roy argued, was "the height of selfishness . . . which is shameful on the part of the people who profess to cherish the high ideals of freedom and progress."[130]

Roy vilified Congress leadership. He considered Gandhi a counterrevolutionary charlatan that sustained class inequality by impeding revolutionary violence: "With all its pompous verbiage, the theory essentially is: 'Let us spin and pray (at the shrine of the Mahatma): once the fat is one fire, something will happen by itself.' It will not."[131] Roy similarly denounced Nehru as an ideological dilettante—an opportunist willfully co-opted by Gandhian spiritualism. In 1926, the World Congress of the League against Imperialism—an auxiliary to the Comintern to which Roy belonged—elected Nehru president. "That accident (it was an accident)," Roy argued during the Second World War, "won for Nehru the reputation of being a Communist, and as such held in high esteem in Moscow."[132] In practice, however, "Nehru's 'progressive Socialism' is hardly to be distinguished from Hitler's National-Socialism."[133] Roy alleged that Nehru safeguarded Gandhian traditionalism by shrouding it in progressivism. This synthesis between nationalism (Gandhi) and socialism (Nehru) animated

Congress politics, and attracted Indians too timorous to incite a violent proletarian revolution.[134]

Roy also denounced those Indians—Subhas Bose, in particular—who supported the Axis powers. If the Nazis conquered England, Roy argued, it would not destroy the Raj. In an emergency, colonial administrators would declare themselves "Indian" and defend the imperial state against foreign invaders. It was preposterous, Roy contended, to presume that colonialists would simply relinquish the machinery of imperialism: "[British India] will be weakened only to the extent of being isolated from the Metropolis. That will be no weakening, much less a break-down. Because, for all practical purposes, the Imperialist State in India is an independent power. For defending itself, particularly against an internal revolt, it does not count upon any help from England."[135] Roy maintained that all freedom-loving Indians, rather than support the Axis powers or practice noncooperation, should support the British war effort. Democracy and revolution were not antithetical. The age of capitalist exploitation was near its end. Britain would evolve—embrace true democracy—or perish. "We do not propose to defend India for British imperialism," Roy contended, "all these considerations are not matters of intellectual gymnastics, but of practical politics. It is a matter of life and death."[136]

~

While a member of the Comintern, Roy developed a theory of decolonization— he was one of the first to use the word—which informed his criticisms of Gandhi and the Congress. He contended that as British imperial hegemony attenuated, and the export of Indian capital declined, colonialists would vouchsafe the imperial leviathan into the neocolonial hands of the Indian bourgeoisie. Congress-led independence, he argued, would not be revolutionary—nor even emancipatory—merely a transfer of power:

> In due course a peaceful transfer of political power to Indian hands would take place—not through the magic of soul-force nor out of the democratic convictions of the British ruling class, but by virtue of a shift of economic power. And it followed that as regards the real problem of the revolution, that transfer of power would mean nothing. The old order would remain, only the personnel at the top would change.[137]

Roy believed that the Congress was anti-British but not revolutionary. Nehru, in particular, manipulated Gandhi's popularity in order to accumulate political power. He created, Roy argued, "a beautiful synthesis . . . between the spiritualist philosophy of Gandhism and the secular politics of the Parliamentary Board."[138] Roy maintained that this synthesis sought dominance, not hegemony.[139] Led by the Congress, India would not attain independence, but instead bear witness as the neocolonial "parliamentary chariot" guided "Marwari merchants and Gujarati cotton manufacturers . . . into the paradise of prosperity."[140]

After the failed China expedition, Roy submitted his decolonization thesis to the Comintern. It was criticized at the Sixth Congress of the Comintern (1928) and led in part to his expulsion from the Soviet Union. More than a decade later, during the Second World War, Roy believed the Congress had (once again) substantiated his theory. For nearly two years, he had contended that even as its belligerents were imperialist, the Anglo-German War would shatter European imperial hegemony and precipitate Indian independence. Operation Barbarossa, Roy maintained, further evinced the war's emancipatory character. Discounting—problematically, to be sure—Stalinist autocracy, Roy argued that after extirpating Nazism, the Soviet Union would support progressive movements such as Indian anti-imperialism.[141] The Congress, however, espoused nationalist isolationism. The Quit India campaign, Roy contended, precluded a revolutionary Indo-Soviet alliance, and was thus counterrevolutionary: "But to continue that policy of non-co-operation even now [after Operation Barbarossa], will be helping Fascism against the Soviet Union. Are there Indians who would claim the distinction of being fighters for freedom, and yet place themselves in that position of shame?"[142] Roy alleged that the Congress had forsaken its revolutionary mandate. It had betrayed a righteous war against counterrevolution, just as it would inevitably betray Indian independence.

Lie-Hunting Is My Profession

While in Mexico, Roy frequented a café along the Avenida de Madero, in Mexico City.[143] In his memoirs, he recounted an incident in which "a tall handsome Negro walked in, accompanied by a young woman belonging to the white race."[144] Roy later discovered this was Jack Johnson—the brilliant American pugilist who had fled the United States to avoid prosecution under the Mann Act.[145] After locating a seat in the bustling café, the couple sat down. "They sat for quite some time," Roy later recalled, "but none came to serve them."[146] Eventually, they beckoned a server. After a prickly exchange, the couple departed. Incensed, Roy resolved to boycott the café. However, as he rose from his table, a group of police officers arrived and demanded that the manager personally serve Johnson. The manager equivocated, until he was reminded that "he was in Mexico where the black man was as good as the whitest of the white."[147] Afterward, Johnson stood up and "with a broad, frank smile that must have shamed the insolent white man, shook [the manager's] hand and said: 'Pardon me for all the trouble, Mr. Sanborn.'"[148] As Johnson exited the café, a "riotously cheering crowd"[149] hoisted him atop its shoulders.[150]

Roy had all the trappings of an outstanding Indian revolutionary. He was imaginative, incisive, and profound. A contemporary of Lenin, Gandhi, Horkheimer, Stalin, and Mao, he served on the presidium of the Comintern and helped found both the Mexican Communist Party and the Communist Party of India. While imprisoned (1931–6), an "international campaign for his release drew support from Jawaharlal Nehru, Albert Einstein, and Roger Baldwin, the founder of the ACLU."[151] Roy, however, never captured the imagination of subaltern India. He "would struggle for decades to gain power in India and fail";[152] Gandhi, meanwhile "acquired authority quickly and kept it."[153] Together, Roy and Gandhi inhabited antipodal ends of the anti-colonial spectrum. A brash, cerebral communist, Roy pursued a violent proletarian revolution. Gandhi, by contrast, anchored his conception of independence (swaraj) in nonviolent religious traditionalism. Roy has popularly—and in my opinion, unjustly—been forgotten, while Gandhi is universally—and occasionally problematically—adored. Of course, Roy's political, popular, and cultural marginalization was often his own fault. He was obdurate, astringent, and at least until later in life, supercilious. He was never hoisted atop the shoulders of his contemporaries. "Lie-hunting," he once argued, "is my profession. This is a thankless job. . . . It has not won me popularity."

Upon the outbreak of the Second World War, Roy inhabited the radical periphery of the Indian independence movement. He wrote penetrating, often trenchant, critiques of the Indian National Congress, yet never attracted a mass following—particularly after he declined to join Subhas Bose's Forward Bloc. Many of Roy's wartime dialectics were erroneous, if not specious. We must be cautious not to elevate one particularly incisive strand of Roy's oeuvre while, at the same time, ignoring the balance. Roy mischaracterized fascism as a reactionary phenomenon and misrepresented its relationship with imperialism. Additionally, his contention that the Second World War pitted revolutionary interests against capitalist-imperialist hegemony oversimplified several of the belligerents. The Allies, in particular, were both an opportunistic imperialist alliance and a revolutionary international coalition. Finally, the divergent wartime paths of Indian anti-colonialists did not necessarily reflect reactionary politics, nor vainglory—though in specific instances those elements existed—but rather the larger difficulty of navigating a war between fascism and liberal-imperialism. Seen from India, there appeared only three approaches to the conflict. Loyalists, including the Princes and the Muslim League, fortified the British Empire in its Manichean war against Nazism; Bose and other opportunists allied with fascism in an abortive attempt to topple liberal-imperialism; and the Congress, rather than support either of Europe's "blood brothers,"[154] protested the conflict. In each instance, these were difficult decisions, not—as Roy contended—a consequence of megalomania.

Despite these and other limitations, Roy propounded a compelling interpretation of the Anglo-German War. He supported Britain, confident that a pyrrhic British victory would debilitate the Raj and precipitate Indian independence. It was a controversial, audacious hypothesis that was ultimately corroborated by postwar events. Until recently, scholarship examining the outbreak of the Second World War has characterized it as a "good war," or—as Marxists have argued—an internecine imperialist conflict. Roy's analysis should be considered alongside these narratives. Seen from the outside-in, the Anglo-German War pitted Europe's imperialist great powers against one another, yet was still revolutionary insomuch as it augured an era of decolonization. In the years before the Second World War, European empires often appeared unassailable. A "futuristic novel set in 1957, in which maniac Indians turned on their British masters 100 years after the mutiny, only to be crushed by the power of aerial bombardment, could still be published without any irony in Britain in the 1930s."[155] Independence appeared on the horizon but was far from the inexorable march depicted in popular literature. In this context, Roy urged all Indians to support the British war effort in order to destroy the British Empire.

Notes

1 M. N. Roy, "Circular to the League of Radical Congressmen," August 17, 1940, M. N. Roy Papers, Nehru Memorial Museum and Library (hereafter NMML), Part I Section I, 90/1/1940-1942, 2.

2 Rabindranath Tagore, *Crisis in Civilization* (Calcutta: Visva-Bharati, 1950), 2. Tagore's writing is in the public domain.

3 Sheila Fitzpatrick, *The Russian Revolution* (Oxford: Oxford University Press 1982), 94–120.

4 Samaren Roy, *M.N. Roy: A Political Biography* (New Delhi: Orient Longman, 1997), 3–7.

5 Ibid., vii.

6 Ibid., 89. After giving Roy the preliminary draft, Angelica Balavanova—the first General Secretary of the Communist International—told Roy: "Young man, you have reason to be proud: but don't lose your head. I wish you luck." Roy, *M.N. Roy*, 89.

7 Ibid.

8 Ibid.

9 M. N. Roy, *Nationalism: An Antiquated Cult* (Bombay: Radical Democratic Party, 1942), xvi.

10 M. N. Roy, *M.N. Roy's Memoirs* (New York: Allied Publishers, 1964), 379.

11 Ramachandra Guha, *Gandhi: The Years That Changed the World, 1914–1948* (New York: Alfred A. Knopf, 2018), 618–700.

12 M. N. Roy, *Nationalism: An Antiquated Cult*, xvi.

13 Ali Raza, *Revolutionary Pasts: Communist Internationalism in Colonial India* (Cambridge: Cambridge University Press, 2020), 86–98.

14 Winston Churchill, *The Second World War, Volume 1: The Gathering Storm* (New York: Houghton Mifflin Company, 1948); Alan Bullock, *Hitler: A Study in Tyranny* (New York: Harper Perennial, 1952); Paul Kennedy, *The Rise and Fall of the Great Powers* (New York: Random House, 1989); R. J. Q. Adams, *British Politics and Foreign Policy in the Age of Appeasement, 1935–39* (Stanford University Press, 1993); Tim Kirk and Anthony McElligott, *Opposing Fascism: Community, Authority and Resistance in Europe* (Cambridge: Cambridge University Press, 1999); Robert Caputi, *Neville Chamberlain and Appeasement* (Selinsgrove, PA: Susquehanna University Press, 2000); Jon Lake, *The Battle of Britain* (Leicester: Silverdale, 2000). Ian Kershaw, *Making Friends with Hitler: Lord Londonderry, the Nazis, and the Road to War* (New York: The Penguin Group, 2004); Peter Neville, *Hitler and Appeasement: The British Attempt to Prevent the Second World War* (London: Hambledon & London, 2007); Mark Mazower, *Dark Continent: Europe's Twentieth Century* (London: Penguin Books, 2008); Ashley Jackson, *The British Empire and the Second World War* (London: Hambledon Continuum, 2008); Andrew D. Stewart, *Empire Lost Britain, the Dominions and the Second World War* (London: Continuum, 2008); Frank McDonough, *Hitler, Chamberlain and Appeasement* (Cambridge: Cambridge University Press, 2011); Susan R. Grayzel, *At Home and Under Fire: Air Raids and Culture in Britain from the Great War to the Blitz* (Cambridge: Cambridge University Press, 2012); Andrew Roberts, *The Holy Fox: The Life of Lord Halifax* (London: Head of Zeus, 2014); Robin Prior, *When Britain Saved The West: The Story of 1940* (Yale: Yale University Press, 2015); Garry Campion, *The Good Fight: Battle of Britain Propaganda and the Few* (London:

Palgrave Macmillan, 2016); David Reynolds, "Britain, the Two World Wars, and the Problem of Narrative," *The Historical Journal* 60, no. 1 (2017): 197–231; Alexander, Amanda. "The 'Good War': Preparations for a War against Civilians," *Law, Culture and the Humanities* 15, no. 1 (2019): 227–52; Jonathan Fennell, *Fighting the People's War: The British and Commonwealth Armies and the Second World War* (Cambridge: Cambridge University Press, 2019).

15 Joseph Stalin, *On the Great Patriotic War of the Soviet Union* (Moscow: Foreign Languages Publishing House, 1946); See Nina Tumarkin, *The Living and the Dead: The Rise and Fall of the Cult of World War II in Russia* (New York: Basic Books, 1994); Nurit Schleifman, *Russia at a Crossroads: History, Memory and Political Practice* (London: Frank Cass, 1998); Tim Rees, and Andrew Thorpe, *International Communism and the Communist International, 1919–1943* (Manchester: Manchester University Press, 1999); Catherine Merridale, *Ivan's War: Life and Death in the Red Army, 1939–1945* (New York: Picador, 2007); Robert Service, *Comrades: A History of World Communism* (Cambridge: Harvard University Press, 2007); Chris Bellamy, *Absolute War: Soviet Russia in the Second World War* (New York: Vintage Books, 2008); Geoffrey Roberts, *Stalin's Wars: From World War to Cold War, 1939–1953* (Yale University Press, 2008); Teddy Uldricks, "War, Politics and Memory: Russian Historians Reevaluate the Origins of World War II," *History and Memory* 21, no. 2 (2009): 60–82; Laurence Rees, *World War II Behind Closed Doors: Stalin, the Nazis and the West* (New York: Vintage Books, 2010); Lee Baker, *The Second World War on the Eastern Front* (Abingdon: Routledge, 2013); Silvio Pons, and Allan Cameron, *The Global Revolution: A History of International Communism 1917–1991* (Oxford: Oxford University Press, 2014); Jeff Rutherford, *Combat and Genocide on the Eastern Front: The German Infantry's War, 1941–194* (Cambridge: Cambridge University Press, 2014); B. Gorbachevskiĭ, David M. Glantz, and Stuart Britton, *Through the Maelstrom: A Red Army Soldier's War on the Eastern Front, 1942–1945* (Lawrence: University Press of Kansas, 2015).

16 Francis G. Hutchins, *India's Revolution, Gandhi, and the Quit India Movement* (Cambridge: Harvard University Press, 1973); Johannes H. Voigt, *India in the Second World War* (Atlantic Highlands, NJ: Humanities Press International, 1988); Peter Ward Fay, *The Forgotten Army: India's Armed Struggle for Independence, 1942–1945* (Ann Arbor: University of Michigan Press, 1993); Shashi Tharoor, *Nehru: The Invention of India* (New York: Arcade Publishers, 2003); Ashley Jackson, *The British Empire and the Second World War* (London: Hambledon Continuum, 2007); Joyce Lebra, *The Indian National Army and Japan* (Singapore: Institute of Southeast Asian Studies, 2008); Madhusree Mukerjee, *Churchill's Secret War: The British Empire and the Ravaging of India during World War II* (New York: Basic Books, 2010); Mithi Mukherjee, *India in the Shadows of Empire: A Legal and Political History (1774–1950)* (New Delhi: Oxford University Press, 2012);

Kaushik Roy, *The Indian Army in the Two World Wars* (Leiden, The Netherlands: Brill, 2012); Yasmin Khan, *India at War: The Subcontinent and the Second World War* (Oxford: Oxford University Press, 2015); Warren Dockter, *Churchill and the Islamic World Orientalism, Empire and Diplomacy in the Middle East* (London: Tauris, 2015); Srinath Raghavan, *India's War: World War II and the Making of Modern South Asia* (New York: Basic Books, 2016); Kaushik Roy, *India and World War II: War, Armed Forces, and Society, 1939–45* (New Delhi: Oxford University Press, 2016); Srinath Raghavan, "Building the Sinews of Power: India in the Second World War," *Journal of Strategic Studies* 42, no. 5 (2019): 577–99; Urvi Khaitan, "Women Beneath the Surface: Coal and the Colonial State in India during the Second World War," *War & Society* 39, no. 3 (2020): 171–88; Ananta Kumar Giri, ed. *Mahatma Gandhi and Sri Aurobindo* (New Delhi: Routledge, 2021); Dinyar Patel, "'One Man Lobby'? Propaganda, Nationalism in the Diaspora, and the India League of America During the Second World War," *The Journal of Imperial and Commonwealth History* 49, no. 6 (2021): 1110–40.

17 Richard Overy, *Blood and Ruins: The Great Imperial War, 1931–1945* (London: Penguin Books, 2021).

18 M. N. Roy, *War and Revolution: International Civil War* (Madras: Radical Democratic Party, 1942), 37–8. Although published in 1942, Roy wrote much of *War and Revolution* before Operation Barbarossa.

19 Yasmin Khan, *The Great Partition: The Making of India and Pakistan* (New Haven: Yale University Press, 2007); Amales Tripathi and Amitava Tripathi, *Indian National Congress and the Struggle for Freedom, 1885–1947* (Oxford: Oxford University Press, 2014); Durba Ghosh, *Gentlemanly Terrorists: Political Violence and the Colonial State in India, 1919–1947* (Cambridge: Cambridge University Press, 2017).

20 Eleanor Rathbone, "Some Indian Friends," May 27, 1941, British Library (hereafter BL), Various Private and Demi-Official Papers of Sir Maurice Hallet; Copies of Intercepted Letters from Jawaharlal Nehru to Eleanor Rathbone MP, Mss Eur E251/62. See also Antoinette Burton, *Burdens of History: British Feminists, Indian Women, and Imperial Culture* (Chapel Hill: University of North Carolina Press, 1994), 203; Susan Pedersen, *Eleanor Rathbone and the Politics of Conscience* (New Haven: Yale University Press, 2004), 323.

21 Ronald Storrs, *A Record of the War* (Bloomington: Indiana University Press, 1940), 44.

22 Rathbone. See also Pedersen, *Eleanor Rathbone and the Politics*, 323.

23 Rabindranath Tagore, "Reply to Miss Rathbone," in *The English Writings of Rabindranath Tagore: Volume Three; A Miscellany*, ed. Sisir Kumar Das (New Delhi: Sahitya Akademi, 1994), 1007.

24 Ibid., 852.

25 Ibid.

26 Madhusree Mukerjee, *Churchill's Secret War: The British Empire and the Ravaging of India during World War II* (New York: Basic Books, 2010), 103–238.

27 Yasmin Khan, *The Raj at War: A People's History of India's Second World War* (London: Bodley Head, 2014), xvi.

28 Ibid., xii.

29 Johannes H. Voight, "Co-operation or Confrontation? War and Congress Politics, 1939–1942," in *Congress and the Raj: Facets of the Indian Struggle, 1917–1947,* ed. D. A. Low (London: Heinemann, 1977), 350.

30 Ibid., 349.

31 Ibid.

32 Jawaharlal Nehru, *What India Wants* (London: The India League, 1942), 9.

33 Srinath Raghavan, *India's War: World War II and the Making of Modern South Asia* (New York: Basic Books, 2016), 1.

34 Viceroy Linlithgow, "Declaration Made by Viceroy in Response to Working Committee Invitation to Clarify British War Aims," Declaration of British War Aims, BL, India Office Records and Private Papers, 29/FD-46/1147/1939.

35 Quoted in Khan, *The Raj at War,* 5.

36 Reflecting on the outbreak of war, Nehru contended: "We had bitter memories of the war of 1914–1918 and what followed it . . . . So as early as 1927, the Congress declared that the Indian people could not permit the exploitation of Indian resources for the furtherance of imperialist aims and that they would not cooperate in any imperialist war. Year after year this policy was reiterated and developed. With the growth of the Nazi power, the Congress condemned Fascism and Naziism and disapproved of their theory and practice. We approved of collective security to check aggression and noticed that British policy, in spite of occasional declarations to the contrary, was deliberately sabotaging this idea, on which the League of Nations had been based, and was often encouraging aggression. Munich came as a terrible shock, and the so-called nonintervention and betrayal of Spain were a tragedy which affected us deeply." Jawaharlal Nehru, "India's Demand and England's Answer," in *The Unity of India: Collected Writings 1937–1940* (London: L. Drummond, 1941), 359–60.

37 The Muslim League and other interest groups opposed to Congress rule declared a "Day of Deliverance" in support of the British war effort. Raghavan, 25.

38 Quoted in Khan, *The Raj at War,* 6.

39 Fennell, *Fighting the People's War,* 6.

40 Voight, "Co-operation or Confrontation?" 351.

41 Abul Kalam Azad, *India's Choice: Abul Kalam Azad's Presidential Address to the Indian National Congress* (London: India League, 1940), 5.

42 Khan, *The Raj at War,* 6.

43 Ibid.

44 As Ram Manohar Lohia made clear: "The fascism of Hitler and others which suppressed the freedom of its own population and conquered and enslaved other peoples is to be looked upon with horror but the imperialism of Britain and others must be found to be equally at the root of the world's slavery, violence and wars. In fact, apart from what British imperialism does to the populations subject to it and the standing model and incitement that it is to other well-armed powers to outrival it, British foreign policy must also be held responsible for encouraging the forces of evil as in the Italo-Ethiopian, Spanish and China-Japan wars and, thus, for hastening a world war. India, therefore, can have nothing to do with a war whose object may in any way be the continuance either of imperialism or fascism. The world can be made secure against the crime of wars only if the imperialist and fascism system are destroyed." Ram Manohar Lohia, *Congress and War* (Lucknow: U.P.C.C., 1939), 2.

45 G. S. Chhabra, *Advanced Study in the History of Modern India*, vol. 3 (New Delhi: Sterling Publishers, 1971), 143.

46 Quoted in Khan, *The Raj at War*, 134.

47 Ram Manohar Lohia, *The Mystery of Sir Stafford Cripps* (Bombay: Padma Publications, 1942), 1–2.

48 Quoted in Rob Johnson, *British Imperialism* (London: Palgrave Macmillan, 2002), 176.

49 Mohandas K. Gandhi, "Message to the Country," August 9, 1942, in *The Collected Works of Mahatma Gandhi* (hereafter CWMG), vol. 83 (New Delhi: Publications Division Government of India, 1999), 208.

50 Mohandas K. Gandhi, "Speech at A.I.C.C. Meeting," in *CWMG*, vol 83, 197.

51 Jawaharlal Nehru, "Speech Made by the Indian Leader at His Trial at Gorakhpur Prison on November 3, 1940," *The Daily Worker* (New York, NY), January 9, 1941.

52 Khan, *The Raj at War*, 12.

53 M. N. Roy, *M.N. Roy's Memoirs*, 217. First seen in Roy, *M.N. Roy*, 23.

54 Robert North, "M.N. Roy and the Fifth Congress of the Chinese Communist Party," *The China Quarterly* 8 (1961): 184–9.

55 Roy, *M.N. Roy*, 86.

56 Manabendra Nath Roy, *I Accuse! From the Suppressed Statement of Manabendra Nath Roy on Trial for Treason* (New York City: Roy Defense Committee of India, 1932), 13.

57 Manabendra Nath Roy, *Fragments of a Prisoner's Diary: Letters from Jail, Volume 3* (New York: Renaissance Publications, 1943), 230. Like many in India, Roy believed the Spanish Civil War might develop into a world war: "I am rather confident about the final outcome of what is called the Spanish embroglio. But, of course, there always remains the danger of one of these international gunmen

touching off the powder magazine on the pretext of the events in Spain. It is astounding how these chaps [Hitler and Mussolini] manage to scare the wits out of the democratic statesman, and get away swaggeringly with the loot." Roy, *Fragments*, 222.

58 After his release from prison, Roy found himself "in a rather peculiar position. One section of the Congress looks upon me with suspicion, as a dangerous communist intriguer . . . and another section, the Socialist Section, says that here is a man who is a traitor to communism." Quoted in John Patrick Haithcox, *Communist and Nationalism in India: M.N. Roy and Comintern Policy, 1920–1939* (Princeton: Princeton University Press, 1971), 252.

59 Jawaharlal Nehru, "Presidential Address to the Indian National Congress at Faizpur," in *The Encyclopaedia of the Indian National Congress*, ed. A. Moin Zaidi and Shaheda Gufran Zaid (New Delhi: Chand, 1980), 184.

60 Roy, *M.N. Roy*, 111.

61 Ibid., 412.

62 Quoted in Kris Manjapra, *M.N. Roy, Marxism and Colonial Cosmopolitanism* (London: Routledge, 2016), 116.

63 Quoted in Roy, *M.N. Roy*, 428. After the AICC meeting in Bombay, Nehru criticized Roy: "These views whether one agrees with them or not represent a certain definite outlook which is clearly at variance with anything we have done so far and which means a complete break with the past. I do not agree with this general outlook and approach and I think it is utterly out of touch with reality in India today." Roy, *M.N. Roy*, 429.

64 M. N. Roy, *Gandhism, Nationalism, Socialism* (Calcutta: Bengal Radical Club, 1940), 42.

65 Roy contended that revolution only occurred when class-based social systems exhausted all possibility of human development. Bourgeois ownership inevitably bred class conflict; this "goes on continuously, and breaks out periodically into gigantic convulsions which subvert an established social order. That takes place only after an established order has decayed. In course of that process of decay, forces capable of creating a new order grow. Man's urge for creation asserts itself by bursting limitations on creativeness." M. N. Roy, *From Savagery to Civilisation* (Calcutta: Digest Book House, 1940), 5–6.

66 M. N. Roy, "Stalin Triumphs," July 27, 1930, BL, Manabendra Nath Roy: Differences with Leadership of Communist International; Foundation of New Communist Part in India; Arrest and Detention at Cawnpore, IOR/L/PJ/12/420, 71.

67 Ibid.

68 Helen Graham and Paul Preston, "The Popular Front and the Struggle Against Fascism," in *The Popular Front in Europe* (London: Macmillan, 1987), 2–5.

69 M. N. Roy, *Fascism: Its Philosophy, Professions, and Practice* (Calcutta: D.M. Library, 1938), 10.

70 Ibid., 8–9.

71 Ibid.

72 Michael Ortiz, "'Disown Gandhi or Be Damned': MN Roy, Gandhi and Fascism," *Journal of Colonialism and Colonial History* 21, no. 3 (2020).

73 Ibid.

74 Roy's political philosophy was as dynamic as it was complex. Kris Manjapra has described him as "intermediary between worlds, while not centered in any, that paradoxically contributed both to his forgetting as a political figure, and to the power and widespread influence of his ideas." Manjapra divides Roy's political evolution into several interrelated stages. While in Europe, Roy was caught up in "the rift that developed within early communism between the Bolshevik ascendancy on one hand, and the members of the German Spartakus Bund closely associated with the thought of Rose Luxemburg, who represented an authoritative alternate school of radical Marxism on the other . . . . In the period of the purges and the centralisation of the communist movement after 1928, Roy was easily marginalised within the ranks of left internationalists and labelled a traitor and 'renegade.'" After his return to India (1930), Roy's work "took on a new tack with its turn towards cultural critique. His writings on sexual politics from the prison cell constituted his entrée in Marxist cultural criticism from a standpoint beyond class analysis." Finally, after the Second World Wary, Roy "attempted to distil and preserve the key elements of his postcolonial hope in the context of the unwanted human devastation brought by Partition, as well as the varying degrees of 'covert and overt' authoritarianism in the postcolonial states after 1947." Manjapra, *M.N. Roy, Marxism and Colonial Cosmopolitanism*, xvi–xvii.

75 B. K. Mahakul, "Radical Humanism of M.N. Roy," *The Indian Journal of Political Science* 66, no. 3 (2005): 609.

76 M. N. Roy, "Thesis Adopted by the Radicals in the Middle of October, 1939," in *India and War* (Lucknow: Dr. A.P. Singh, 1942), 4–5.

77 Ibid., 4.

78 Thomas Christofferson and Michael Christofferson, *France during World War II: From Defeat to Liberation* (New York: Fordham University Press, 2006), 1–33.

79 Winston Churchill, "War," September 3, 1939, in *Never Give In: Winston Churchill's Speeches,* ed. Winston S. Churchill (London: Bloomsbury Academic, 2004), 163.

80 Quoted in Geoffrey Roberts, *Stalin's Wars: From World War to Cold War, 1939–1953* (Yale University Press, 2008), 36.

81 Roy, "Thesis," 6.

82 Ibid.

83 Ibid., 9.

84 Roy, "Thesis," 8.

85 Louise Young, *Japan's Total Empire: Manchuria and the Culture of Wartime Imperialism* (Berkely: University of California Press, 1998); Stein Ugelvik Larsen, *Fascism Outside Europe: The European Impulse against Domestic Conditions in the Diffusion of Global Fascism* (New York: Columbia University Press, 2001); Federico Finchelstein, *Transatlantic Fascism; Ideology, Violence, and the Sacred in Argentina and Italy, 1919–1945* (Durham: Duke University Press, 2009); Shelley Baranowski, *Nazi Empire: German Colonialism and Imperialism from Bismarck to Hitler* (Cambridge: Cambridge University Press, 2011); Daniel Hedinger, "Universal Fascism and its Global Legacy: Italy's and Japan's Entangled History in the Early 1930s," *Fascism* 2, no. 2 (2013): 141–60; Birthe Kundrus, "Colonialism, Imperialism, National Socialism: How Imperial Was the Third Reich?" In *German Colonialism in a Global Age*, ed. Geoff Eley and Bradley Naranch (Durham: Duke University Press, 2014); Benjamin Zachariah, "A Voluntary Gleichschaltung? Indian Perspectives Towards a Non-Eurocentric Understanding of Fascism," *Journal of Transcultural Studies* 2014, no. 2 (2014): 63–100; Reto Hofmann, *The Fascist Effect: Japan and Italy, 1915–1952* (Ithaca, NY: Cornell University Press, 2015); Jens Steffek, "Fascist Internationalism," *Millennium: Journal of International Studies* 44, no. 1 (2015): 3–22; Jacoby, "Global Fascism: Geography, Timing, Support, and Strategy"; Madeleine Herren, "Fascist Internationalism," in *Internationalism: A Twentieth Century History*, ed. Glenda Sluga and Patricia Clavin (Cambridge: Cambridge University Press, 2017).

86 Roy, "Thesis," 9.

87 Ibid.

88 Ibid., 11.

89 Ibid., 12.

90 Ibid., 13.

91 Ibid., 19.

92 Ibid., 27. Roy contended that the tumultuous outbreak of the Second World War paralleled that of the First.

93 A. J. P. Taylor, *The Origins of the Second World War* (London: Simon & Schuster, 1961).

94 Roy, "Thesis," 66.

95 Ibid., 19.

96 Roy, *War and Revolution,* 20.

97 Roy, "Circular to the League of Radical Congressmen," 2.

98 Roy, "Thesis," 28.

99 Ironically, Roy's support of the British war effort led "to his dismissal as a viable political ally for colonial administrators. By late 1940, British officials had a low estimation of Roy as an intermediary, a non-Indian Indian, who did not belong

squarely in any of the representative camps of Indian political identity." Manjapra, *M.N. Roy, Marxism and Colonial Cosmopolitanism*, 125.

100 Roy, *War and Revolution*, 8.

101 Ibid., 9.

102 M. N. Roy, "A Statement Regarding My Differences with the Present Leadership of the Communist International," Manabendra Nath Roy: Differences with Leadership of Communist International; Foundation of a New Communist Party in India; Arrest and Detention at Cawnpore, BL, India Office Records and Private Papers, IOR/L/PJ/12/420: August 1930–December 1931, 8.

103 M. N. Roy, "Stalin Triumphs," 71. After his expulsion from the Soviet Union, Roy contended that the proletarian revolution transcended the Soviet Union: "The Communist movement has become too great, its tasks have become too complicated, its scope of action has become too sweeping to remain still under the exclusive leadership of the Russian comrades who on their part, are so much occupied in the entirely different task of building up socialism on the basis of a victorious revolution. Further development of the movement demands a collective internationally leadership in which the Russian comrades will have the place of honour as the first among equals. For this we are fighting." M. N. Roy, "When the Communists Differ Among Themselves," in Differences with Leadership of Communist International; Foundation of a New Communist Party in India; Arrest and Detention at Cawnpore, BL, India Office Records and Private Papers, IOR/L/PJ/12/420: August 1930–December 1931, 9.

104 B. K. Basu, *Call of Yanan: The Story of the Indian Medical Mission to China 1938–1943: Yin Du Yuan Hua Yi Liao Dui De Gu Shi* (Beijing: Foreign Language Press, 2003), 139.

105 Ibid.

106 Sourendra Ganguly, *Leftism in India: M. N. Roy and Indian Politics 1920–1948* (Calcutta: Minerva Publishers, 1984); Satyabrata Rai Chowdhuri, *Leftism in India, 1917–947* (New York: Palgrave Macmillan UK, 2007).

107 Dennis Dalton, *Mahatma Gandhi: Nonviolent Power in Action* (Columbia University Press, 2012), 79.

108 Prior, *When Britain Saved the West*, 1–19.

109 Christian Hartmann, *Operation Barbarossa: Nazi Germany's War in East, 1941–1945* (Oxford: Oxford University Press, 2013), 1.

110 Ibid.

111 Churchill, *Never Give In*, 289–93.

112 Only weeks after Operation Barbarossa, the Soviet Union entered into a military alliance with Britain. Roy celebrated the union: "July 14 [Bastille Day] is a memorable day. The events occurring on that day a century and a half ago determined the course of world events for a whole period of history. In future, July

12, the day on which the Anglo-Soviet Agreement was signed, will be regarded as a still more memorable day, for it heralds a revolution which will be even greater because it promises to be less painful." M.N. Roy, *War and Revolution*, 34–5.

113 Khan, *The Raj at War*, 3.

114 Ibid.

115 Nehru, *What India Wants*, 6–7.

116 Ashley Jackson and James E. Kitchen, "The British Empire and the First World War: Paradoxes and New Questions," in *The British Empire and the First World War*, ed. Ashley Jackson (London: Routledge, 2016), 11.

117 J. B. Kripalani, *Congress and War Crisis* (Allahabad: All India Congress Committee, 1940), 1.

118 Lohia, *Congress and War*, 2.

119 Anti-imperialists around the world largely supported the Congress. Afro-Trinidadian Marxist C. L. R. James similarly urged anti-colonialists to boycott the war: "Ethiopia was the last piece of Africa left free. Mussolini decided that he wanted it. The League of Nations had sworn to defend it Every Negro with a spark of pride knows what happened, and remembers it with justified bitterness. Not only did they not protect Ethiopia as they had sworn to do, but instead they prevented arms from going to her while they bargained with Mussolini. They stabbed Ethiopia in the back—Britain, France, America, these great 'democracies.' (And Stalin, who claims to be a friend of Negroes, sold oil to Italy all through the Italian campaign.) Now Roosevelt comes running, to tell all good Americans (Negroes included of course) that they must fight against aggression. And who is going to do the fighting against this aggression ? The workers as always. Roosevelt, Hull and Landon are getting ready to push the workers of America into the war. These are the very men who actively collaborated with Mussolini in destroying the last independent African state." C. L. R. James (J.R. Johnson), "Why Negroes Should Oppose the War," *Pioneer Publishers*, 1939.

120 Jawaharlal Nehru, "India and the War," in *India, Spain and the War* (Allahabad: Kitabistan, 1940), 153–4.

121 Subhas Bose, "The Axis Powers and India: Broadcast from Berlin," May 1, 1942, in *Selected Speeches of Subhas Chandra Bose* (New Delhi: Publications Division, Ministry of Information and Broadcasting, 1974), 144.

122 Sugata Bose, *His Majesty's Opponent: Subhas Chandra Bose and India's Struggle against Empire* (Cambridge, MA: Belknap Press of Harvard University Press, 2011), 1–14.

123 For scholarship examining Bose and the Indian National Army, see Gurbachan Singh Mangat, *Indian National Army, Role in India's Struggle for Freedom* (Ludhiana: Gagan Publishers, 1991); Anuradha Jaiswal, *Subhash Chandra Bose and Indian National Army* (Delhi: Globus Press, 2013); Raghavan, *India's War*.

124 Roy, "Thesis," 66.

125 Kunwar Anand Singh, "Letter of Resignation," October 15, 1940, M.N. Roy Papers, NMML, Part I Section II, 90/1/1940–1942, 8.

126 Jawaharlal Nehru to Kunwar Anand Singh, 28 October 1940, M.N. Roy Papers, NMML, Part I Section II, 90/1/1940–1942, 35.

127 Roy contended that Gandhi and the Congress only superficially understood the materialist anatomy of fascism and imperialism, and oversimplified a complicated international situation. See Roy, "Thesis," 6–7.

128 M. N. Roy, "A New Lead: Summary of a Speech at a Public Meeting at Coconada, February 6, 1941," in *India and War*, 310–11.

129 Jawaharlal Nehru, July 17, 1938, "Speech at a Demonstration Held at Trafalgar Square to Mark the Second Anniversary of Hostilities in Spain," Pandit Jawaharlal Nehru: Reports on Activities 1936–1938, BL, India Office Records and Private Papers, L/PJ/12/293, File 295/26.

130 Roy, *War and Revolution*, 26.

131 M. N. Roy, *Problems of the Indian Revolution: Lecture Delivered on June 3, 1940 in the All-India Summer Camp for Political Study Held at Dehradun in May 1940* (Bombay: R. Panday, 1941), 9.

132 M. N. Roy, *Jawaharlal Nehru* (Delhi: Radical Democratic Party, 1945), 26.

133 Ibid., 16.

134 Roy similarly decried Nehruvian anti-fascism: "As a full-blooded nationalist, he must oppose anything done by the British Government. For the passionate nationalist Nehru, victory of Fascism, disappearance of the very possibility of Socialism, even a possible destruction of the Soviet Union, the Mecca of all revolutionaries—were utterly irrelevant considerations. Only one emotion influenced his judgment and it was fear. Nehru held that it was an imperialist war, and that if the United Nations won it, British imperialism would be aggrandised. The Socialist, anti-fascist, Nehru was not prepared to pay that imaginary price for the defeat of the Axis Powers, and subsequently for the defence of the land of Socialism." Roy, *Nehru*, 28–9.

135 Roy, *Problems of the Indian Revolution*, 11.

136 M. N. Roy, "World Crisis: Speeches by M.N. Roy during the Discussion on the International Situation in the Radical Summer Camp for Political Study, Dehradun, May 24, 1940," in *India and War*, 134–5.

137 Quoted in Prakash Chandra, *The Political Philosophy of M.N. Roy* (New Delhi: Sarup & Sons, 1992), 39–40. See also Partha Chatterjee, *Nationalist Thought and the Colonial World: A Derivative Discourse?* (Minneapolis: University of Minnesota Press, 1986); Gayatri Chakravorty Spivak, *"Can the Subaltern Speak?"* In *Can the Subaltern Speak?: Reflections on the History of an Idea* (New York: Columbia University Press, 2010).

138 Roy, *Gandhism*, 6.

139 Ranajit Guha, *Dominance without Hegemony: History and Power in Colonial India* (Cambridge: Harvard University Press, 1997).

140 M. N. Roy and K. K. Sinha, *Royism Explained* (Calcutta: Saraswati Library, 1938), 7.

141 In 1936, long after his expulsion from the Soviet Union, Roy praised Stalin in a private letter: "You see, after all, I still remain a personal admirer of my ex-friend [Stalin], who used to pride over our racial affinity, and called me 'gold.' Now, he won't appreciate me even as copper! But I have the weakness of giving the devil his due. And in my account, his due is very considerable. I was publicly castigated for this weakness once at Weimar." Roy, *M.N. Roy*, 90.

142 Roy, *War and Revolution*, 26.

143 Roy, *Memoirs*, 116.

144 Ibid.

145 Randy Roberts, *Papa Jack: Jack Johnson and the Era of White Hopes* (New York: The Free Press, 1983), 138–54.

146 Roy, *Memoirs*, 116.

147 Ibid., 117.

148 Ibid.

149 Ibid.

150 Ibid.

151 Manjapra, *M.N. Roy, Marxism and Colonial Cosmopolitanism*, xiii.

152 Dalton, *Mahatma Gandhi*, 79.

153 Ibid.

154 Jawaharlal Nehru, *Fascism and Empire* (London: Spain-India Committee, 1937), 1–2.

155 Khan, *The Raj at War*, 5.

Conclusion

"Before They Were Its Victims, They Were Its Accomplices"[1]

On May 15, 1940, Winston Churchill received an early morning phone call from French prime minister Paul Reynaud. "He spoke in English," Churchill recalled in *Their Finest Hour*, "and evidently under stress."[2] Five days earlier, Adolf Hitler had initiated *Fall Gelb* (Case Yellow)—the German invasion of France, Belgium, Luxembourg, and the Netherlands. Outmaneuvering the puissant—albeit ponderous—French defense, the Wehrmacht poured through the Ardennes. After crossing the river Meuse, near Sedan—site of Moltke the Elder's famous "mousetrap"[3] during the Franco-Prussian War—German forces stormed north, toward the English Channel. "We have been defeated," Reynaud told Churchill, "We are beaten; we have lost the battle. . . . The front is broken near Sedan; they are pouring through in great numbers with tanks and armoured cars."[4] Five days later, German soldiers reached the Channel, circumscribing advancing Allied forces in Belgium. Nothing "stood between the German armies and the French capital."[5] "It is midnight in Europe," observed Canadian prime minister Mackenzie King. On June 22, France formally surrendered—the "most terrible collapse in all the long story of our national life."[6]

After the Second Armistice at Compiègne, France was bifurcated into Nazi-occupied and Vichy-occupied zones. The celerity of conquest, and the subsequent trauma of occupation, isolated Paris—the imperial metropole—from its vast colonial empire. Many colonial governors faced a difficult decision between supporting Nazi-controlled France or the Free French government-in-exile of Charles de Gaulle. With the exception of Chad, the New Hebrides (Vanuatu), and French-India, colonialists unilaterally supported the collaborationist Vichy regime.[7] The fall of Paris nevertheless undermined French imperial hegemony. French West Indians—colonial subjects since the seventeenth century and "racial colonial citizens (certainly not full citizens)"[8] since the Second Republic (1848)—were burdened with subsistence living after centuries of depredatory colonization.[9] At the same time, "new cultural consciousness, social sensibilities, and political praxes were quickly coupled with the ethical imperative of concrete choices, either for or against Vichy, which had been the major issues of daily existence during the Occupation years."[10]

Amid this political maelstrom, Aimé Césaire returned home to Martinique. Together with his partner Suzanne Césaire and several colleagues, he founded the literary and cultural journal *Tropiques* to resist fascist tyranny and raise "consciousness of and pride in Martinique's repressed Creole culture, by foregrounding folk tales, expressions, African religious traces, and the unique flora and fauna of the Caribbean island."[11] Over the course of his illustrious career, Césaire published critically acclaimed poetry, popularized Négritude literary theory, and mentored anti-imperialist intellectuals—most famously, Frantz Fannon. Although scholars and intellectuals such as Raphaël Confiant have critiqued problematic facets of Césaire's Weltanschauung—his "obfuscation of the history of plantation society, his aspiration towards universality, and above all what [Confiant] conceives as his political betrayal in helping to implement the departmentalisation of Martinique in 1946"[12]—Césaire remains an essential colonial and postcolonial theorist.

Césaire had long grappled with the choler of imperial subjugation. Francis Abiola Irele has characterized him as "the Nietzschean man of Resentment."[13] Césaire's most famous poem, *Cahier d'un retour au pays natal* (1939), explored the ways in which French imperialism had despoiled black history, identity, language, and culture. Invoking the imprisonment of Haitian revolutionary Toussaint Louverture, Césaire argued:

> a lone man imprisoned in whiteness
> a lone man defying the white screams of white death
> (TOUSSAINT, TOUSSAINT LOUVERTURE)
> a man who mesmerizes the white sparrow hawk of white death
> a man alone in the sterile sea of white sand.[14]

In 1950, five years after the end of the Second World War, Césaire published *Discours sur le colonialisme* (*Discourse on Colonialism*). At the same time the postwar French Fourth Republic repudiated Vichy collaboration— and trumpeted republican shibboleths such as *liberté, égalité, fraternité*—it reconstituted, or fortified, predatory imperialisms in Martinique, Algeria, and Vietnam. For Césaire, this hypocrisy exhibited the vacuousness of the *mission civilisatrice*. Echoing Indian anti-colonialists (or perhaps vice-versa), he contended that imperialism prefigured Nazism: "The crowning barbarism that sums up all the daily barbarisms; that it is Nazism, yes, but that before they were its victims, they were its accomplices; that they tolerated that Nazism before it was inflicted on them, that they absolved it, shut their eyes to it, legitimized it, because, until then, it had been applied only to non-European peoples."[15] Césaire argued that as Europeans increasingly promulgated racial antipathy to advance their expansionist interests, they inevitably turned on one another. Violence "practiced outside the continent in the form of colonization, returned with a vengeance in the form of fascism."[16]

One year after Césaire released *Discourse on Colonialism*, Hannah Arendt published *The Origins of Totalitarianism* (1951). It was, and remains, an exceptional analysis of the fascist phenomenon. In recent years, scholars have rediscovered Arendt's "Boomerang Thesis," which, similar to Césaire, contends that German colonial conquest—the Herero and Namaqua Genocide,[17] in particular—presaged Nazism:

> When the European mob discovered what a "lovely virtue" a white skin could be in Africa, when the English conqueror in India became an administrator who no longer believed in the universal validity of law, but was convinced of his own innate capacity to rule and dominate, when the dragon-slayers turned into either "white men" of "higher breeds" or into bureaucrats and spies ... the stage seemed to be set for all possible horrors. Lying under anybody's nose were many of the elements which, gathered together, could create a totalitarian government on the basis of racism.[18]

The Boomerang Thesis has since inspired several analyses of the interrelation between fascism and liberal-imperialism.[19] Enzo Traverso, for example, has contended that "The notion of 'living space' was not a Nazi invention. It was simply the German version of a commonplace of European culture at the time of imperialism."[20] Critics of the Boomerang Thesis have argued that, due to its ephemerality, the *Deutsches Kolonialreich* scarcely imprinted upon Germany's collective (or cultural) conscience, and that Hitler—obsessed, as he was, with continental *lebensraum*—was largely disinterested in overseas empires.[21] Arendt, moreover, possessed problematic racial beliefs and too often idealized the British Empire.[22] Nevertheless, the Boomerang Thesis—and *Origins of Totalitarianism* more broadly—remain indispensable to understanding the origins of fascism.

Together, Arendt and Césaire identified profound similarities between fascism and liberal-imperialism. Until recently, however, their scholarship has been sequestered. Arendt (inside-out) has been revivified—immortalized once again with the sobriquet "Boomerang Thesis"—while Césaire (outside-in) has only recently been taken up in mainstream fascist narratives.[23] This discrepancy underscores the intellectual, epistemological, and geographical palisades insulating fascist and imperialist historiographies. Too often, they are treated as hermetic analytical categories. Hitler menaced England, while Gandhi imperiled the Raj. This dichotomization of "Europe" and "empire" precludes analyses of their intersections—of the ways in which Gandhi understood Hitler. Situated firmly within "Europe," fascism is reified as a centrifugal European discourse that, as Benjamin Zachariah has argued, "struggles with what I might call an 'original' and 'copy' problem: the original is in Europe and the outside world copies it, either properly and correctly, in which case it is fascist (in our case), or imperfectly (in which case it is not fascist, though it might have similarities)."[24]

Modern Europe was made in the image of a colonizing power. "[It] is literally the creation of the Third World,"[25] Frantz Fannon famously argued. Fascism was not something to be copied outside of Europe, but rather a protean ideology formed in part by non-Western, imperialist, and anti-colonial discourses. With this in mind, I believe that the Boomerang Thesis, widely cited as the archetype of fascist-imperialist analysis, should be reframed as the "anti-imperialist critique." Indian anti-colonialists associated fascism with liberal-imperialism more than a decade before Arendt published *Origins,* yet their perspectives have been excluded from mainstream fascist narratives. This is not to say that Arendt should be disavowed, merely that her renascence reflects the primacy of inside-out perspectives. The Boomerang Thesis is the argument of Césaire—of Jawaharlal Nehru, George Padmore, Kamaladevi Chattopadhyay, C. L. R. James, and others. For too long, non-Western politicians and intellectuals have been labeled "anti-colonialist," rather than "anti-fascist." They were both.

~

To date, inside-out (or centrifugal) narratives have monopolized Western understandings of fascism. In this book, I have endeavored to broaden our apperception of interwar Europe by analyzing it from the outside-in. My approach is not meant to rehabilitate fascist regimes, nor minimize the atrocities committed by fascists and their collaborators, merely to provincialize Eurocentric narratives.[26] Nehru, Gandhi, and Indian anti-fascists were at the political and intellectual epicenter of the crises of interwar fascism. To be sure, they often misunderstood, or willfully mischaracterized, elements of fascist ideology. Nehru, in particular, too often conflated fascism with liberal-imperialism; he was, moreover, quixotic and often supercilious—more concerned with European political developments than subaltern India. Despite these and other limitations, I believe that the arguments of Nehru and other

Indian anti-fascists have reconceptualized, and ultimately, enriched, our understanding of interwar Europe.

Seen from India, the Second Italo-Ethiopian War resuscitated Europe's New Imperialist covenant; the Spanish Civil War was a struggle between national self-determination and Europe's satisfied and unsatisfied imperial powers; the Second Sino-Japanese War evinced the extent to which British imperial hegemony influenced Japanese expansionism; the Munich Agreement was yet another instance of Europe's imperial powers negotiating the sovereignty of smaller nations; and finally, the outbreak of the Second World War pitted Europe's imperialist great powers against one another, but was nevertheless revolutionary insomuch as it augured an era of decolonization. These conclusions, although largely irreconcilable with inside-out narratives of Europe, are nevertheless meant to be understood alongside them. There were multiple Europes—many of which were incongruous or even paradoxical. Examining the interrelation between fascism and liberal-imperialism was inconceivable within Europe and indisputable within its empires. Such malleability underscores the ways in which Europe often looked different from the outside.

While geographically diverse, my analytical framework has explored only a fragment of the political, intellectual, and cultural networks that animated fascist and colonial anti-fascist movements. The crises that precipitated the Second World War were international phenomena that inspired individuals from around the world to fight for freedom and self-determination.[27] In the years to come, I look forward to reading scholarship that challenges, supports, and refutes my own contentions. Just as inside-out narratives have competed for narrative predominance, there are, and will be, competing outside-in narratives. Europe was, and remains, an idea, rather than a place.

~

In 1930, as he resigned from the government to form his New Party (eventually the British Union of Fascists), Oswald Mosley invoked the decline and fall of the Spanish Empire: "What I fear much more than a sudden crisis is a long, slow crumbling through the years until we sink to the level of a Spain, a gradual paralysis, beneath which all the vigour and energy of this country will succumb."[28] Mosley and other arch-imperialists lamented the dissolution—both real and imagined—of the British Empire. During the Spanish Civil War, they "drew inspiration from Franco's Nationalists,"[29] particularly as Whitehall appeared increasingly "weak on imperial issues, especially India, and misguided in refusing to align with authoritarian anti-communist states."[30] After Bolshevik intervention in the Spanish Civil War, many imperialists deemed the Republic a Soviet satellite. Samuel Hoare's definition of neutrality was: "'On no account must we do anything to bolster up Communism in Spain' (as it might spread to Portugal and threaten British imperial interests)."[31] Similarly, in the early stages of the conflict, Prime Minister Stanley Baldwin's only known instructions to Anthony Eden were: "On no account, French or other, must he bring us in to the fight on the side of the Russians."[32] Imperialists raised the specter of communism to justify British nonintervention in Spain. As the First Sea Lord, Ernle Chatfield, explained: "Franco's was a 'much nobler cause than the Reds.'"[33]

Six years after retiring from the government, Mosley led his blackshirted British Union on a march in the East End of London. During the subsequent Battle of Cable Street, anti-fascists shouted: "They shall not pass!"[34]—a tribute to the defenders of Madrid. After several clashes—most with the Metropolitan Police—protestors ultimately repulsed British fascism. Never again "were the blackshirts to sally forth en masse."[35] The Battle of Cable Street has since come to symbolize anti-fascism. Mosley and the British Union were popularly repudiated, never to remerge as a serious movement. In India, anti-fascists celebrated the defenders of Cable Street. Yet while this event largely invalidated fascism in the form of Mussolini, British imperial regimes—the Raj, in particular—perpetuated the racism, exploitation, and repression endemic to fascist ideologies. Thwarted in London, did fascism thrive within its empire?

It is a difficult question to answer. The relationship between fascism in Europe and colonialisms across Afro-Eurasia was multivalent, and frustratingly nebulous. This book has contended that the crises of interwar fascism were yet another paroxysm of imperial cupidity analogous (though not identical) to the Scramble for Africa and the Treaty of Versailles—but to what extent? Is there a rubric? Or perhaps an equation? Such questions inevitably lead back to debates over the fascist minimum. Yet as many scholars have argued, propounding a taxonomy of fascist-imperialist interrelation tends to infix their dynamic, ever-evolving consanguinity. Nevertheless, at the risk of proposing a reductive framework, I will try.

Borrowing from Arendt, I believe that European colonial brutality produced a "boomerang effect," in which frustrated nationalists (or fascists) deployed colonial violence within their own nation-states. As Césaire argued nearly seventy-five years ago, imperialism ultimately destroyed European civilizations: "A nation which colonizes, that a civilization which justifies colonization— and therefore force—is already a sick civilization, a civilization that is morally diseased, that irresistibly, progressing from one consequence to another, one repudiation to another, calls for its Hitler, I mean its punishment."[36] For centuries, liberal-imperialists espoused democracy within Europe and colonial oppression across Africa, Asia, and the Americas. In the aftermath of the First World War, embittered nationalists like Mussolini rejected this circumscription and propagated a radicalized colonialism within Europe. "Fascism," Raul Carstocea, has argued, "was intended from the outset as an insurgency against the Western hegemonic narrative of liberal progress, yet one that was synthetically grounded in its racist and colonial tenets."[37] To be sure, fascism possessed unique characteristics—fanatical paramilitarism and its "mobilizing passions,"[38] to name just two.[39] Fascists, moreover, did not simply import colonial violence into Europe.[40] Yet much of what we associate with fascism—organic nationalism, ferocious expansionism, the exaltation of violence, and racio-religious persecution—drew upon European colonial ideologies, even if, as was the case with Nazi Germany, fascists transformed these tenets into something unprecedented.[41]

I believe that European fascisms should be understood in part as radicalized—often transmogrified—forms of liberal-imperialist violence. Put simply, imperial expansion and colonial repression were essential components of fascist ideologies. They should be analyzed, and understood, in conjunction. This is not necessarily a new argument. Yet to date many inside-out narratives of interwar Europe have discounted (or ignored) the essentiality of empire, to say nothing of non-European and outside-in perspectives. At the very least, I hope that this book has conveyed the fundamental interrelation between fascism and liberal-imperialism. They were intertwined in kaleidoscopic, often bewildering, ways.

Notes

1 Aimé Césaire, *Discourse on Colonialism* (New York: New York University Press, 2001), 36.

2 Winston Churchill, *Their Finest Hour: Volume 2* (London: Cooperation Publishing Company, 1949), 42.

3 Geoffrey Wawro, *The Franco-Prussian War: The German Conquest of France in 1870–1871* (Cambridge: Cambridge University Press, 2005), 211.

4 Churchill, *Their Finest Hour: Volume 2*, 42.

5 Julian Jackson, *The Fall of France: The Nazi Invasion of 1940* (Oxford: Oxford University Press, 2003), 9.

6 Quoted in William Shirer, *The Collapse of the Third Republic: An Inquiry into the Fall of France in 1940* (New York: Simon and Schuster, 1969), 17.

7 Nick Nesbitt, "Aimé Césaire and the Logic of Decolonization," *Caribbean Critique: Antillean Critical Theory from Toussaint to Glissant* 26, no. 1 (2013): 88. In due course, additional territories came to support the Free French Government: "The trickle of imperial defections to Charles de Gaulle's Free French—and hence to the Allies—in 1940 turned to a steady stream by 1942." Eric T. Jennings, *Vichy in the Tropics* (Stanford: Stanford University Press, 2004), 3.

8 Reiland Rabaka, *The Negritude Movement: W.E.B. Du Bois, Leon Damas, Aime Cesaire, Leopold Senghor, Frantz Fannon, and the Evolution of an Insurgent Idea* (Lanham, MD: Lexington Books, 2015), 158.

9 Ibid.

10 Ibid.

11 Ronnie Scharfman, "Homage to Aimé Césaire," *Callaloo* 31, no. 4 (2008): 976.

12 Jane Hiddleston, *Decolonising the Intellectual: Politics, Culture, and Humanism at the End of the French Empire* (Liverpool: Liverpool University Press, 2014), 3.

13 Francis Abiola Irele, "Homage to Aimé Césaire," *Présence Africaine* Nouvelle Série, no. 174 (2006): 92.

14 Aimé Césaire, *Notebook of a Return to the Native Land*, trans. Annette Smith (Middletown, CT: Wesleyan University Press, 2001), 16.

15 Césaire, *Discourse*, 36.

16 Irina Dzero, "Meanings of Hybridity in Aimé Césaire's "Discours Sur Le Colonialisme," *The French Review* 85, no. 1 (2011): 108.

17 Jürgen Zimmerer, *Genocide in German South-West Africa: The Colonial War (1904–1908) in Namibia and Its Aftermath* (Monmouth, Wales: Merlin Press, 2008). See also Isabel V. Hull, *Absolute Destruction; Military Culture and the Practices of War in Imperial Germany* (Ithaca: Cornell University Press, 2005), 31–57; David Ciarlo, *Advertising Empire: Race and Visual Culture in Imperial Germany* (Cambridge: Harvard University Press, 2011), 271–3.

18 Hannah Arendt, *The Origins of Totalitarianism* (London: Penguin Classics, 1951), 221.

19 A. Dirk Moses, *Genocide and Settler Society: Frontier Violence and Stolen Indigenous Children in Australian History* (New York: Berghahn Books, 2004); A. Dirk Moses and Dan Stone, *Colonialism and Genocide* (London: Routledge, 2006); Jacques Semelin, *Purify and Destroy: The Political Uses of Massacre and Genocide* (New York: Colombia University Press, 2007); A. Dirk Moses, *Empire, Colony, Genocide: Conquest, Occupation, and Subaltern Resistance in World History* (New York: Berghahn Books, 2008); Zimmerer, *Genocide in German South-West Africa*; Robert Gerwath and Stephan Malinowski, "Hannah Arendt's Ghosts: Reflections on the Disputable Path from Windhoek to Auschwitz," *Central European History* 42, no. 2 (2009): 279–300.

20 Enzo Traverso, *The Origins of Nazi Violence,* trans. Janet Lloyd (New York: New Press, 2003), 39.

21 Richard H. King and Dan Stone, "Introduction," in *Hannah Arendt and the Uses of History,* ed. Richard H. King and Dan Stone (New York: Berghahn Books, 2007), 9–13.

22 Ibid.

23 For some exceptions, see Kathryn Gines, "Race Thinking and Racism in Hannah Arendt's The Origins of Totalitarianism," in *Hannah Arendt and the Uses of History*; Stef Craps, *Postcolonial Witnessing: Trauma Out of Bounds* (London: Palgrave Macmillan, 2013); Enzo Traverso, *The New Faces of Fascism: Populism and the Far Right* (New York: Verso, 2019); Connor Woodman, "The Imperial Boomerang: How Colonial Methods of Repression Migrate Back to the Metropolis" *Verso Blog,* Verso Books, 2020; Mullen Bill and Christopher Vials, eds., *The US Anti-fascism Reader* (New York: Verso, 2020).

24 Benjamin Zachariah, "A Voluntary Gleichschaltung? Perspectives from India towards a non-Eurocentric Understanding of Fascism," *Transcultural Studies* 5, no. 2 (2014): 66.

25 Frantz Fanon, *The Wretched of the Earth* (New York: Grove Press, 1961), 58.

26 Dipesh Chakrabarty, *Provincializing Europe: Postcolonial Thought and Historical Difference* (Princeton: Princeton University Press, 2000).

27 Marc Matera and Susan Kingsley Kent, *The Global 1930s: The International Decade* (London: Routledge, 2017), 70–98.

28 Robert Skidelsky, *Oswald Mosley* (London: Macmillan, 1976), 215. First seen in Tom Buchanan, *Britain and the Spanish Civil War* (Cambridge: Cambridge University Press, 1997), 4.

29 Buchanan, *Britain and the Spanish Civil War,* 4.

30 Ibid.

31 Ibid., 43.

32 Ibid., 48.

33 Ibid., 39.

34 Nigel Copsey, *Anti-Fascism in Britain* (London: Macmillan, 2000), 49.

35 Roger Eatwell, *Fascism: A History* (New York: Penguin Books, 1995), 238.

36 Césaire, *Discourse,* 39.

37 Raul Carstocea, "Debate: Decolonising Fascist Studies," *Fascism* 10, no. 2 (2021): 329.

38 Robert Paxton has argued that fascism "is more plausibly linked to a set of 'mobilizing passions' that shaped fascist action than to a consistent and fully articulated philosophy. At the bottom is a passionate nationalism. Allied to it is a conspiratorial and Manichean view of history as a battle between the good and evil camps, between the pure and the corrupt, in which one's own community or

nation has been the victim. In this Darwinian narrative, the chosen people have
been weakened by political parties, social classes, unassimilable minorities, spoiled
rentiers, and rationalist thinkers who lack the necessary sense of community."
Robert Paxton, *The Anatomy of Fascism* (New York: Vintage Books, 2004), 41.

39 Michael Mann has contended that paramilitarism "was both a key value and the key
organizational form of fascism. It was seen as 'popular,' welling up spontaneously
from below, but it was also elitist, supposedly representing the vanguard of the
nation." Michael Mann, *Fascists* (Cambridge: Cambridge University Press), 16.

40 Understanding fascism in this way discounts the influence of events like the First
World War and the Bolshevik Revolutions: "Adolf Hitler and Benito Mussolini
openly stated that war constituted their most meaningful experience. After the war,
these two former soldiers found violence and war to be political elements of the first
order. When this ideology of violence fused with extreme right-wing nationalism
and imperialism and non-Marxist leftist tendencies of revolutionary syndicalism,
fascism as we know it today crystallized." Federico Finchelstein, "On Fascist
Ideology," *Constellations* 15, no. 3 (2008): 321.

41 As Finchelstein has argued: "Without fascism, there would be no Nazism as we
know it. Nazism represented a radical outcome of transnational fascist ideology,
an outcome so different from its ideological cousins that some historians argue
that it was something else: a totally unique ideology." Finchelstein, "On Fascist
Ideology," 326.

Selected Bibliography

Adams, Ralph James Quincy. *British Politics and Foreign Policy in the Age of Appeasement, 1935–39*. Stanford: Stanford University Press, 1993.

Adeney, Julia and Geoff Eley, eds. *Visualizing Fascism: The Twentieth Century Rise of the Global Right*. Durham: Duke University Press, 2020.

Arendt, Hannah. *The Origins of Totalitarianism*. London: Penguin Classics, 1951.

Aydin, Cemil. *The Politics of Anti-Westernism in Asia: Visions of World Order in Pan-Islamic and Pan-Asian Thought*. New York: Columbia University Press, 2013.

Baranowski, Shelley. *Nazi Empire: German Colonialism and Imperialism from Bismarck to Hitler*. Cambridge: Cambridge University Press, 2011.

Bhagavan, Manu. *India and the Quest for One World: The Peacemakers*. London: Palgrave Macmillan, 2013.

Bose, Sugata. *His Majesty's Opponent: Subhas Chandra Bose and India's Struggle Against Empire*. Cambridge, MA: The Belknap Press of Harvard University Press, 2011.

Bosworth, Richard. *The Italian Dictatorship: Problems and Perspectives in the Interpretation of Mussolini and Fascism*. New York: Arnold, 2007.

Braskén, Kasper, Nigel Copsey, and David Featherstone, eds. *Anti-Fascism in a Global Perspective: Transnational Networks, Exile Communities, and Radical Internationalism*. London: Taylor and Francis, 2020.

Brown, Judith M. *Nehru: A Political Life*. New Haven: Yale University Press, 2003.

Buchanan, Tom. *Britain and the Spanish Civil War*. Cambridge: Cambridge University Press, 1997.

Burton, Antoinette. *Empire in Question: Reading, Writing, and Teaching British Imperialism*. Durham: Duke University Press, 2011.

Burton, Antoinette. *The Trouble with Empire: Challenges to Modern British Imperialism*. Oxford: Oxford University Press, 2015.

Bush, Barbara. *Imperialism, Race and Resistance: Africa and Britain, 1919–1945*. London: Routledge, 1999.

Cain, Peter. and Antony Hopkin. *British Imperialism, 1688–2000*. London: Longman, 2002.

Casanova, Julián. *The Spanish Republic and Civil War*. Cambridge: Cambridge University Press, 2010.

Ceadel, Martin. *Semi-Detached Idealists: The British Peace Movement and International Relations, 1854–1945*. Oxford: Oxford University Press, 2000.

Césaire, Aimé. *Discourse on Colonialism*. New York: Monthly Review Press, 1950.

Chakrabarty, Dipesh. *Provincializing Europe: Postcolonial Thought and Historical Difference*. Princeton: Princeton University Press, 2000.

Chandra, Sudhir. *Gandhi: An Impossible Possibility*. London: Taylor & Francis, 2016.

Chowdhuri, Satyabrata Rai. *Leftism in India, 1917–1947*. London: Palgrave Macmillan, 2007.

Ciarlo, David. *Advertising Empire: Race and Visual Culture in Imperial Germany*. Cambridge, MA: Harvard University Press, 2011.

Cohn, Bernard. *Colonialism and Its Forms of Knowledge*. Princeton: Princeton University Press, 1996.

Dalton, Dennis. *Mahatma Gandhi: Nonviolent Power in Action*. New York: Columbia University Press, 2012.

Dasgupta, Tapati. *Social Thought of Rabindranath Tagore: A Historical Analysis*. New Delhi: Abhinav Publications, 1993.

Dasgupta, Uma. *Rabindranath Tagore: A Biography*. Oxford: Oxford University Press, 2004.

Dirks, Nicholas. *The Scandal of Empire: India and the Creation of Imperial Britain*. Cambridge, MA: Belknap Press, 2006.

Eley, Geoff. *Nazism as Fascism: Violence, Ideology and the Ground of Consent in Germany 1930–1945*. London: Routledge, 2013.

Evans, Richard. *The Third Reich in Power*. London: Penguin Books, 2005.

Fennell, Jonathan. *Fighting the People's War: The British and Commonwealth Armies and the Second World War*. Cambridge: Cambridge University Press, 2019.

Finchelstein, Federico. *From Fascism to Populism in History*. Berkeley: University of California Press, 2017.

Ganguly, Sourendra. *Leftism in India: M. N. Roy and Indian Politics 1920–1948*. London: Minerva Publishers, 1984.

Ghosh, Durba. *Gentlemanly Terrorists: Political Violence and the Colonial State in India, 1919–1947*. Cambridge: Cambridge University Press, 2016.

Gopal, Priyamvada. *Insurgent Empire: Anti-Colonial Resistance and British Dissent*. London: Verso, 2019.

Goswami, Manu. *Producing India: From Colonial Economy to National Space*. Chicago: University of Chicago Press, 2013.

Graham, Helen. *The Spanish Republic at War 1936–1939*. Cambridge: Cambridge University Press, 2002.

Gregor, A. James. *Interpretations of Fascism*. New York: General Learning Press, 1974.

Griffin, Roger. *Fascism*. Oxford: Oxford University Press, 1995.

Guha, Ramachandra. *Gandhi: The Years That Changed the World, 1914–1948*. New York: Knopf Doubleday, 2018.

Guha, Ranajit. *Dominance Without Hegemony: History and Power in Colonial India*. Cambridge, MA: Harvard University Press, 1998.

Hays, Romain. *Subhas Chandra Bose in Nazi Germany*. New York: Columbia University Press, 2011.

Herman, Arthur. *Gandhi and Churchill: The Epic Rivalry That Destroyed an Empire and Forged Our Age*. New York: Bantam Books, 2008.

Hofmann, Reto. *The Fascist Effect Japan and Italy, 1915–1952*. Ithaca: Cornell University Press, 2015.

Hotta, Eri. *Pan-Asianism and Japan's War 1931–1945*. London: Palgrave Macmillan, 2013.

Howe, Stephen. *Anticolonialism in British Politics: The Left and the End of Empire, 1918–1964*. Oxford: Oxford University Press, 1993.

Hucker, Daniel. *Public Opinion and the End of Appeasement in Britain and France*. London: Routledge, 2011.

Hucker, Daniel, Julie Gottlieb, and Richard Toye. *The Munich Crisis, Politics and the People*. Manchester: Manchester University Press, 2021.

Hughes, Gerald. *The Postwar Legacy of Appeasement*. London: Bloomsbury, 2014.

Hull, Isabel. *Absolute Destruction; Military Culture and the Practices of War in Imperial Germany*. Ithaca: Cornell University Press, 2005.

Imlay, Talbot. *Facing the Second World War: Strategy, Politics, and Economics in Britain and France, 1938–1940*. Oxford: Oxford University Press, 2003.

Jorge, David. *War in Spain: Appeasement, Collective Insecurity, and the Failure of European Democracies Against Fascism*. London: Routledge, 2020.

Keene, Judith. *Fighting for Franco: International Volunteers in Nationalist Spain during the Spanish Civil War, 1936–1939*. Leicester: Leicester University Press, 2007.

Kershaw, Ian. *The Nazi Dictatorship: Problems and Perspectives of Interpretation*. London: Edward Arnold, 1985.

Kershaw, Ian. *Hitler, the Germans, and the Final Solution*. New Haven: Yale University Press, 2008.

Khan, Yasmin. *The Great Partition: The Making of India and Pakistan*. New Haven: Yale University Press, 2007.

Khan, Yasmin. *The Raj at War: A People's History of India's Second World War*. London: Bodley Head, 2014.

Laqueur, Walter. *Fascism: Past, Present, Future*. Oxford: Oxford University Press, 1997.

Larsen, Stein Ugelvik. *Fascism Outside Europe: The European Impulse against Domestic Conditions in the Diffusion of Global Fascism*. New York: Columbia University Press, 2001.

Linehan, Thomas. *British Fascism 1918–39: Parties, Ideology and Culture*. Manchester: Manchester University Press, 2021.

Loomba, Ania. *Colonialism/Postcolonialism*. London: Routledge, 2007.

Louro, Michele. *Comrades against Imperialism: Nehru, India, and Interwar Internationalism*. Cambridge: Cambridge University Press, 2018.

Maclean, Kama. *A Revolutionary History of Interwar India: Violence, Image, Voice and Text*. Oxford: Oxford University Press, 2015.

Maiolo, Joseph. *Cry Havoc: How the Arms Race Drove the World to War, 1931–1941*. New York: Basic Books, 2010.

Makalani, Minkah. *In the Cause of Freedom: Radical Black Internationalism from Harlem to London: 1917–1939*. Chapel Hill, NC: University of North Carolina Press, 2011.

Mallet, Robert. *Mussolini in Ethiopia, 1919–1935: The Origins of Fascist Italy's African War*. Cambridge: Cambridge University Press, 2015.

Manjapra, Kris. *M.N. Roy, Marxism and Colonial Cosmopolitanism*. London: Routledge, 2016.

Mann, Michael. *Fascists*. Cambridge: Cambridge University Press, 2004.

Marcus, Harold. *A History of Ethiopia*. Berkeley: University of California Press, 1994.

Matera, Marc and Susan Kent. *The Global 1930s: The International Decade*. London: Taylor and Francis, 2017.

Mazower, Mark. *Hitler's Empire: How the Nazis Ruled Europe*. New York: Penguin Press, 2008.

McCarthy, Helen. *The British People and the League of Nations: Democracy, Citizenship, and Internationalism, 1918–1945*. Manchester: Manchester University Press, 2013.

McClintock, Anne. *Imperial Leather: Race, Gender, and Sexuality in the Colonial Contest*. London: Routledge, 1995.

McDonough, Frank. *Neville Chamberlain, Appeasement, and the British Road to War*. Manchester: Manchester University Press, 1998.

Mishra, Pankaj. *From the Ruins of Empire: The Intellectuals Who Remade Asia*. London: Farrar, Straus and Giroux, 2012.

Mitter, Rana. *China's War with Japan, 1937–1945: The Struggle for Survival*. New York: Allen Lane, 2013.

Morgan, Philip. *Fascism in Europe, 1919-1945*. London: Routledge, 2002.

Morgan, Philip. *Italian Fascism, 1919–1945*. London: Macmillan, 1995.

Moses, A. Dirk and Dan Stone. *Colonialism and Genocide*. London: Routledge, 2006.

Mosse, George. *The Crisis of German Ideology: Intellectual Origins of the Third Reich*. New York: Grosset & Dunlap, 1964.

Mukherjee, Mithi. *India in the Shadows of Empire: A Legal and Political History, 1774–1950*. Oxford: Oxford University Press, 2012.

Mukherjee, Rudrangshu. *Nehru and Bose: Parallel Lives*. London: Penguin, 2014.

Neville, Peter. *Hitler and Appeasement: The British Attempt to Prevent the Second World War*. London: Hambledon Continuum, 2006.

Overy, Richard. *Blood and Ruins: The Great Imperial War, 1931–1945*. London: Penguin Books, 2021.

Paxton, Robert. *The Anatomy of Fascism*. New York: Vintage Books, 2005.

Payne, Stanley G. *A History of Fascism, 1914–1945*. Madison: University of Wisconsin Press, 1995.

Pedersen, Susan. *The Guardians: The League of Nations and the Crisis of Empire*. Oxford: Oxford University Press, 2015.

Post, Gaines. *Dilemmas of Appeasement: British Deterrence and Defense, 1934–1937*. Ithaca: Cornell University Press, 1993.

Poulantzas, Nicos. *Fascism and Dictatorship: The Third International and the Problem of Fascism*. London: Verso Books, 2019.

Preston, Paul. *The Spanish Civil War; Reaction, Revolution, and Revenge*. New York: W.W. Norton, 2007.

Raza, Ali. *Revolutionary Pasts: Communist Internationalism in Colonial India*. Cambridge: Cambridge University Press, 2020.

Raza, Ali, Franziska Roy, and Benjamin Zachariah, eds. *The Internationalist Moment: South Asia, Worlds, and World Views, 1917–39*. London: Sage, 2015.

Roberts, David, ed. *Fascist Interactions: Proposals for a New Approach to Fascism and its Era, 1919–1945*. New York: Berghahn Books, 2016.

Roy, Kaushik. *India and World War II: War, Armed Forces, and Society, 1939–45*. Oxford: Oxford University Press, 2016.

Roy, Samaren. *M.N. Roy: A Political Biography*. London: Orient Longman, 1997.

Said, Edward. *Orientalism*. New York: Vintage Books, 1979.

Sternhell, Zeev. *The Birth of Fascist Ideology: From Cultural Rebellion to Political Revolution*. Princeton: Princeton University Press, 1995.

Sternhell, Zeev. *Neither Right nor Left: Fascist Ideology in France*. Princeton: Princeton University Press, 1996.

Strivastava, Neelam. *Italian Colonialism and Resistance to Empire, 1930–1970*. London: Palgrave Macmillan, 2018.

Tarling, Nicholas. *The Fall of Imperial Britain in South-East Asia*. Oxford: Oxford University Press, 1993.

Taylor, A. J. P. *The Origins of the Second World War*. London: Touchstone, 1961.

Tharoor, Shashi. *Nehru: The Invention of India*. London: Arcade Publishers, 2003.

Thomas, Hugh. *The Spanish Civil War*. London: Harper and Brothers, 1961.

Traverso, Enzo. *The New Faces of Fascism: Populism and the Far Right*. London: Verso, 2019.

Wildenthal, Lora. *German Women for Empire, 1884–1945*. Durham: Duke University Press, 2001.

Woolf, Stuart. *Fascism in Europe*. North Yorkshire: Methuen, 1981.

Yellen, Jeremy. *The Greater East Asia Co-Prosperity Sphere: When Total Empire Met Total War*. Ithaca: Cornell University Press, 2019.

Young, Louise. *Japan's Total Empire: Manchuria and the Culture of Wartime Imperialism*. Berkeley: University of California Press, 1999.

Zachariah, Benjamin. *Nehru*. London: Routledge, 2004.

Index

www.ingramcontent.com/pod-product-compliance
Lightning Source LLC
Chambersburg PA
CBHW050416280326
41932CB00013BA/1881